There's Math in My Origami!

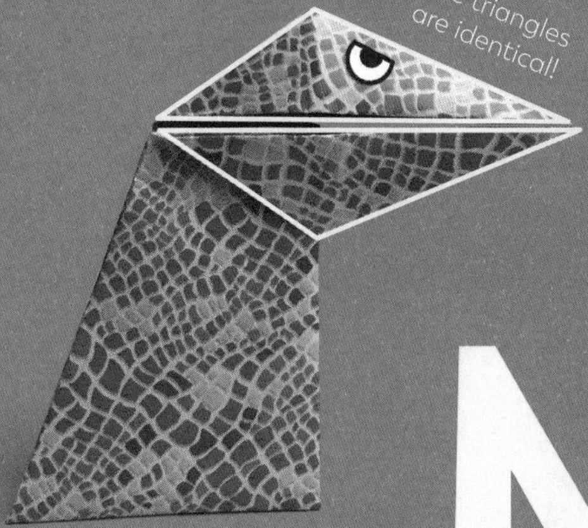
The triangles are identical!

You can fit two yellow rectangles inside the dark green square.

There's Math in My Origami!

35 Fun Projects for Hands-On Math Learning

FUMIAKI SHINGU

Yes, the
ngles are
:he same!
90°

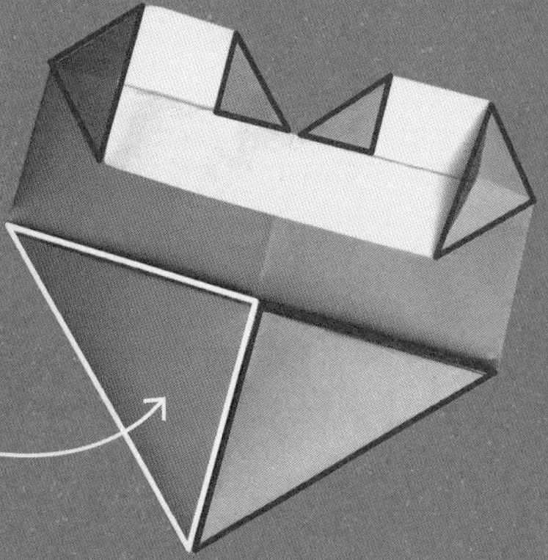
The five triangles outlined in blue are the same shape as the yellow triangle.

THERE'S MATH IN MY ORIGAMI!: *35 Fun Projects for Hands-On Math Learning*

Originally published in Japan as さんすうおり紙 (*Sansu Origami*) by Shogakukan, Inc., in 2009. First published in English in North America in revised form by The Experiment, LLC, in 2021. English translation rights arranged with Shogakukan, Inc., through Paper Crane Agency.

The Experiment, LLC, 220 East 23rd Street, Suite 600, New York, NY 10010-4658
theexperimentpublishing.com

Library of Congress Cataloging-in-Publication Data

Names: Shingū, Fumiaki, author. | Felton, Corinne, illustrator. | Williams, Erica (Translator)
Title: There's math in my origami! : 35 fun projects for hands-on math learning / Fumiaki Shingu ; illustrations by Corinne Felton ; translation by Erica Williams.
Other titles: Sansū origami. English
Identifiers: LCCN 2021009554 (print) | LCCN 2021009555 (ebook) | ISBN 9781615197798 (paperback) | ISBN 9781615197958 (ebook)
Subjects: LCSH: Origami--Juvenile literature.
Classification: LCC TT872.5 .S5413 2021 (print) | LCC TT872.5 (ebook) | DDC 736/.982--dc23
LC record available at https://lccn.loc.gov/2021009554
LC ebook record available at https://lccn.loc.gov/2021009555

ISBN 978-1-61519-779-8
Ebook ISBN 978-1-61519-795-8

Cover, text design, and photographs by Beth Bugler
Illustrations by Corinne Felton
Translation by Erica Williams

Manufactured in China

First printing June 2021
10 9 8 7 6 5 4 3 2 1

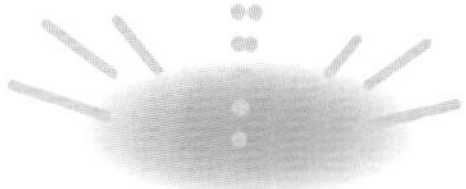

Contents

In the Air

Make It Move

Animal Friends

Play and Decorate

How to Use This Book

Follow along

Use the numbered steps and drawings to help you as you fold.

Difficulty levels

★ Beginner

★ ★ Easy

★ ★ ★ Intermediate

★ ★ ★ ★ Challenging

★ ★ ★ ★ ★ Expert

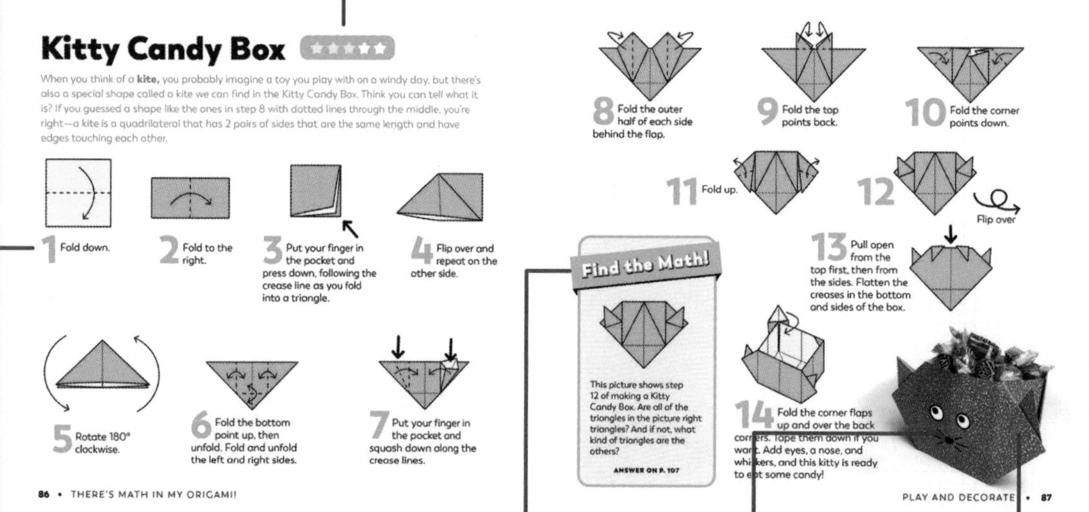

Kitty Candy Box ★★★★★

When you think of a **kite**, you probably imagine a toy you play with on a windy day, but there's also a special shape called a kite we can find in the Kitty Candy Box. Think you can tell what it is? If you guessed a shape like the ones in step 8 with dotted lines through the middle, you're right—a kite is a quadrilateral that has 2 pairs of sides that are the same length and have edges touching each other.

1 Fold down.

2 Fold to the right.

3 Put your finger in the pocket and press down, following the crease line as you fold into a triangle.

4 Flip over and repeat on the other side.

5 Rotate 180° clockwise.

6 Fold the bottom point up, then unfold. Fold and unfold the left and right sides.

7 Put your finger in the pocket and squash down along the crease lines.

8 Fold the outer half of each side behind the flap.

9 Fold the top points back.

10 Fold the corner points down.

11 Fold up.

12 Flip over

13 Pull open from the top first, then from the sides. Flatten the creases in the bottom and sides of the box.

14 Fold the corner flaps up and over the back corners. Tape them down if you want. Add eyes, a nose, and whiskers, and this kitty is ready to eat some candy!

Find the Math!

This picture shows step 12 of making a Kitty Candy Box. Are all of the triangles in the picture right triangles? And if not, what kind of triangles are the others?

ANSWER ON P. 107

86 • THERE'S MATH IN MY ORIGAMI!

PLAY AND DECORATE • 87

Find the math!

Do you have what it takes to be a math master? Give these challenges a try!

Stickers

You can decorate your origami with the eye stickers in this book.

Origami paper

Each project has its own special color of origami paper—or you can choose which color you'd like to use!

Understanding the Instructions

Fold

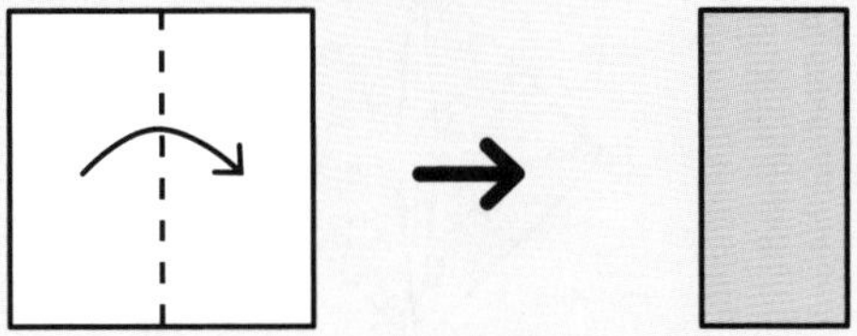

Flip

Fold and unfold

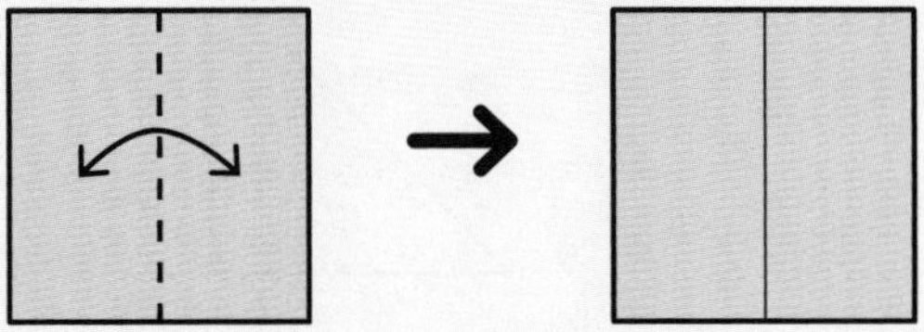

Turn

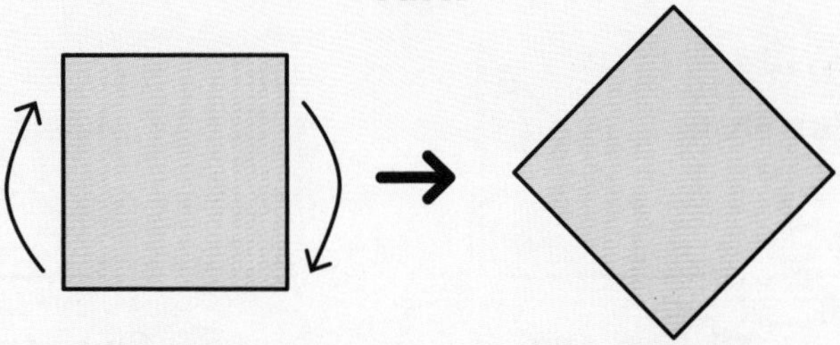

Fold under

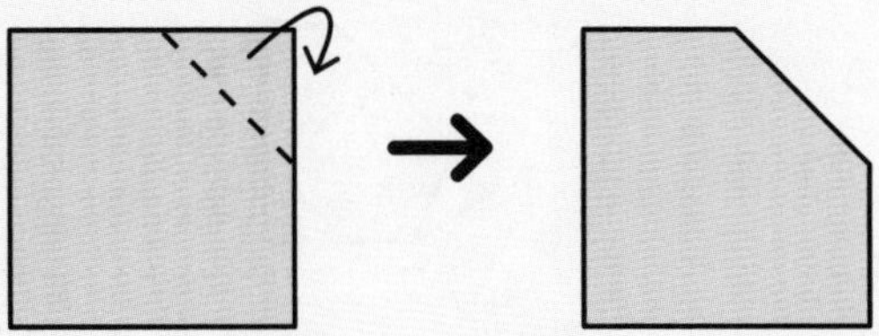

Fold open

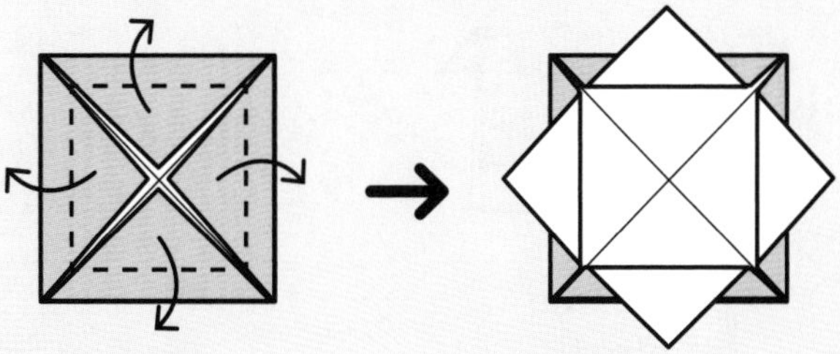

The Basic Folds to Know

Cushion Fold

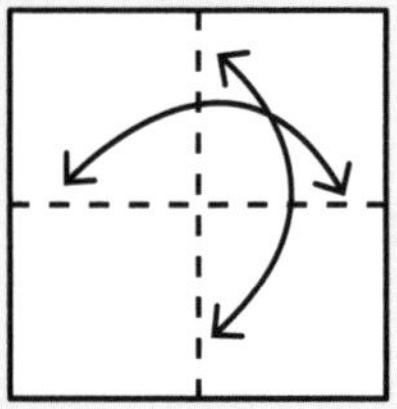

1 Fold and unfold.

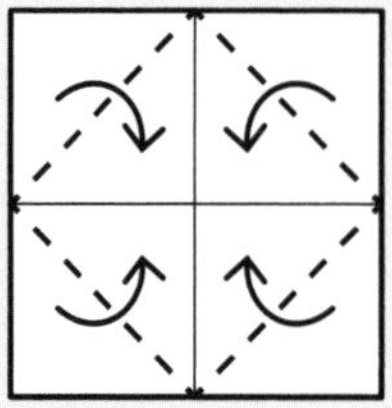

2 Fold the corners to the center.

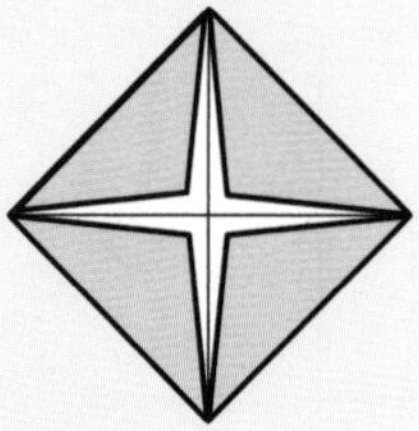

3 Ta-da!

Inside Reverse Fold

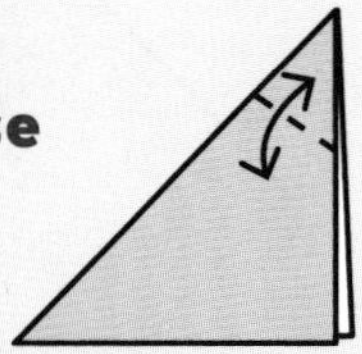

1 Fold and unfold.

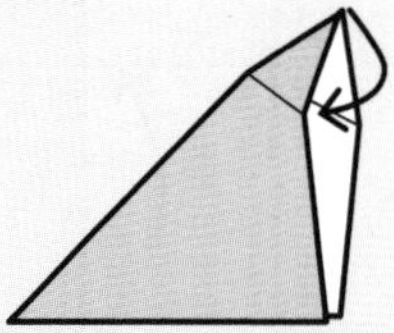

2 Open the paper slightly and fold the flap to the inside.

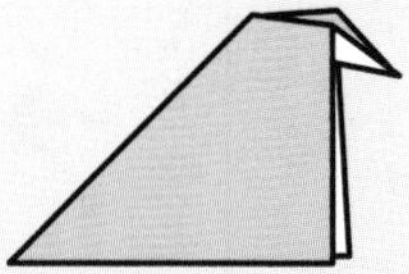

3 Now you've got a bird's head!

Outside Reverse Fold

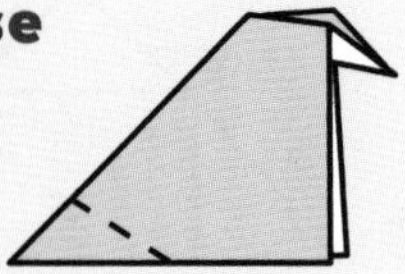

1 Fold and unfold.

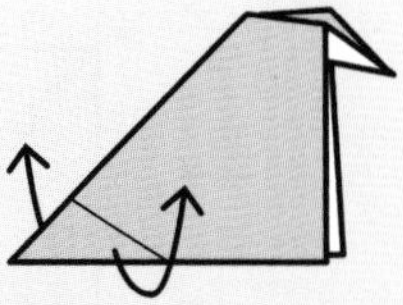

2 Open the flap slightly and fold to the outside.

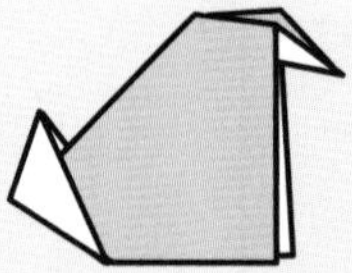

3 A cute bird's tail!

Balloon Fold

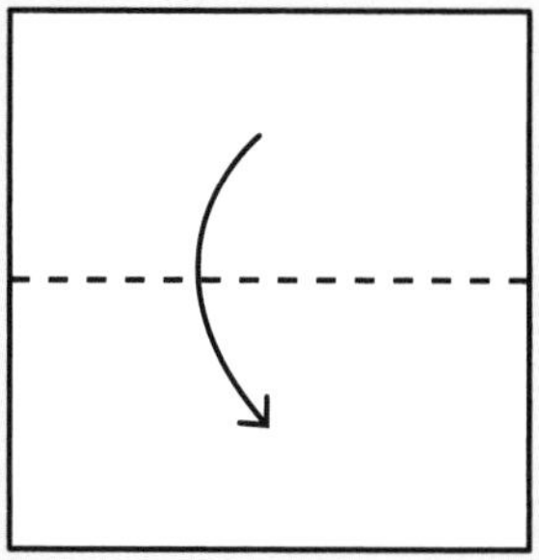

1 Fold in half.

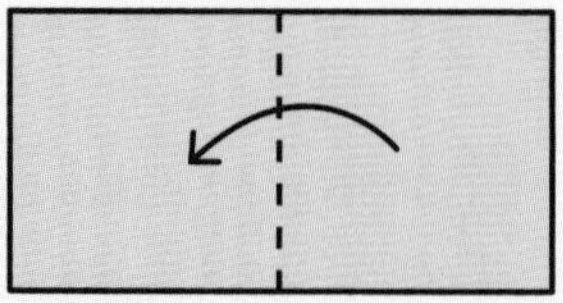

2 Fold in half again.

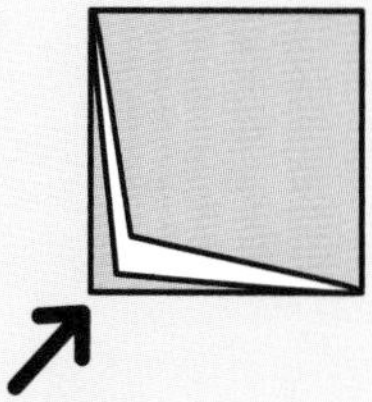

3 Put your finger in the pocket of the top flap.

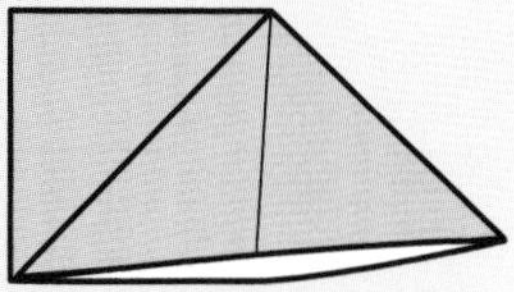

4 Press down to make a triangle.

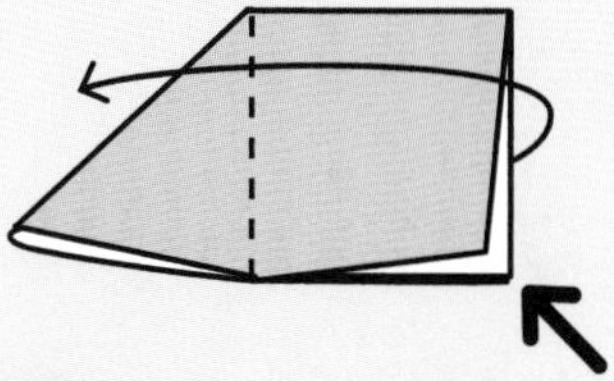

5 Swing the right edge to the left, then put your finger in the pocket.

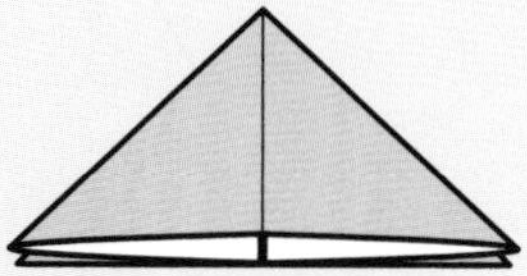

6 Press down to make another triangle.

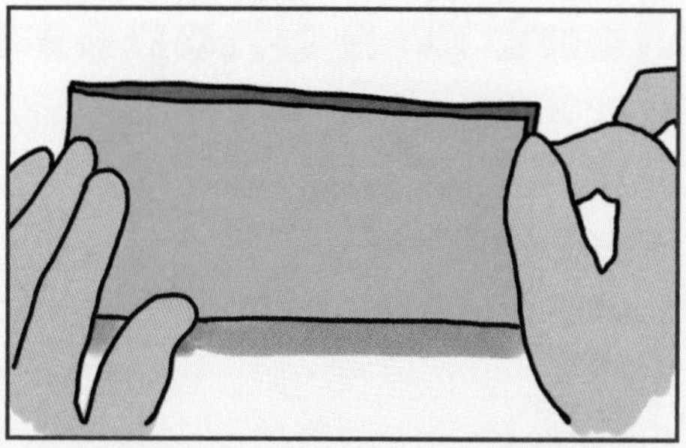

Helpful Hints

1 Fold on a flat surface.

2 Review all the instructions and diagrams before folding your origami.

3 Check the next step as you are folding to see where you are heading.

4 Be sure to match up the corners of the paper exactly!

Meet the Shapes and Numbers

Hello, shapes!

You can figure out a shape's name by counting the number of sides and angles it has.

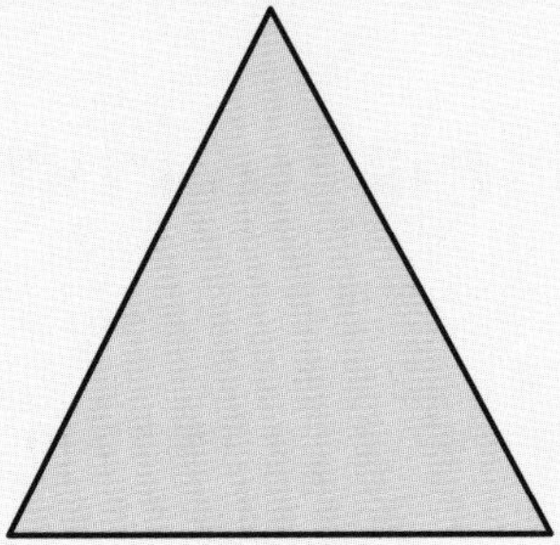

Triangle

3 sides and 3 angles

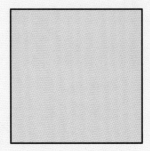

Quadrilateral

4 sides and 4 angles

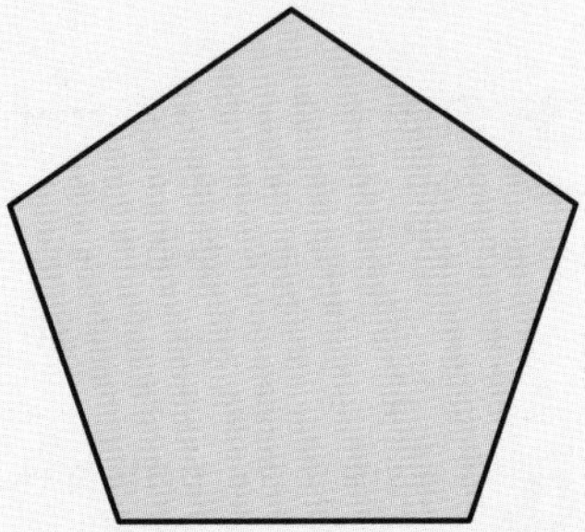

Pentagon

5 sides and 5 angles

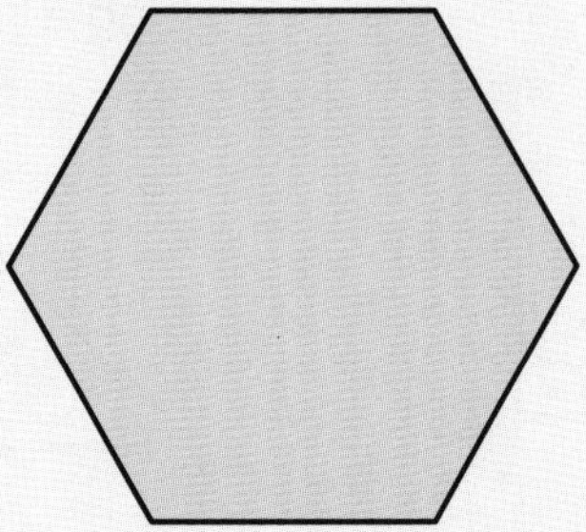

Hexagon

6 sides and 6 angles

The Triangle Family

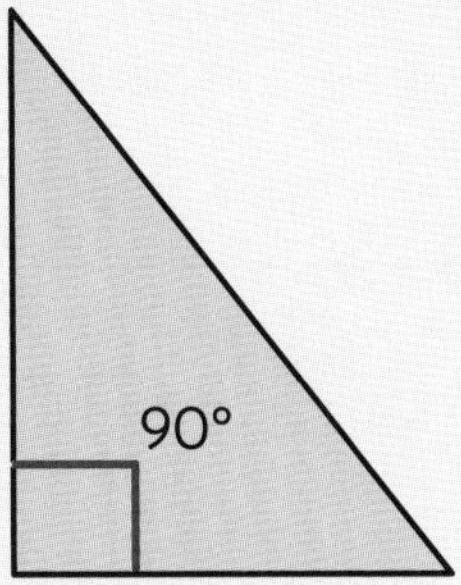

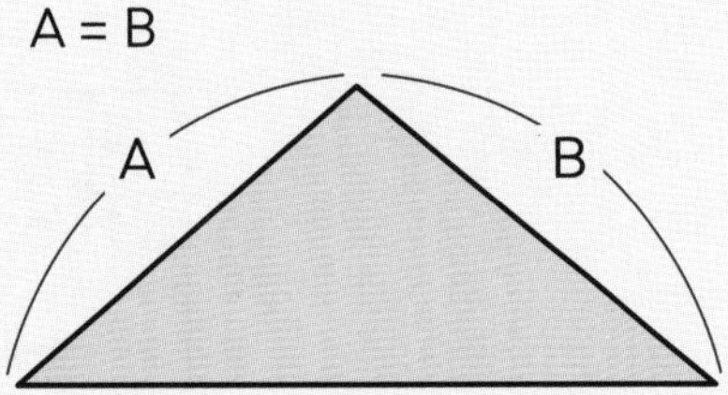

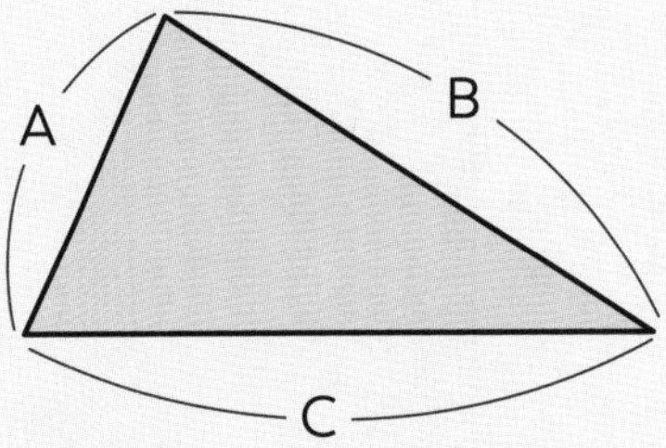

Right Triangle

When 1 of a triangle's 3 angles is a right angle (90°), it's called a right triangle.

Isosceles Triangle

When 2 of a triangle's sides are the same length, it's called an isosceles (eye-SAA-suh-lees) triangle.

Scalene Triangle

When none of a triangle's sides are the same length, it's called a scalene (SKAY-lean) triangle. A, B, and C are all different lenghts.

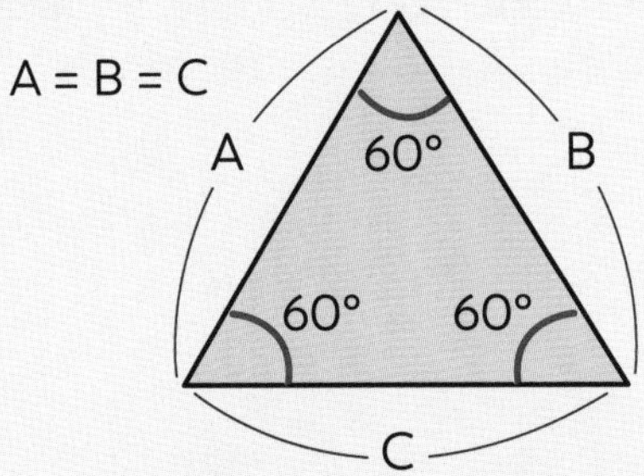

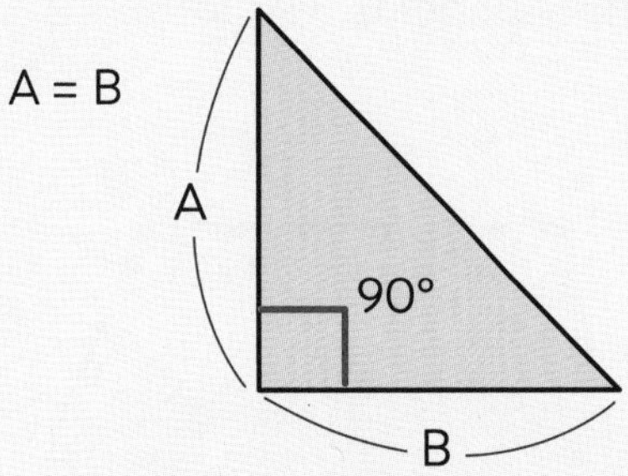

Equilateral Triangle

When all 3 of a triangle's angles are equal and all 3 of its sides are the same length, it's called an equilateral triangle. Each angle in an equilateral triangle measures 60°.

Isosceles Right Triangle

When 1 of a triangle's 3 angles is a right angle (90°), and 2 of its sides are the same length, it's called an isosceles right triangle.

The Quadrilateral Family

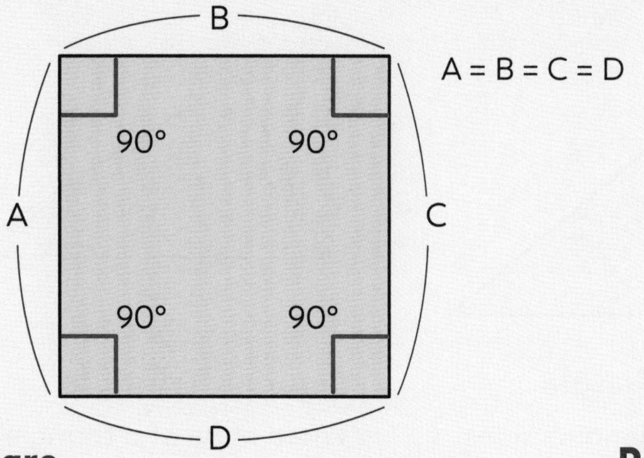

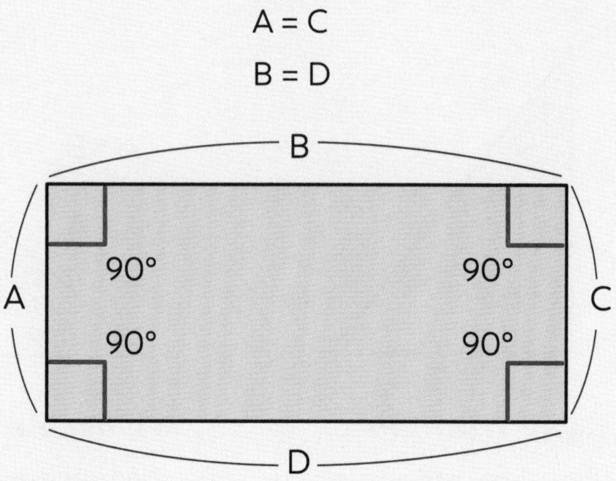

Square

When all 4 of a quadrilateral's sides are the same length and all 4 of its angles are right angles (90°), it's called a square. Each piece of origami paper is a square.

Rectangle

When a quadrilateral is made of 4 sides with 4 corners that form right (90°) angles, but 1 pair of opposite sides is longer than the other pair of opposite sides, it's called a rectangle. A piece of origami paper folded in half is a rectangle.

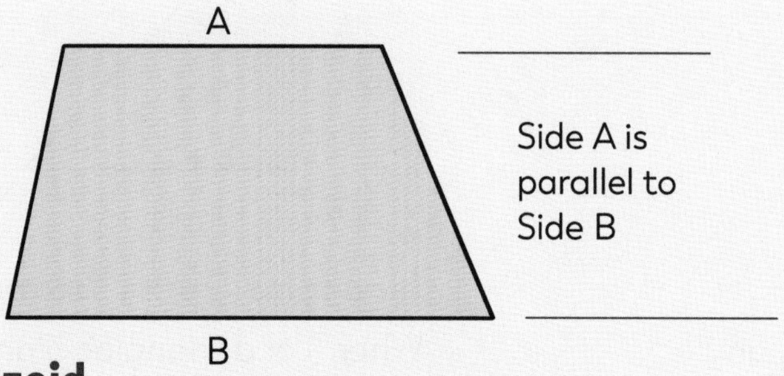

Trapezoid

When a quadrilateral's corners don't form right (90°) angles, but at least 1 pair of its opposite sides is parallel, it's called a trapezoid.

Comparing Shapes

2 shapes are **congruent** if they have the exact same shape and size.

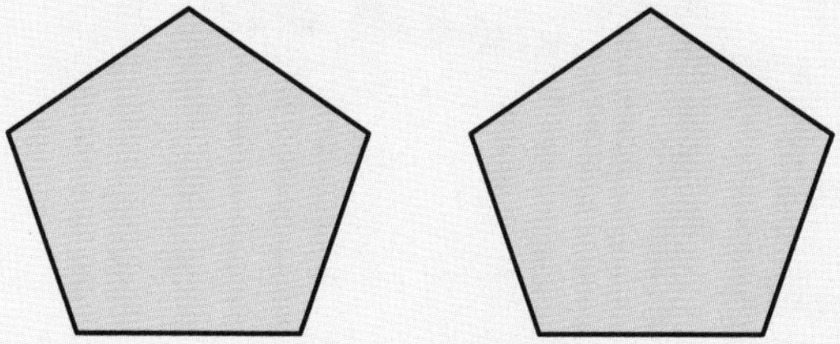

2 shapes are **similar** if they have the same shape but different sizes.

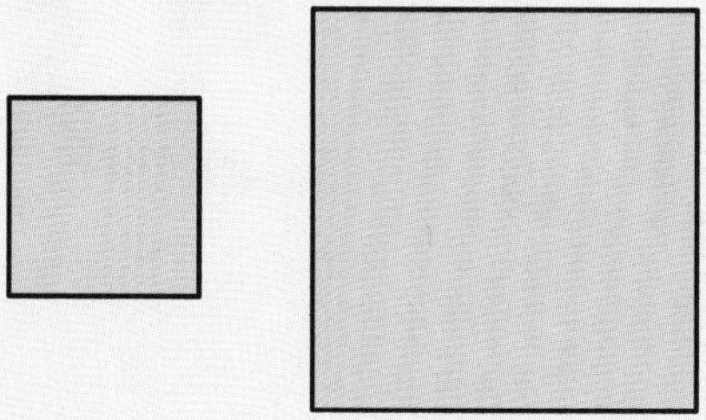

Fantastic Fractions

Fractions help us divide things into equal parts (like we sometimes do when we fold origami paper). We can write them like this:

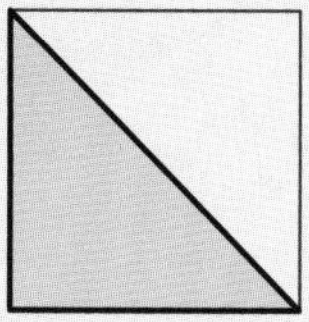

One half
(or 1 part out of 2 parts)
$= \frac{1}{2}$

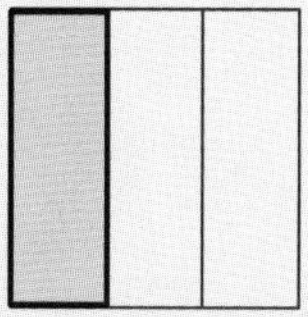

One third
(or 1 part out of 3 parts)
$= \frac{1}{3}$

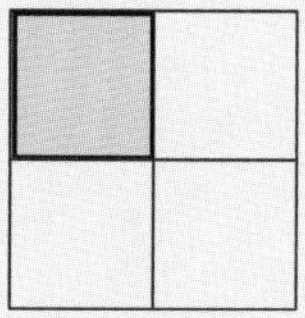

One fourth/one quarter
(or 1 part out of 4 parts)
$= \frac{1}{4}$

"Half" means $\frac{1}{2}$. The isosceles right triangle above is made by folding a square in half. In other words, an isosceles right triangle is $\frac{1}{2}$ a square.

We can put even higher numbers on the bottom part of the fraction to divide into more parts. For example, 1 part out of 5 parts is $\frac{1}{5}$, or one fifth. Look for different kinds of fractions as you fold!

In the Air

Planes, squids, and balloons can all sail through the air with the help of symmetry and shapes.

Have fun flying!

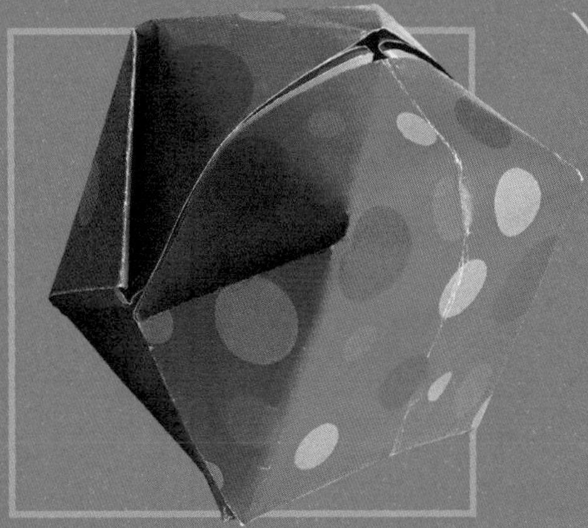

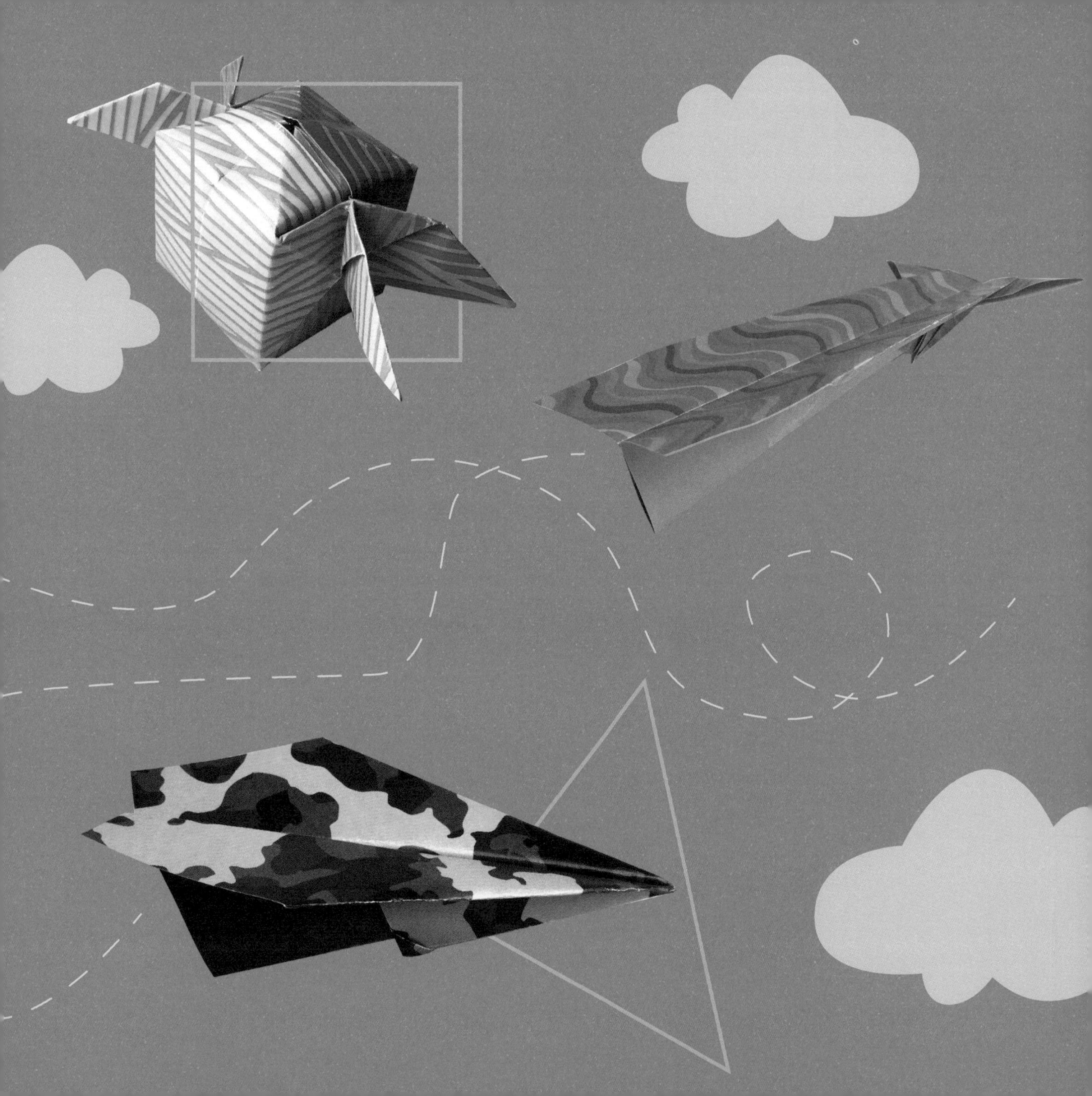

Airplane ★☆☆☆☆

If you've ever flown a paper airplane, you probably know that they work best when both of their wings are the same shape. When something is the same on both sides like this, we say it's **symmetrical.** Look closely at these steps—the Airplane is symmetrical after each new fold!

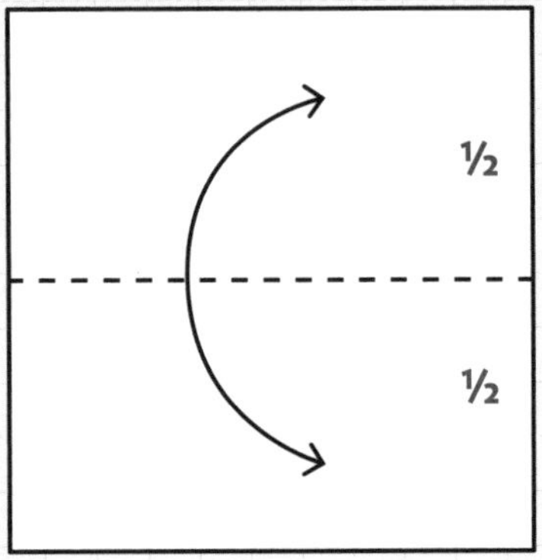

1 Fold in half and unfold.

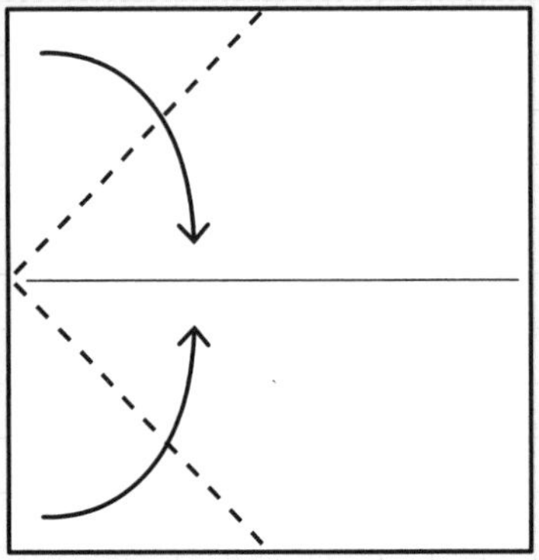

2 Fold the corners to the center crease.

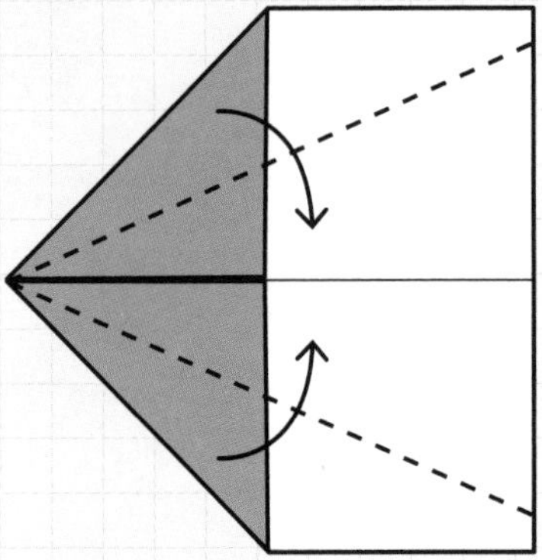

3 Fold the outside edges to the center crease.

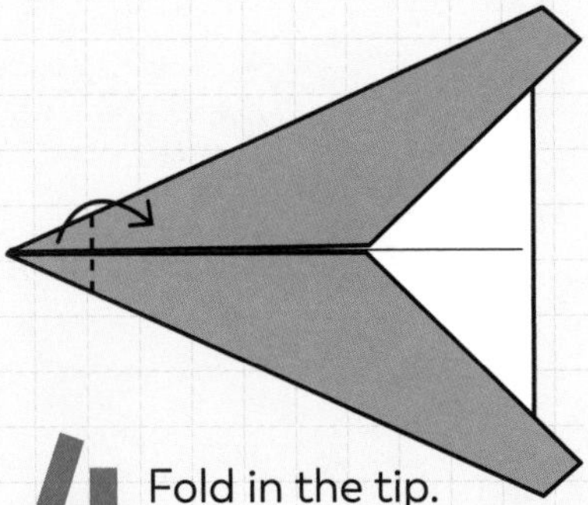

4 Fold in the tip.

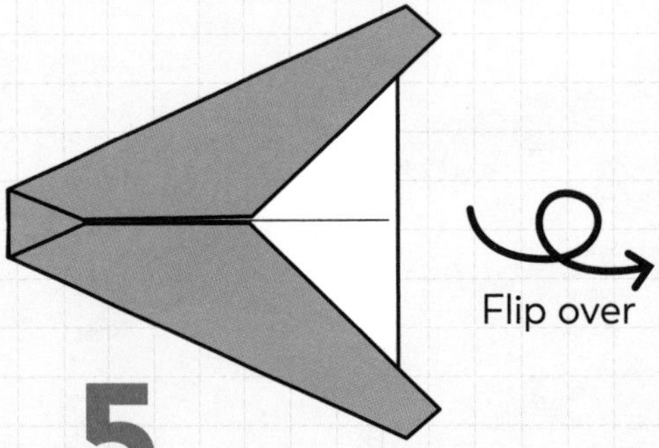

5 Flip over

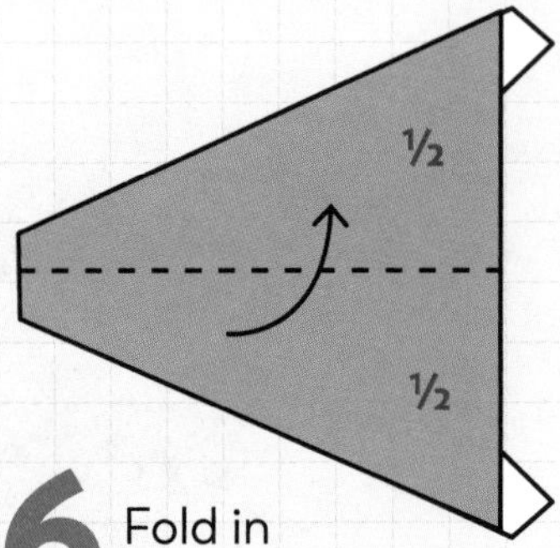

6 Fold in half up.

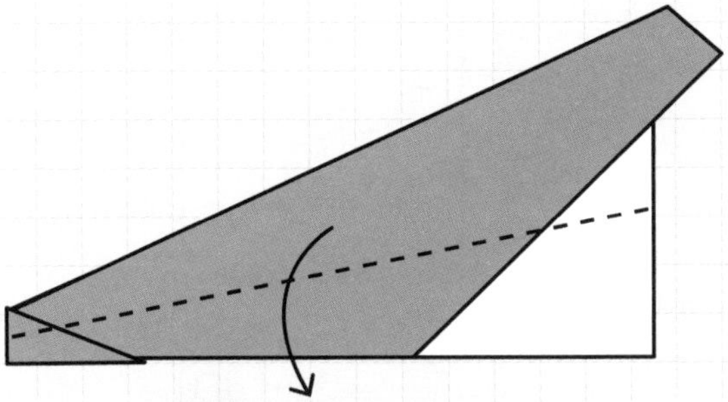

Flip over

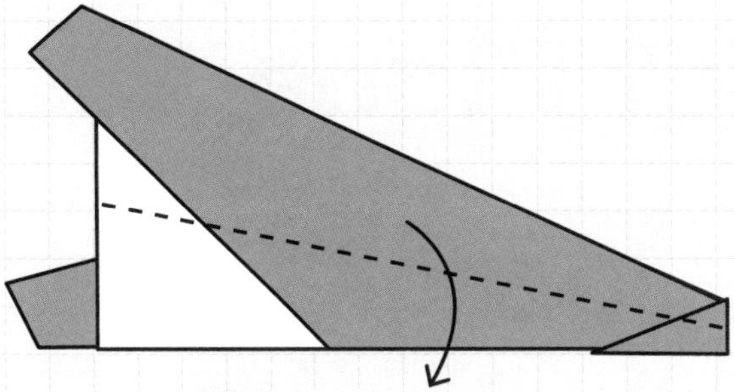

7 Fold the top flap down.

8 Fold the other flap down.

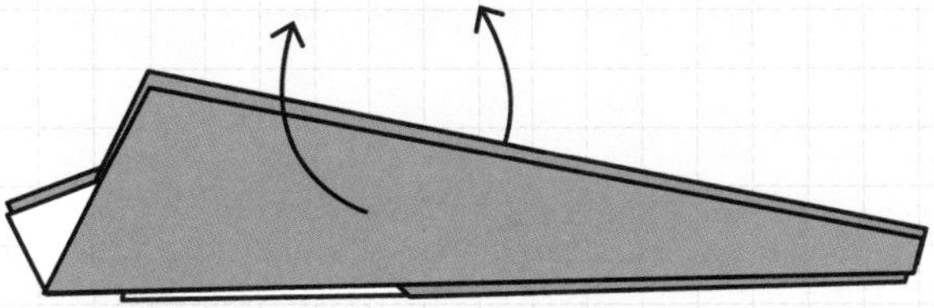

9 Fold the wings upward to make them flat and even. Spread the wings wider by pinching the flat part of the airplane at the nose and underneath the wings. Now your plane's ready to fly!

Find the Math!

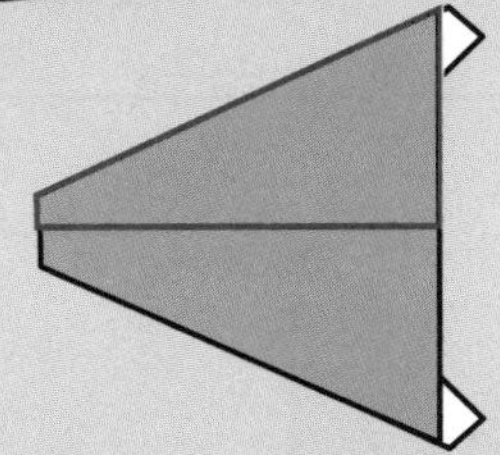

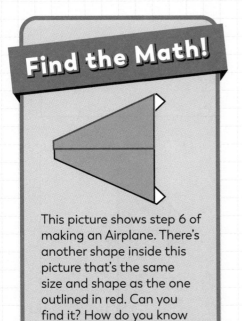

This picture shows step 6 of making an Airplane. There's another shape inside this picture that's the same size and shape as the one outlined in red. Can you find it? How do you know it's the same?

ANSWER ON P. 102

Jet Plane

The Jet Plane is different from the Airplane (p. 12) because its wings are larger—both planes' wings are the same length, but the Jet Plane's are a greater width. This means these wings have more **surface area,** which is the amount of space a shape takes up. Does more surface area make a paper airplane fly better? Try building both planes and having a flying competition to find out!

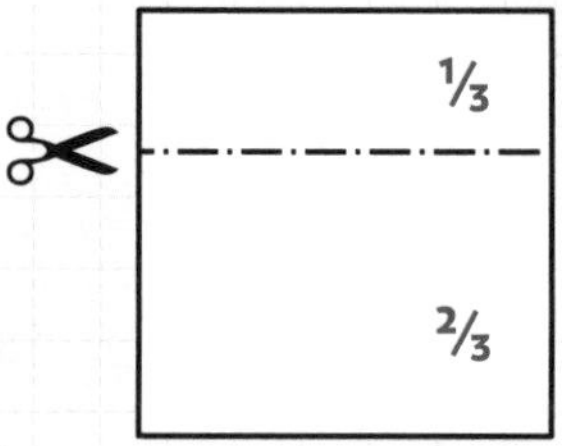

1 Fold the top of the paper down one third of the way, then cut along the fold. Use the bottom two thirds of the paper for the next step.

2 Fold in half and unfold.

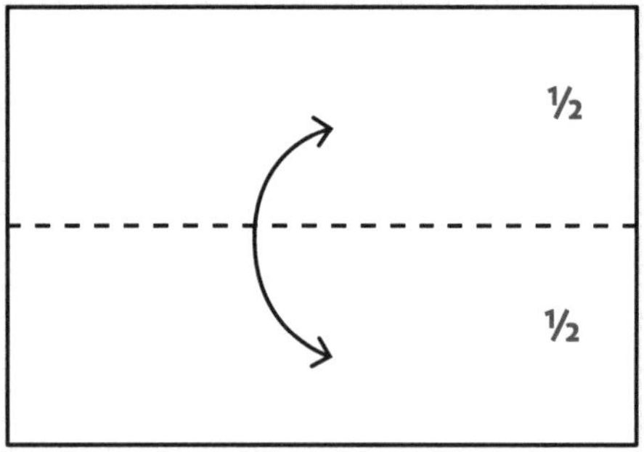

3 Fold the corners to the center crease.

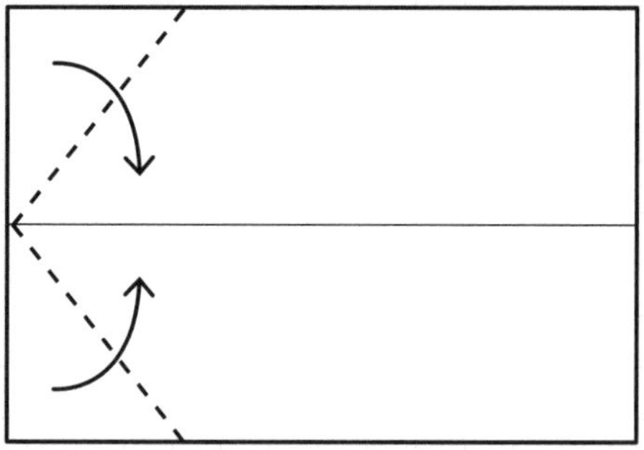

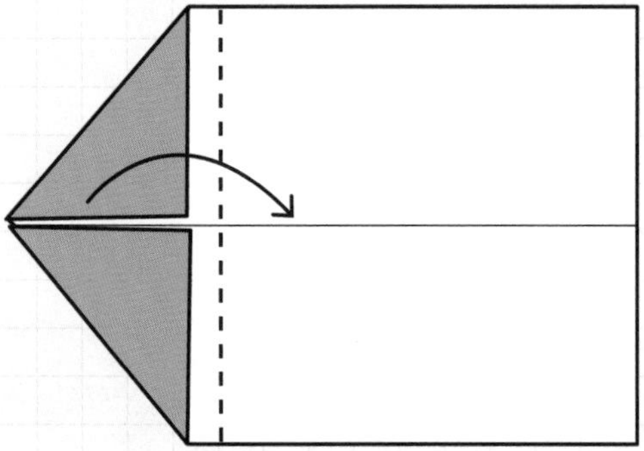

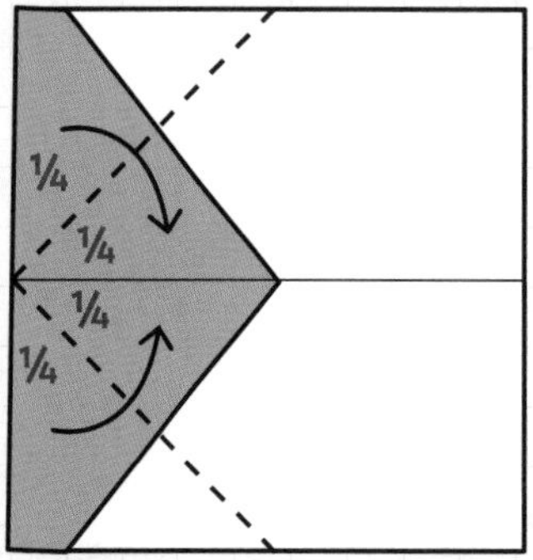

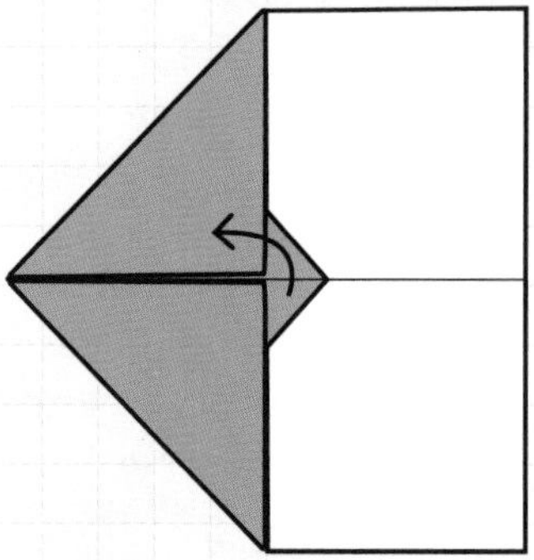

4 Fold the tip to the center.

5 Fold the corners to the center crease.

6 Fold the tip on top of the flaps.

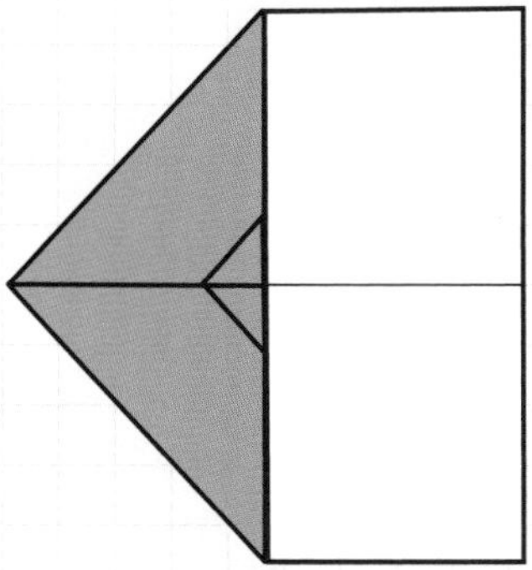

7

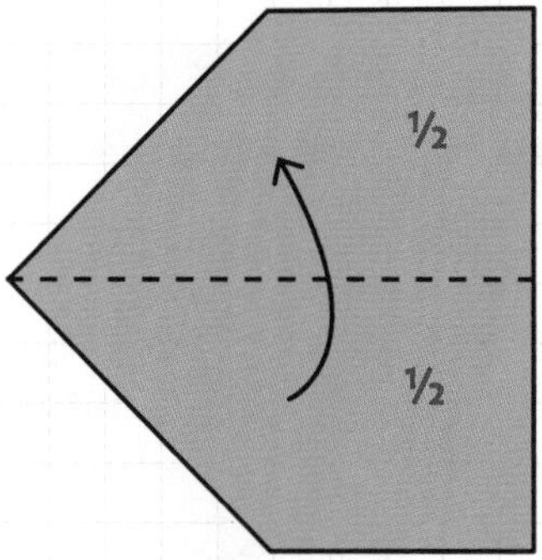

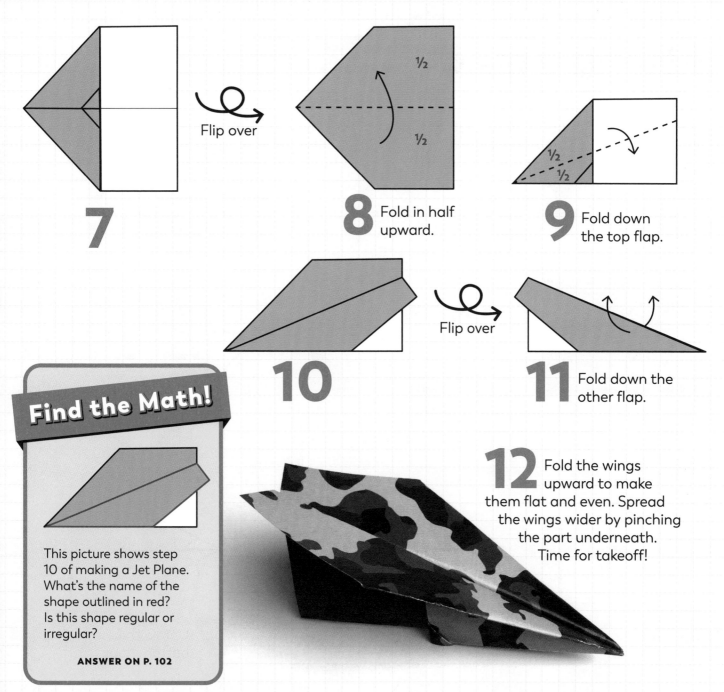

8 Fold in half upward.

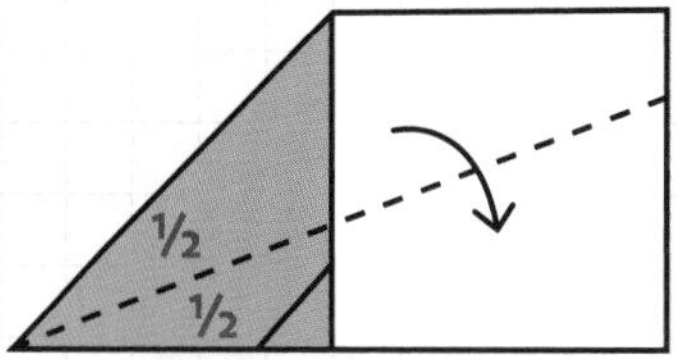

9 Fold down the top flap.

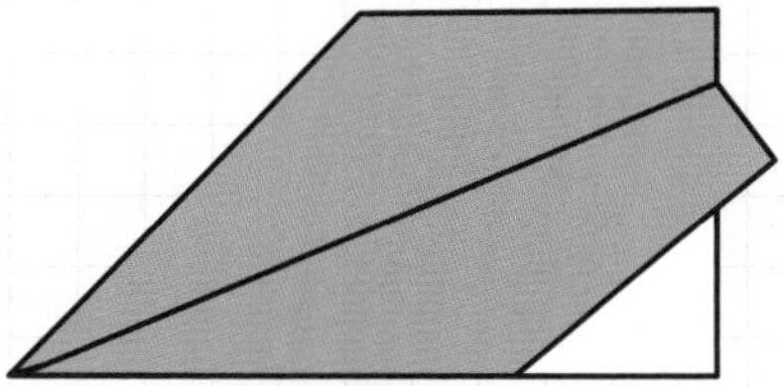

10

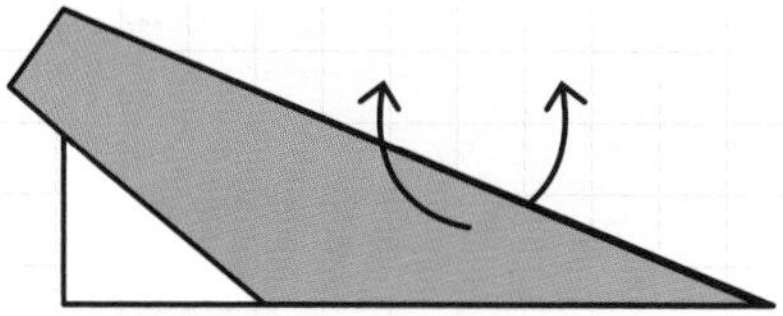

11 Fold down the other flap.

12 Fold the wings upward to make them flat and even. Spread the wings wider by pinching the part underneath. Time for takeoff!

Find the Math!

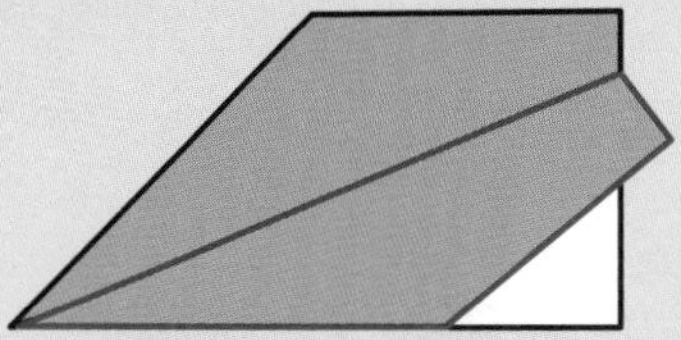

This picture shows step 10 of making a Jet Plane. What's the name of the shape outlined in red? Is this shape regular or irregular?

ANSWER ON P. 102

Flying Squid

Step 1 of making a Flying Squid requires turning a square sheet of origami paper into a rectangle. Squares and rectangles are both types of quadrilaterals, but did you know they have another special relationship? Every square is a rectangle (because all squares have four sides and four right angles) but not all rectangles are squares (because not every rectangle has four sides that are all the same length).

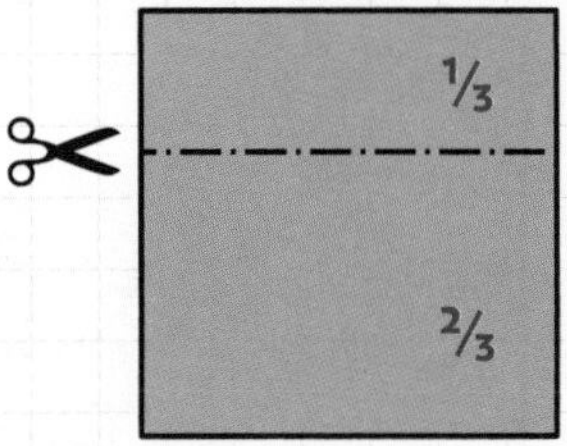

1 Fold the top of the paper down one third of the way, then cut along the fold. Use the bottom two thirds of the paper for the next step.

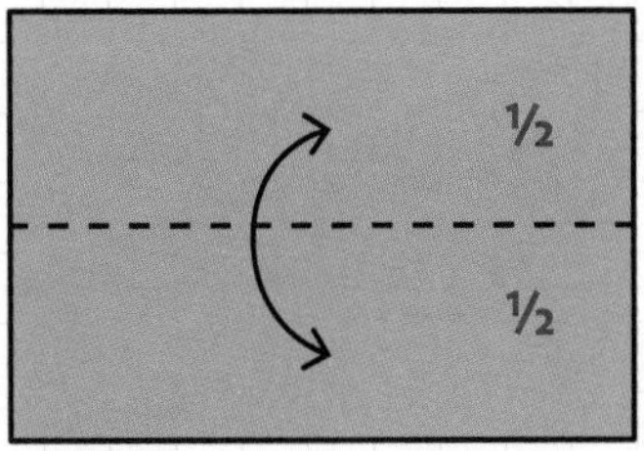

2 Fold in half and unfold.

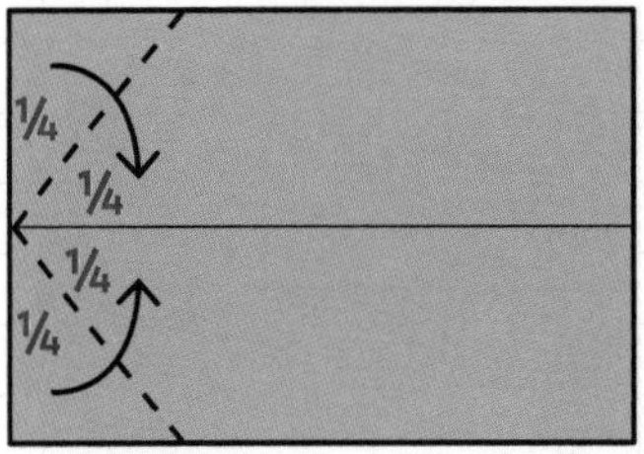

3 Fold the corners to the center crease.

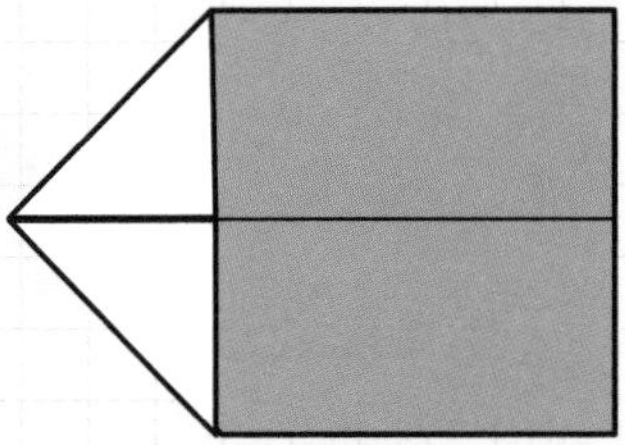

4

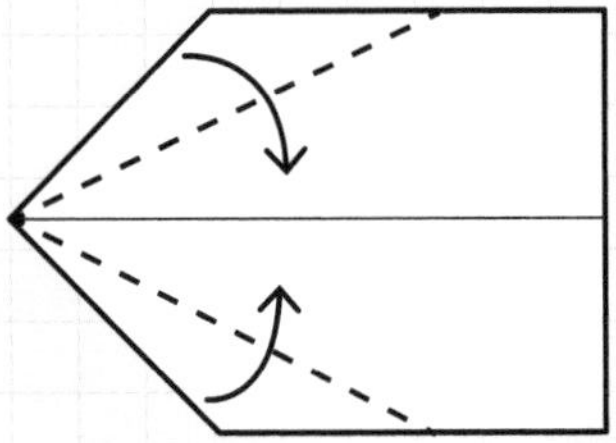

5 Fold the edges to the center crease.

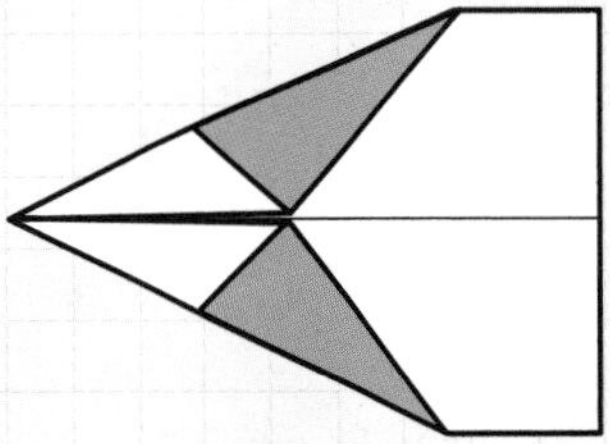

6

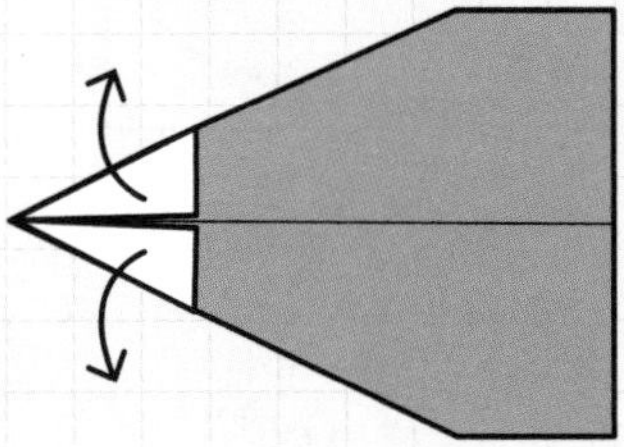

7 Unfold the top and bottom flaps.

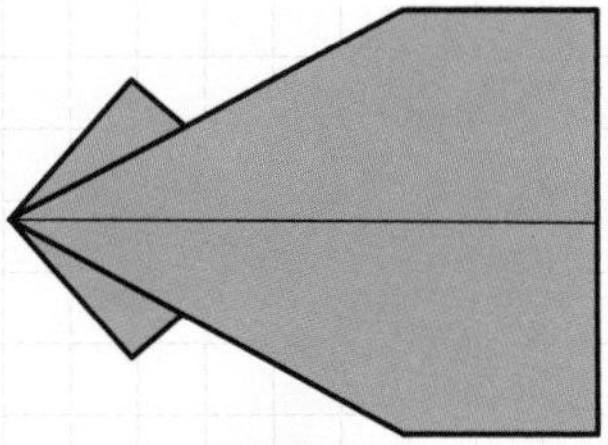

8

Flip over

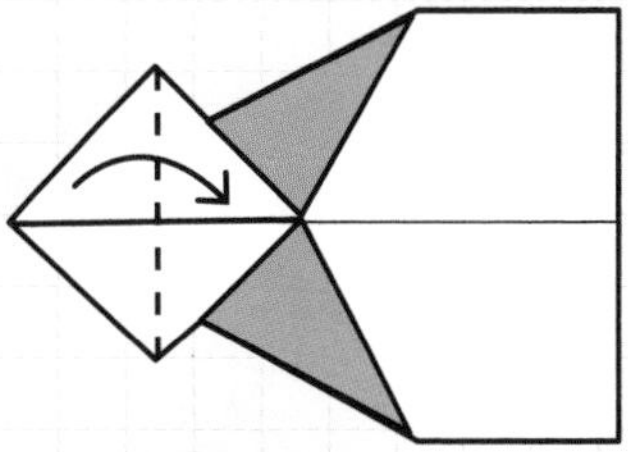

9 Fold into a triangle.

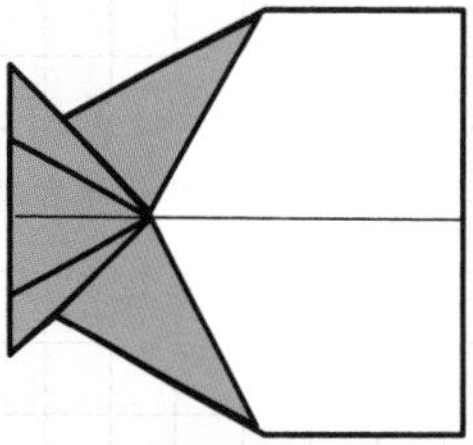

10

Flip over

11 Fold in half up.

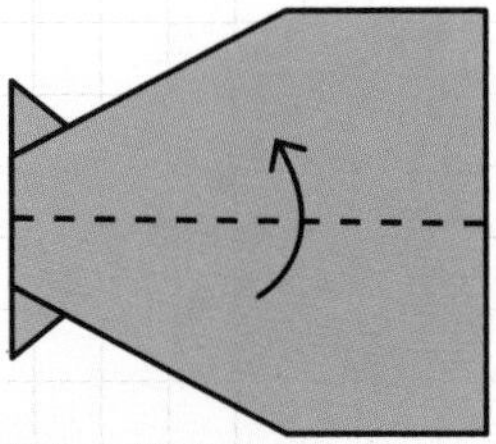

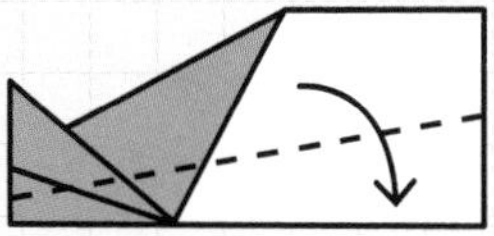

12 Fold the top flap down.

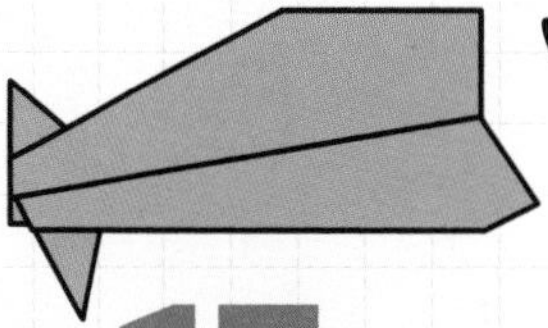

Flip over

13

Find the Math!

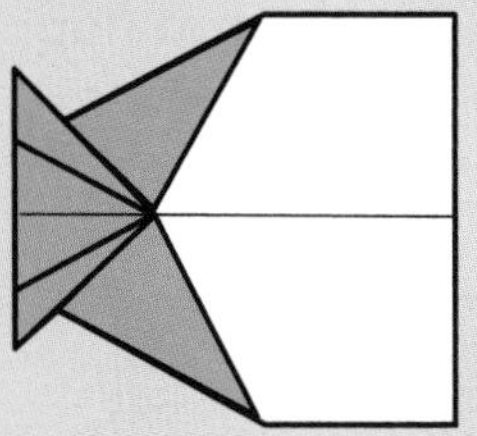

This picture shows step 10 of making a Flying Squid. There are 2 pairs of identical triangles here. Can you find them?

ANSWER ON P. 102

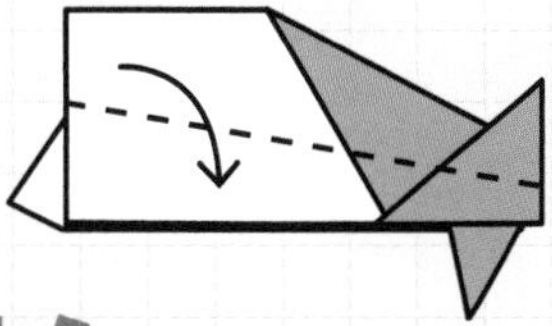

14 Fold the other flap down.

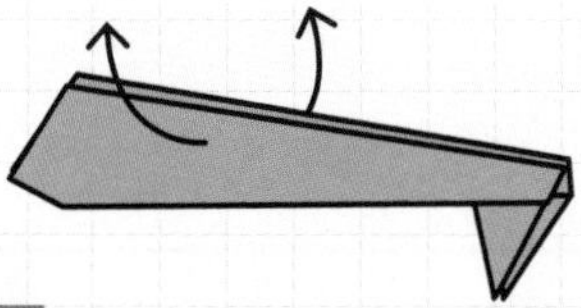

15 Fold the wings up to make them flat and even. Spread the wings wider by pinching the part underneath, and your squid is all set to swim through the sky!

Boxy Balloon ★★★★★

The squares and triangles we've talked about so far are **two-dimensional** (or **2D**), meaning they're flat like a piece of paper. But check out the finished Boxy Balloon—it's much thicker and takes up space! That's because it's a **three-dimensional** (or **3D**) shape called a **cube,** which is made up of 6 square faces combined.

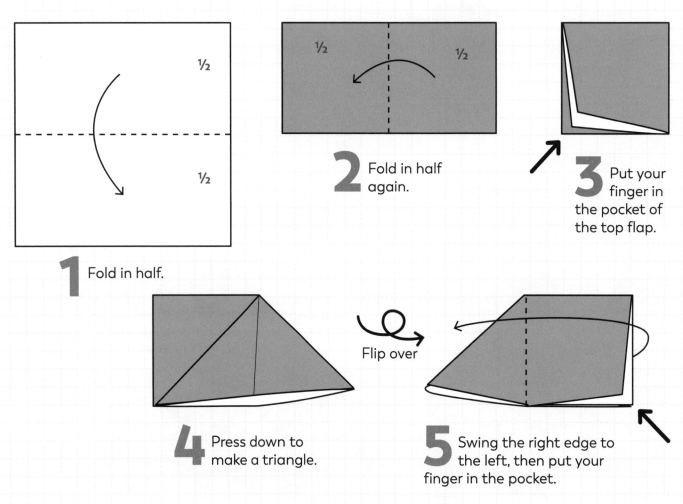

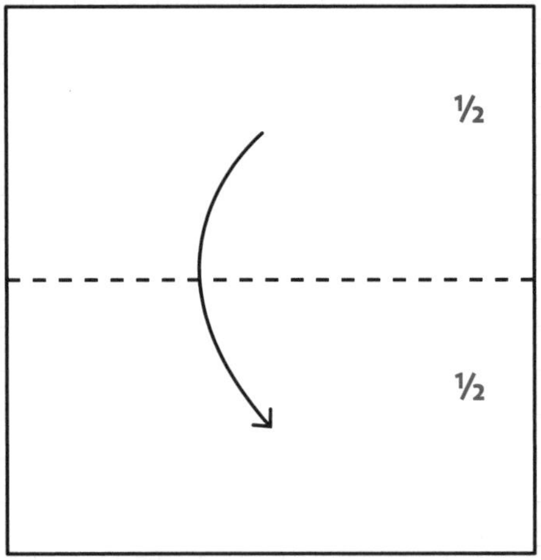

1 Fold in half.

½
½

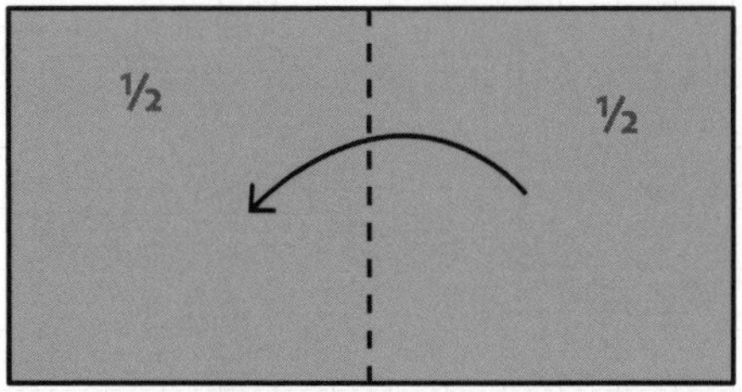

2 Fold in half again.

½   ½

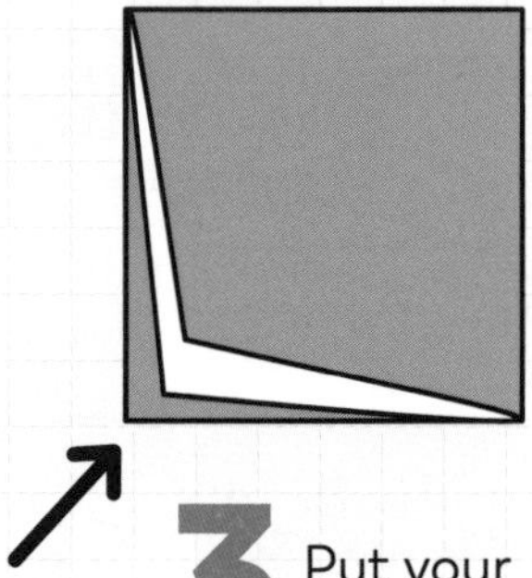

3 Put your finger in the pocket of the top flap.

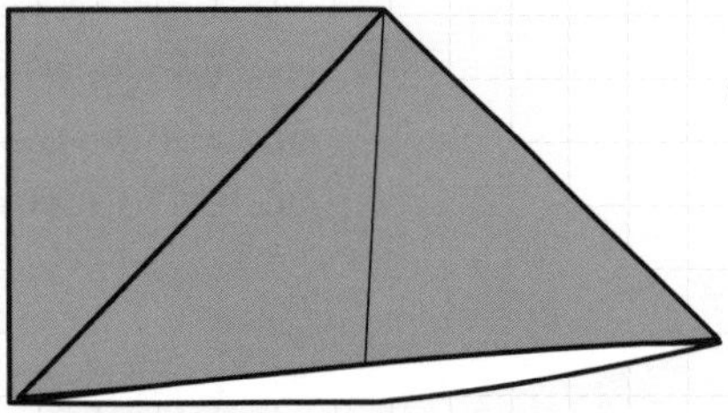

4 Press down to make a triangle.

Flip over

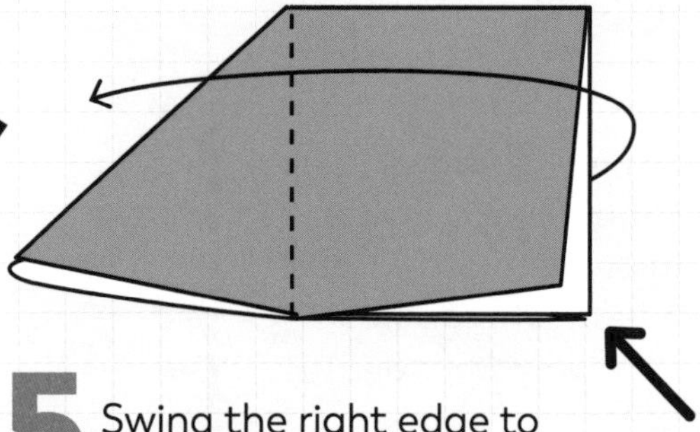

5 Swing the right edge to the left, then put your finger in the pocket.

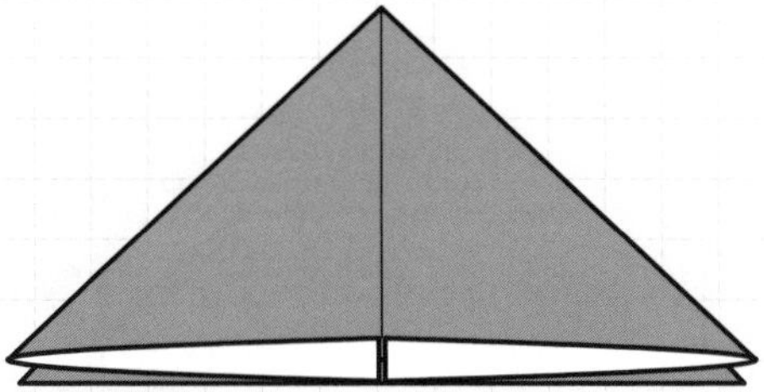

6 Press down to make another triangle.

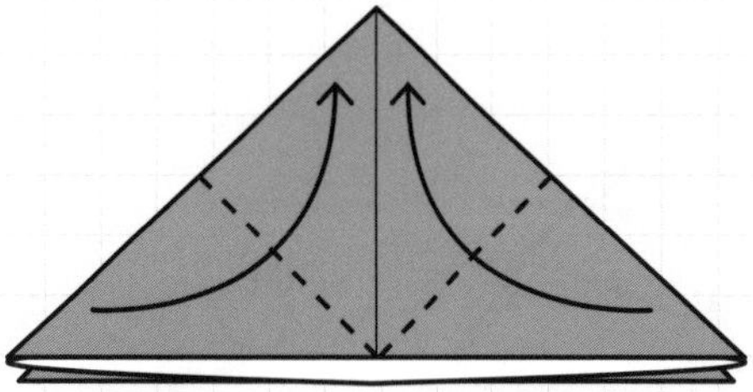

7 Bring the first layer of the bottom corners to the top point and fold.

Find the Math!

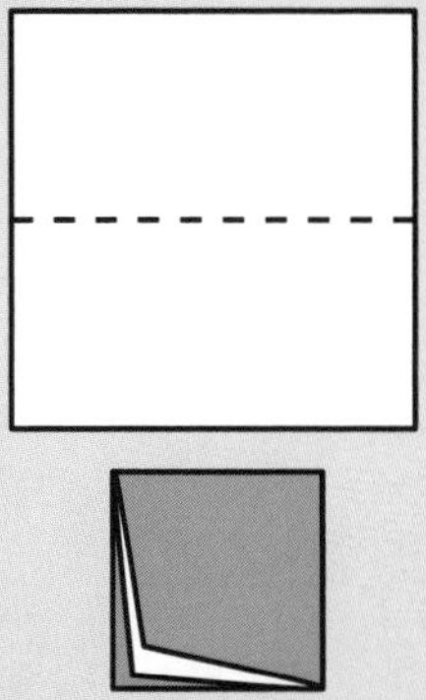

These pictures show steps 1 and 3 of making a Boxy Balloon. What fraction of the unfolded paper in step 1 is the smaller shape in step 3?

ANSWER ON P. 102

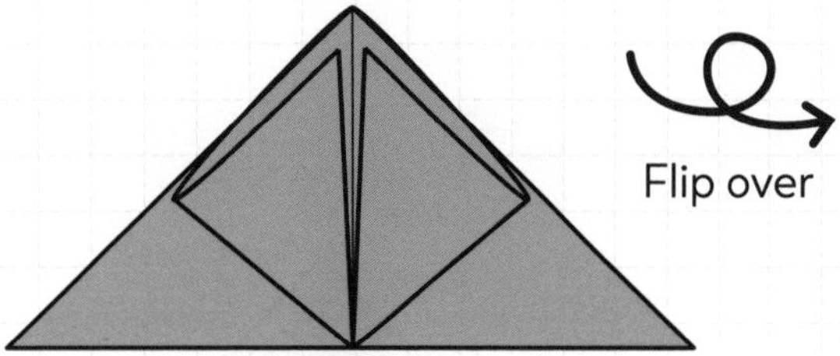

8

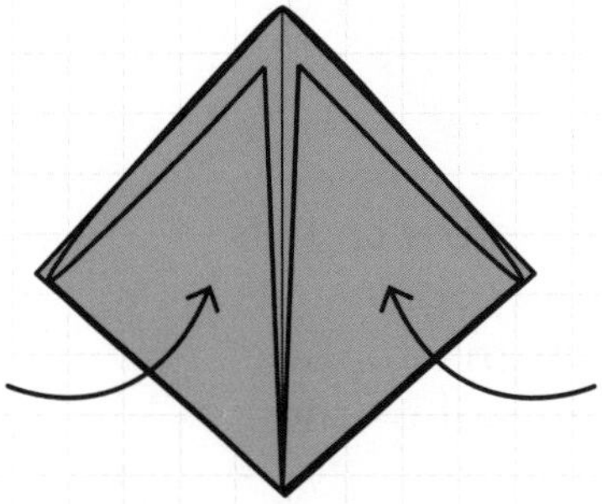

9 Bring the other corners to the top and fold.

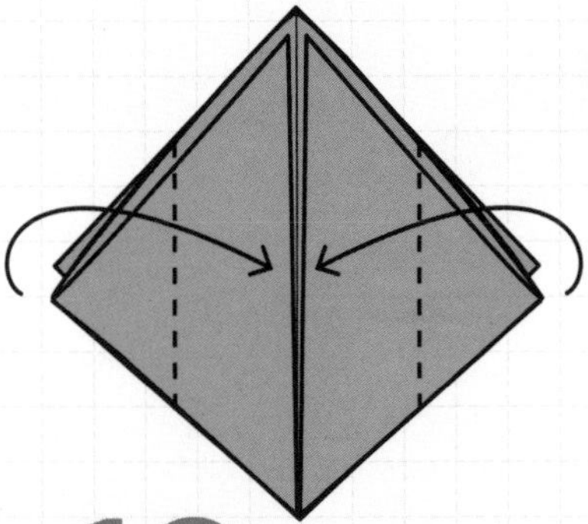

Flip over

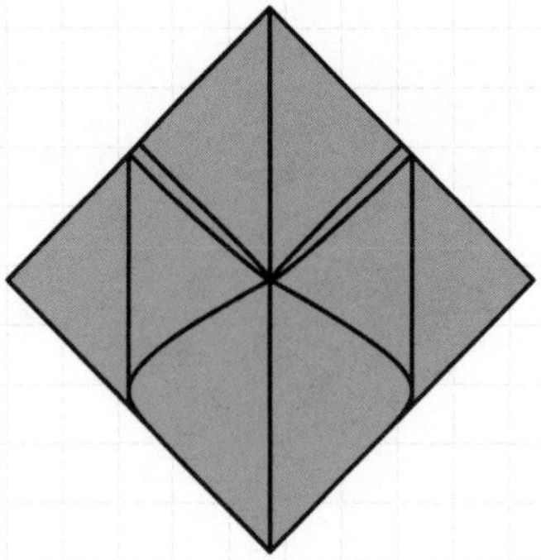

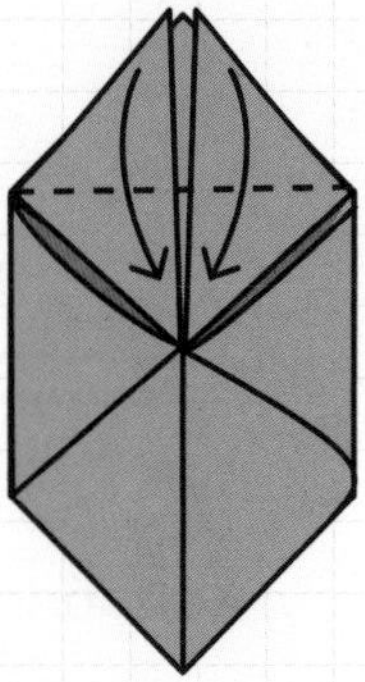

10 Bring the first layer of the side corners to the center and fold.

11 Repeat on the other side.

12 Fold the top corners down.

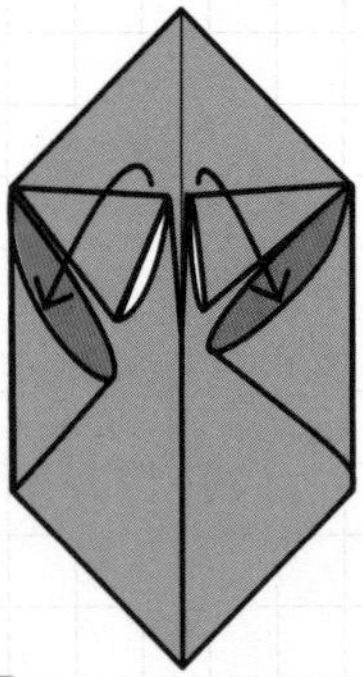

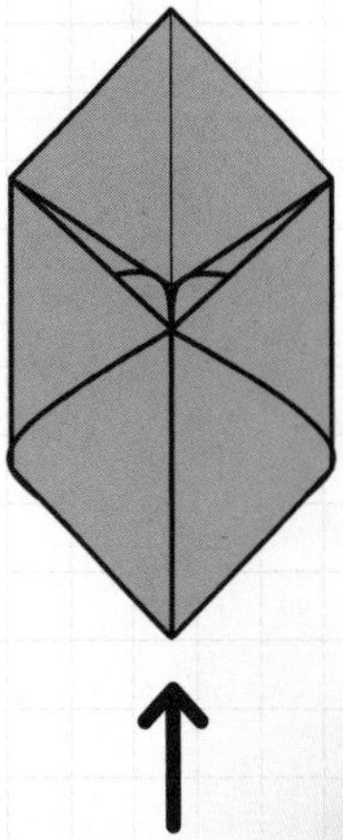

13 Fold the corners over again and tuck them into the pockets. Repeat on the other side.

14 Blow air here to inflate your balloon!

Winged Balloon

We've mostly been looking at shapes with 3, 4, or 5 sides, but a shape can have an infinite number of sides! Shapes with higher numbers of sides have so many crazy names that it would be pretty hard to know all of them—eventually, it's easier to just start describing how many sides they have. The shape made by the whole paper in step 22 has 10 sides, and you can amaze your friends by telling them that a 10-sided shape is called a **decagon.**

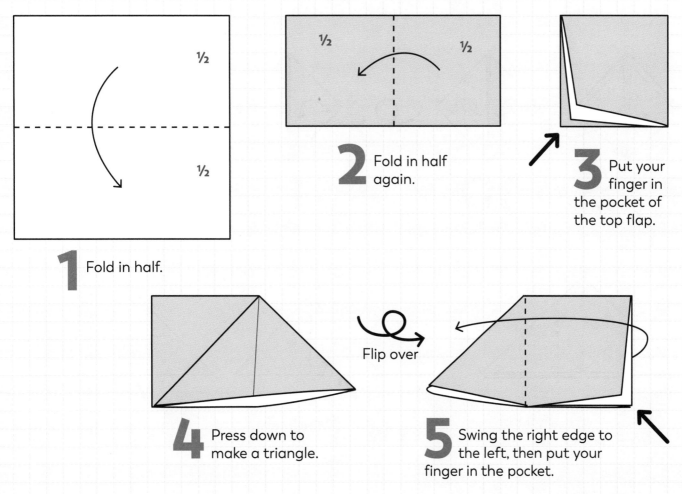

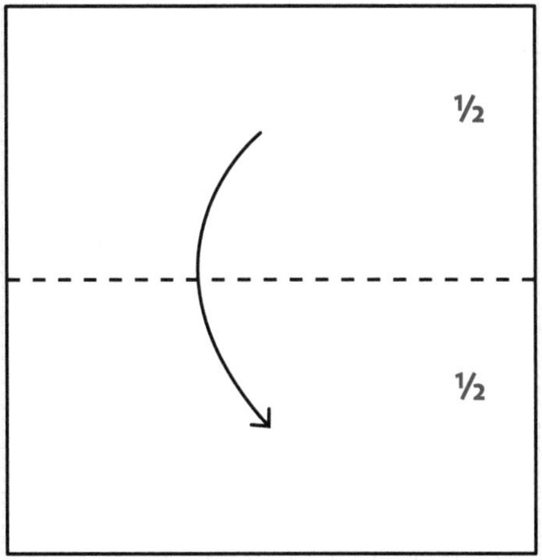

1 Fold in half.

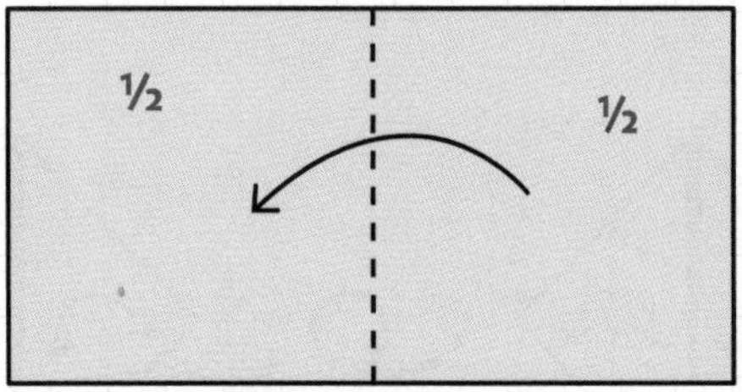

2 Fold in half again.

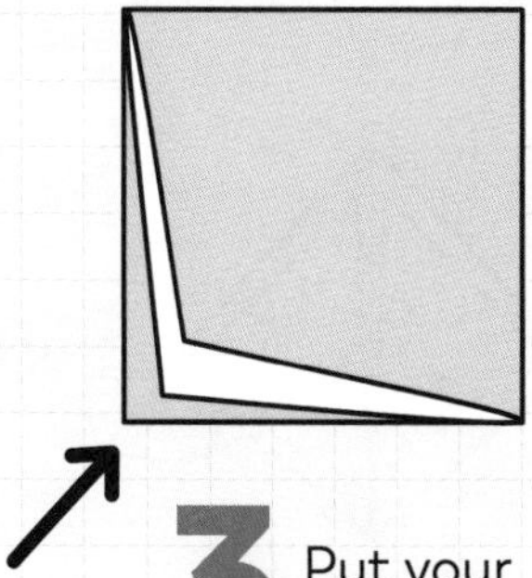

3 Put your finger in the pocket of the top flap.

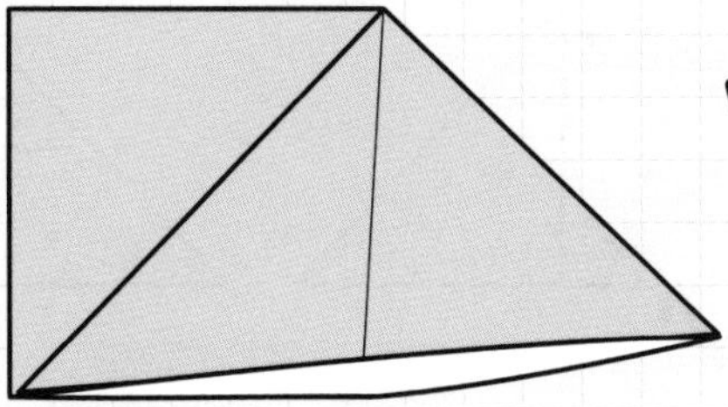

4 Press down to make a triangle.

Flip over

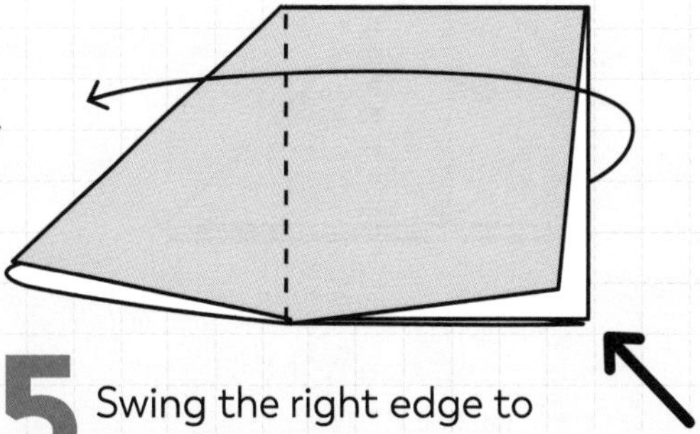

5 Swing the right edge to the left, then put your finger in the pocket.

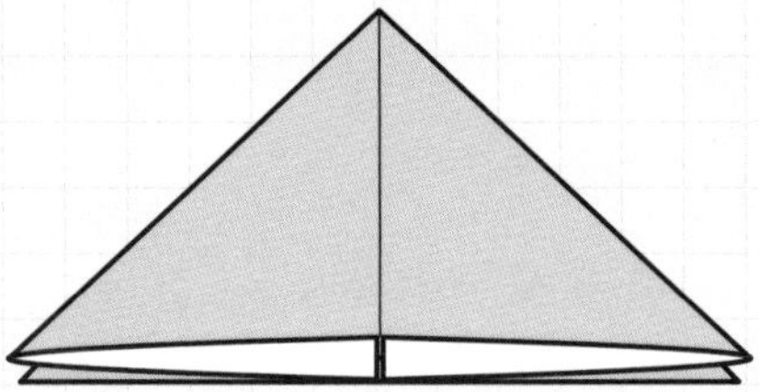

6 Press down to make another triangle.

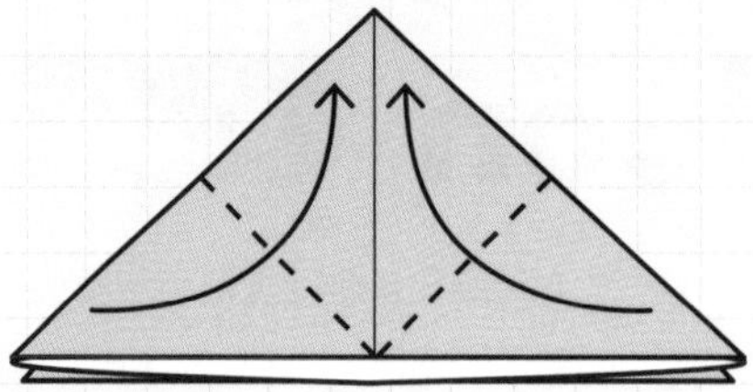

7 Bring the bottom corners of the top layer to the top point and fold.

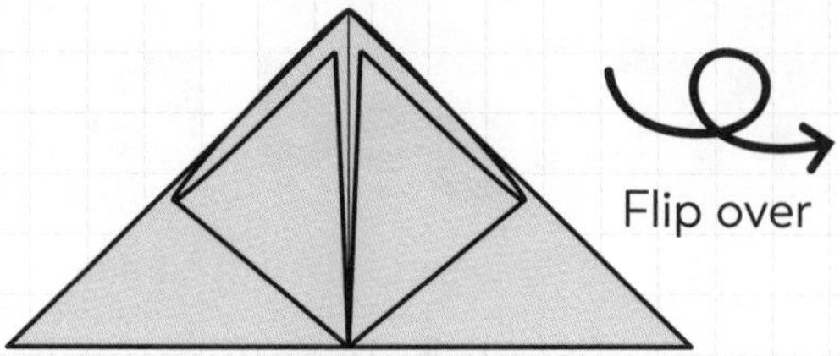

8

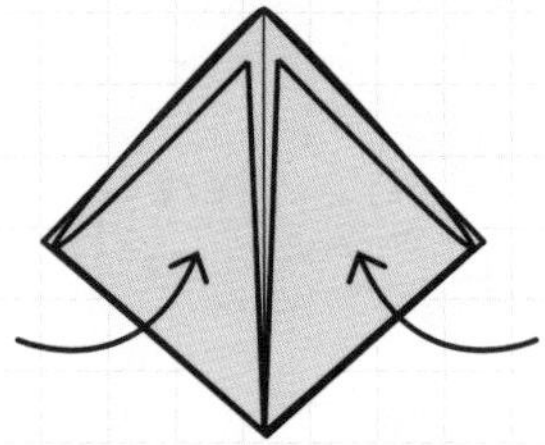

9 Bring the other corners to the top point and fold.

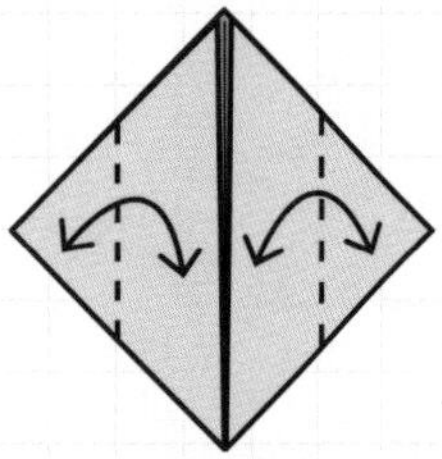

10 Fold and unfold.

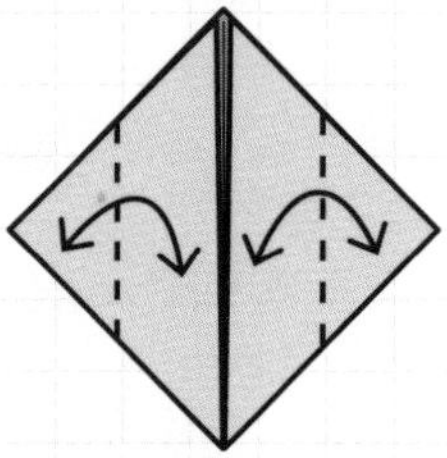

11 Fold and unfold on the other side.

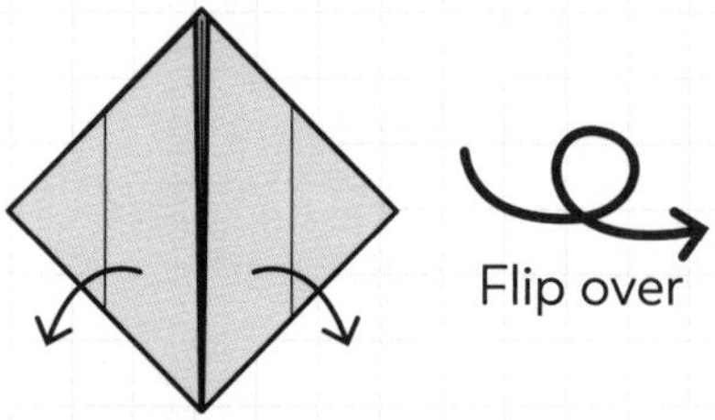

12 Unfold the top flaps down. Repeat on the other side.

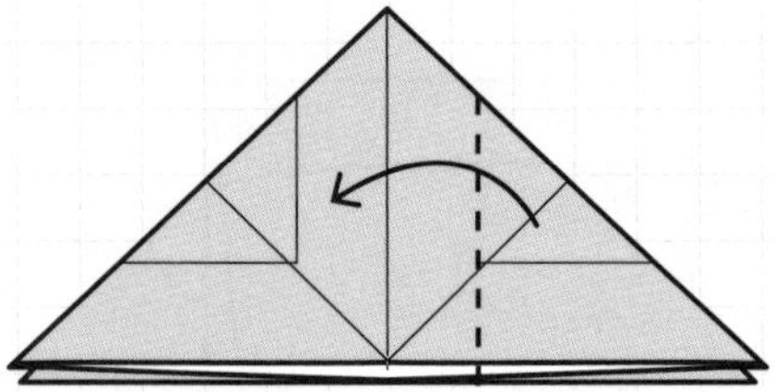

13 Fold the right point of the top layer to the left.

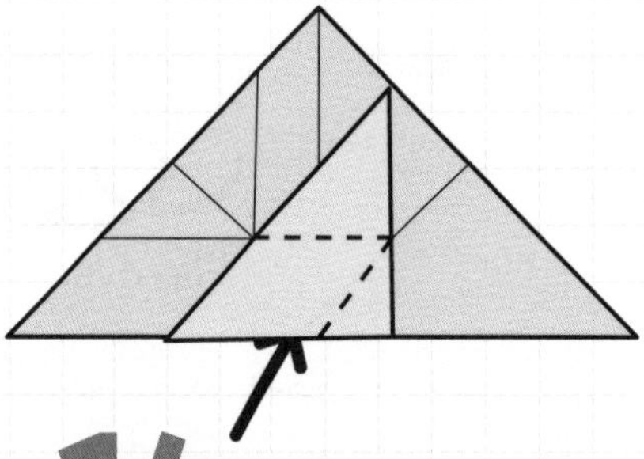

14 Put your finger under the flap.

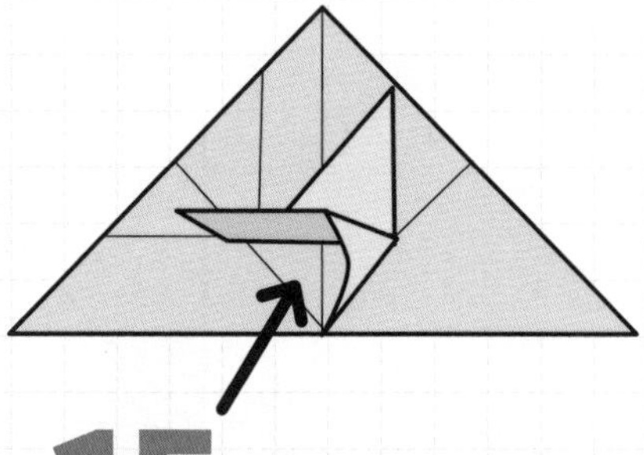

15 Lift and press down.

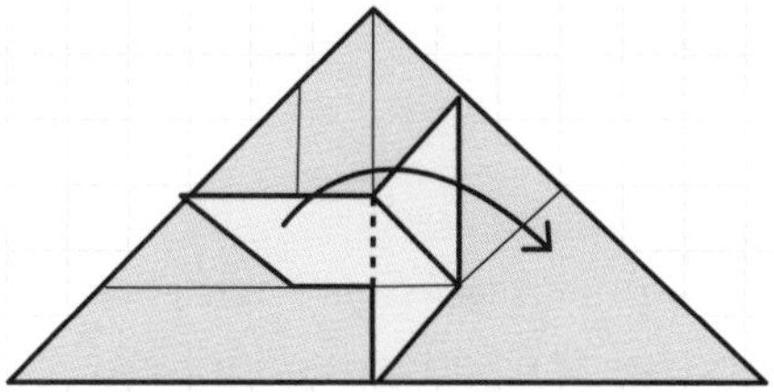

16 Fold the left point to the right.

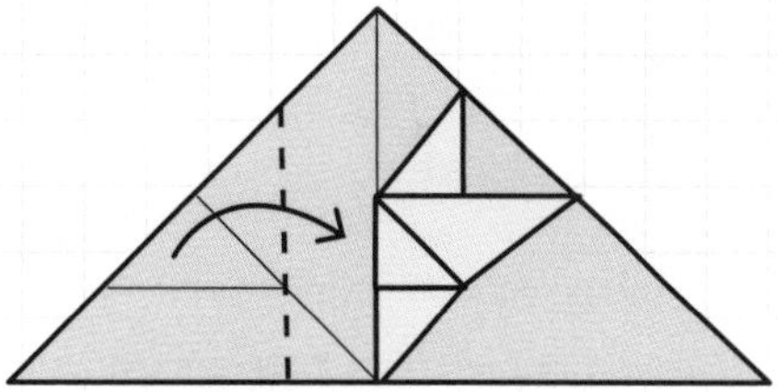

17 Fold the left point to the right.

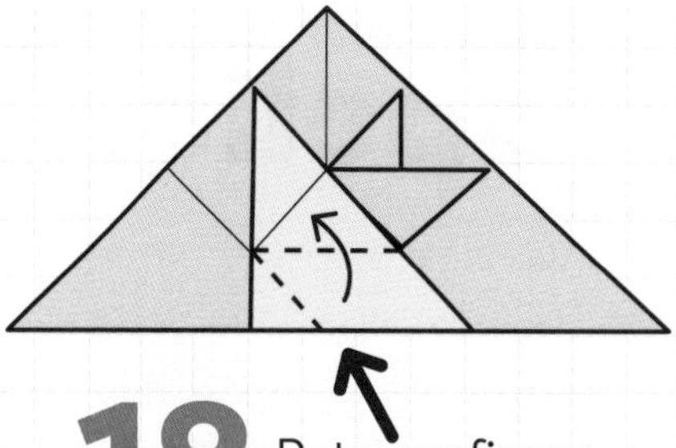

18 Put your finger under the flap, then lift and press down.

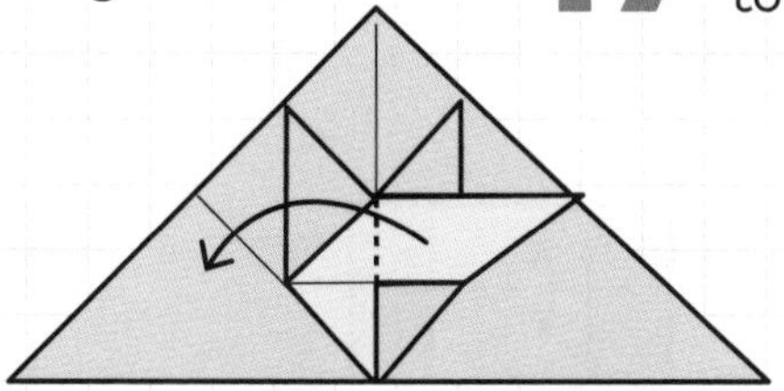

19 Fold the top right flap to the left.

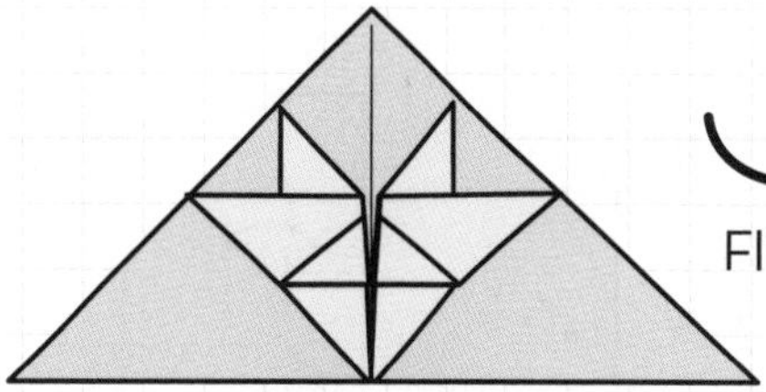

20

Flip over

Find the Math!

This picture shows step 22 of making a Winged Balloon. How many of the triangles outlined in red would it take to fill up the whole area outlined in blue?

ANSWER ON P. 102

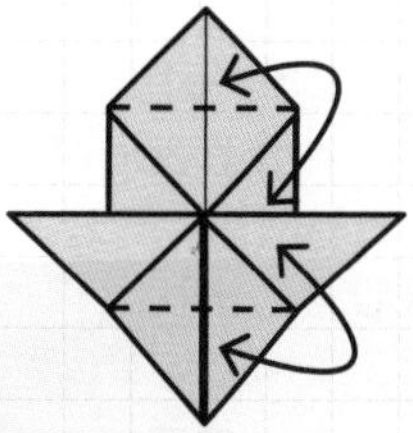

21 Repeat steps 13 through 17 on the other side. Then, fold and unfold.

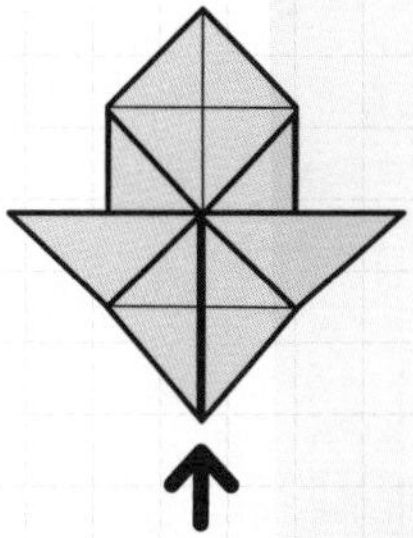

22 Blow air here to inflate your balloon!

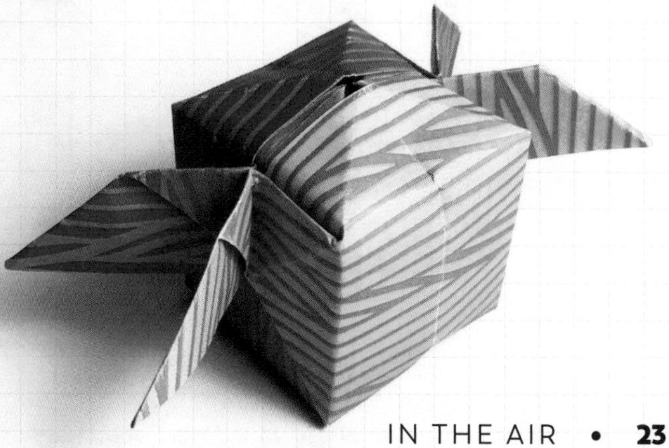

Propeller

When we turn a shape around (like when we're changing which way a piece of origami is facing to do the next step) we have to know which direction to turn it. We often use the idea of a clock's hands spinning to talk about this. Turning a shape **clockwise** means moving it in the same direction as a clock's hands go (or spinning it to the right), and turning it **counterclockwise** means moving it in the opposite direction (or spinning it to the left). When you finish your Propeller, see if you can spin it both ways!

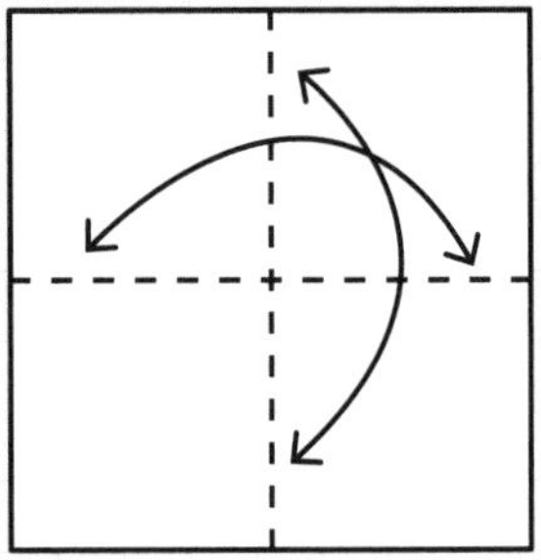

1 Fold and unfold.

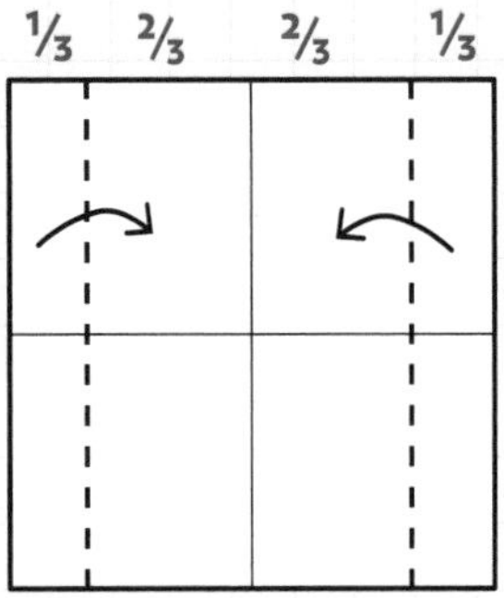

2 Fold the left and right edges one third of the way toward the center.

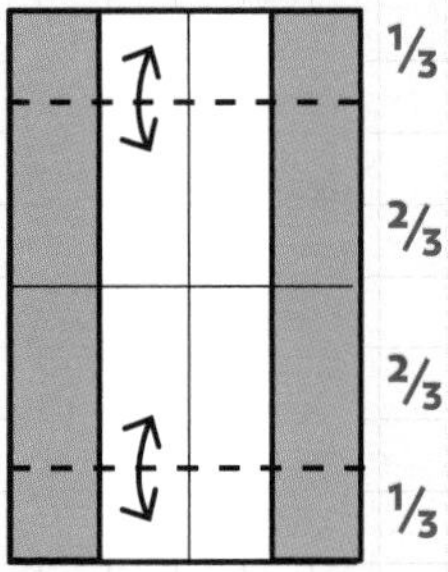

3 Fold one third of the way toward the center and unfold.

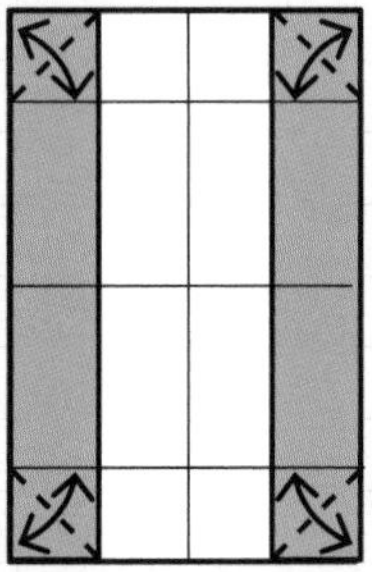

4 Fold and unfold the corners.

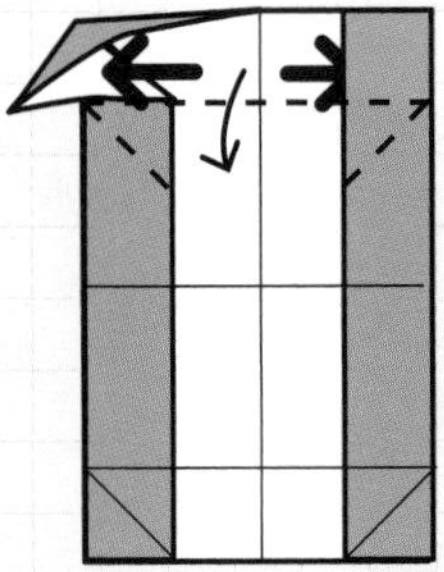

5 Pull the flaps open at the top, then put your finger in the corner pockets and squash flat.

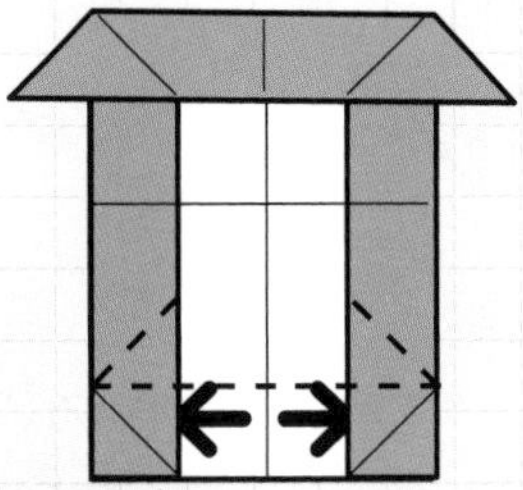

6 Repeat step 5 on the bottom.

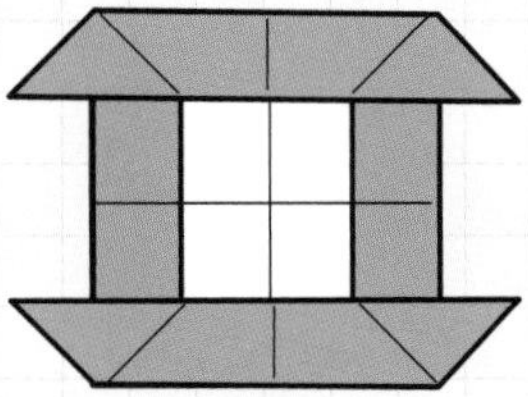

7

Flip over

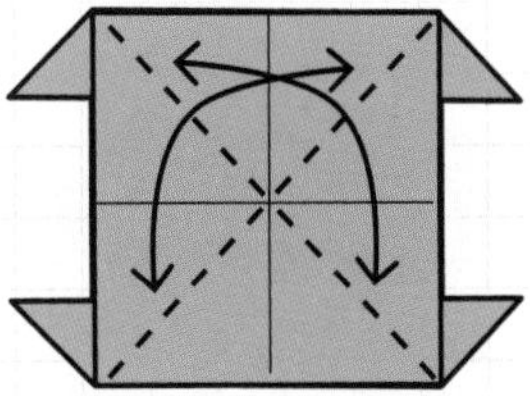

8 Fold and unfold diagonally.

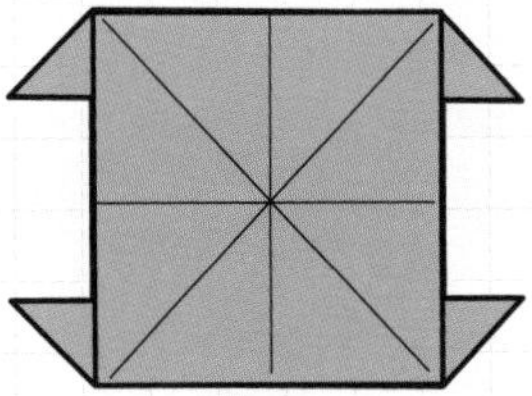

9

Flip over

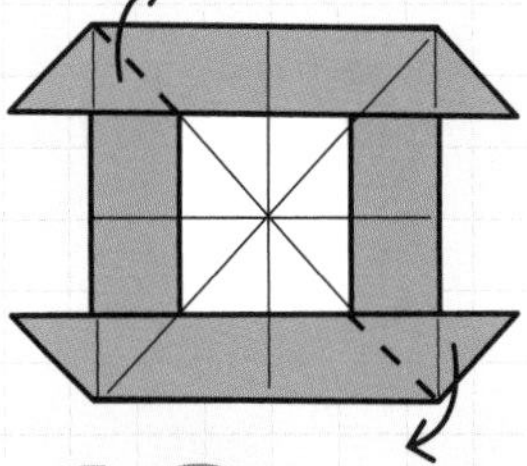

10 Fold the top left and bottom right corners out.

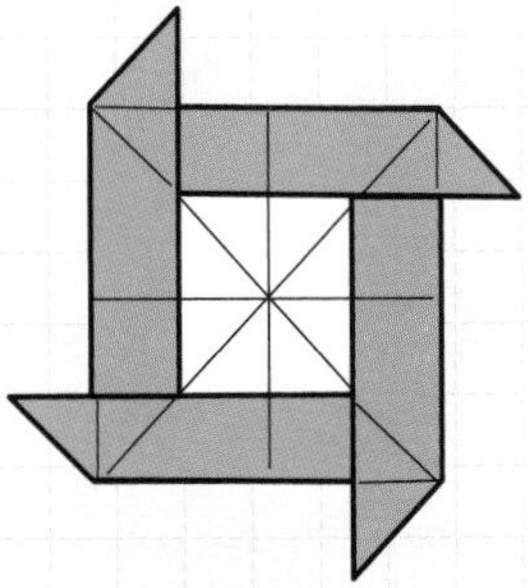

11 Press the sides in.

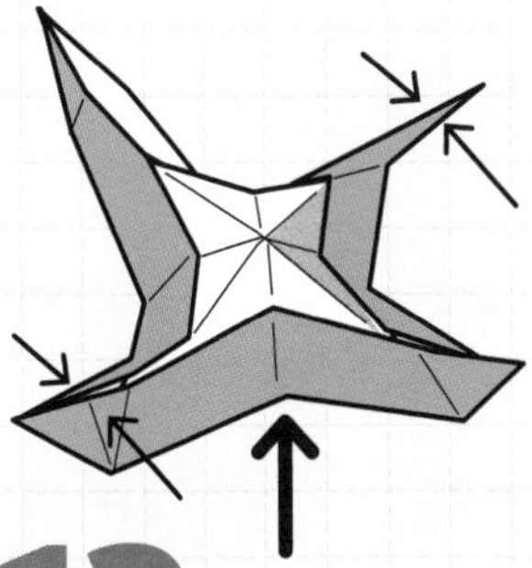

12 Push the middle up while pushing the wings to the side.

Find the Math!

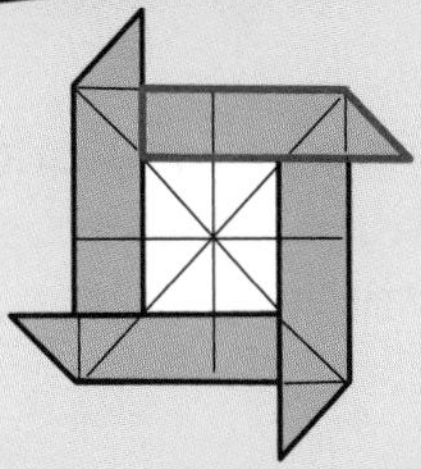

This picture shows step 11 of making a Propeller. How many other shapes can you find that are the same shape as the one outlined in red? It doesn't matter what direction they're facing as long as they're the same shape.

ANSWER ON P. 102

13 Balance the Propeller on top of your finger, then blow air at it to make it spin around and around!

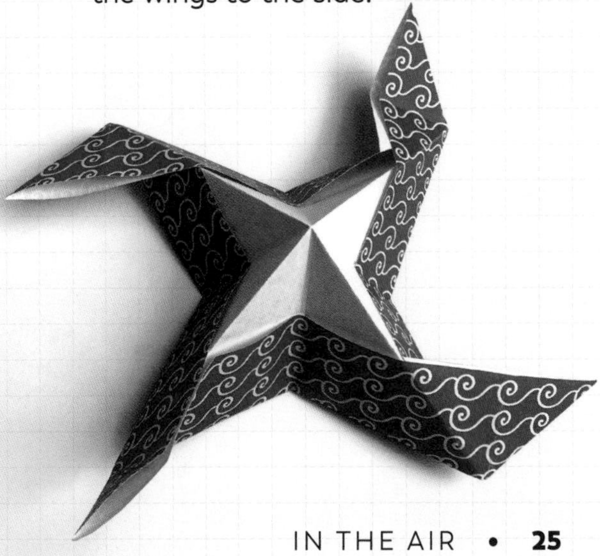

Catapult

If you loaded up the Catapult with a flat piece of paper, it probably wouldn't fly very far. So we need to introduce our second 3D shape—the **sphere.** Spheres are special 3D shapes that don't have any flat faces. Instead, they're round all over. They're great for throwing and launching, as you'll see when you let the Catapult loose.

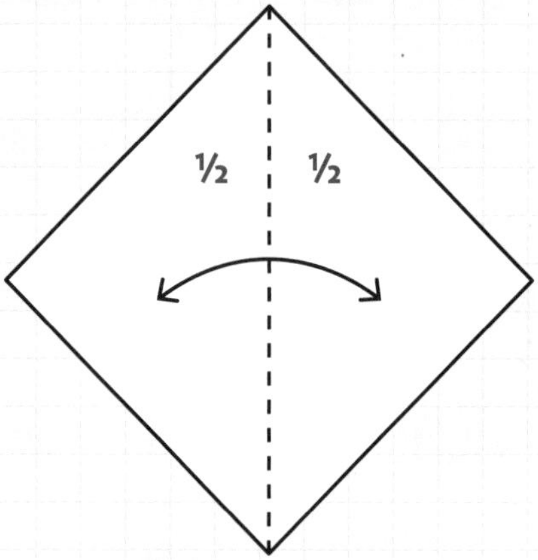

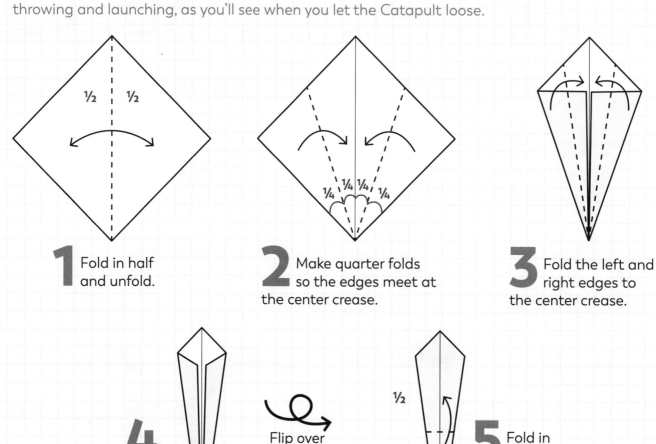

1 Fold in half and unfold.

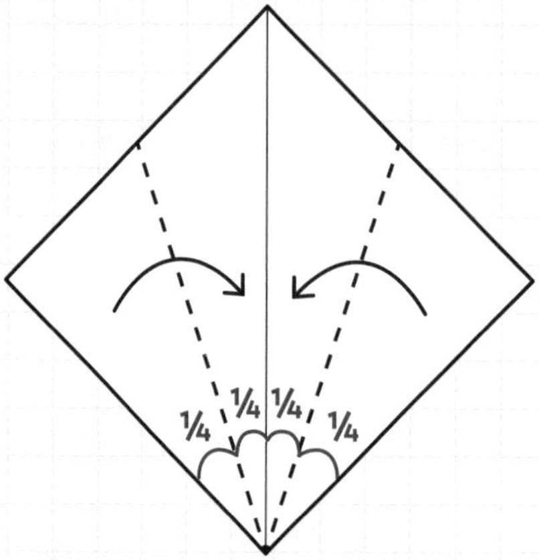

2 Make quarter folds so the edges meet at the center crease.

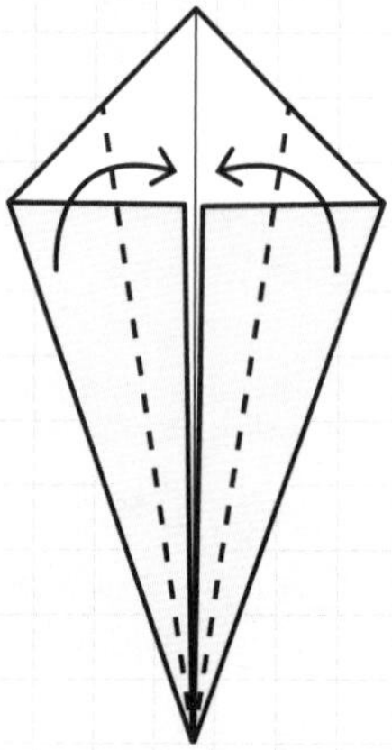

3 Fold the left and right edges to the center crease.

4

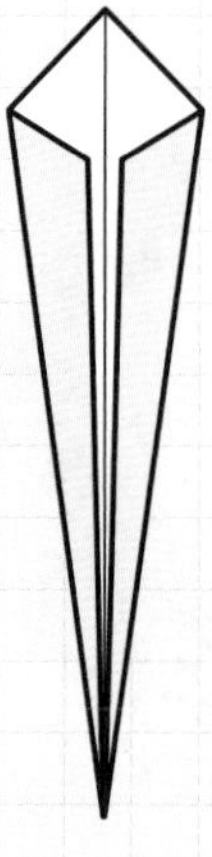

Flip over

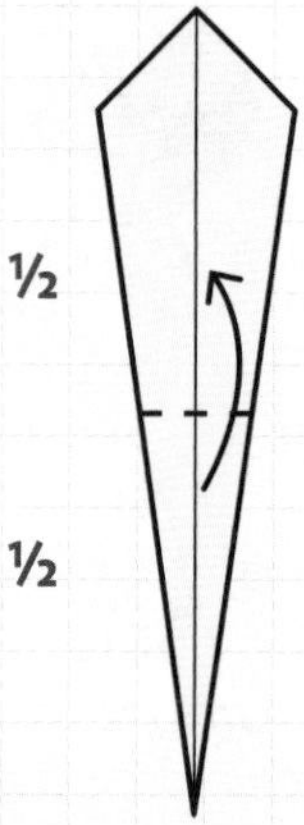

5 Fold in half.

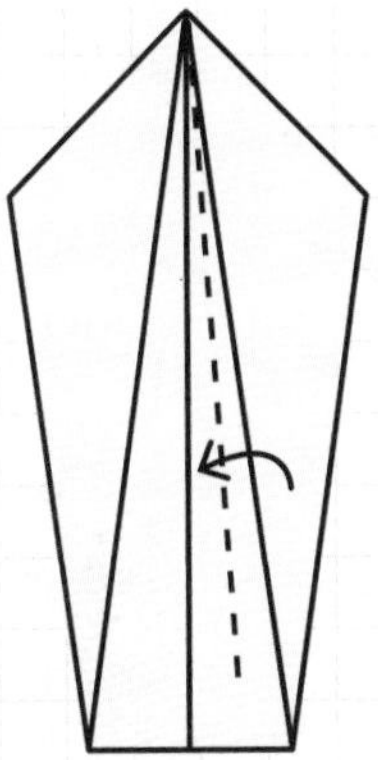

6 Lift the right edge of the flap and fold in half toward the center.

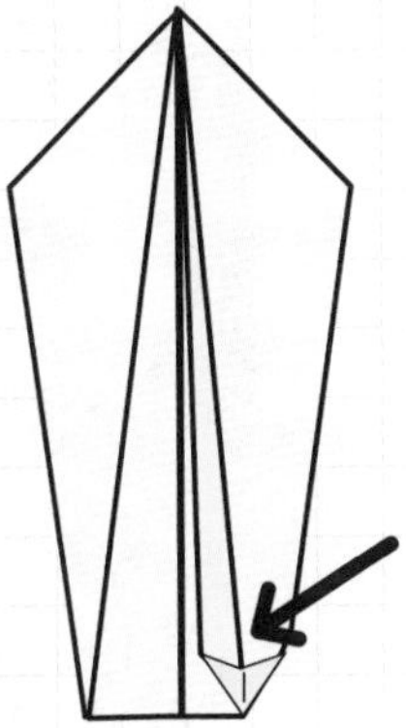

7 Put your finger in the pocket and press down to make a triangle.

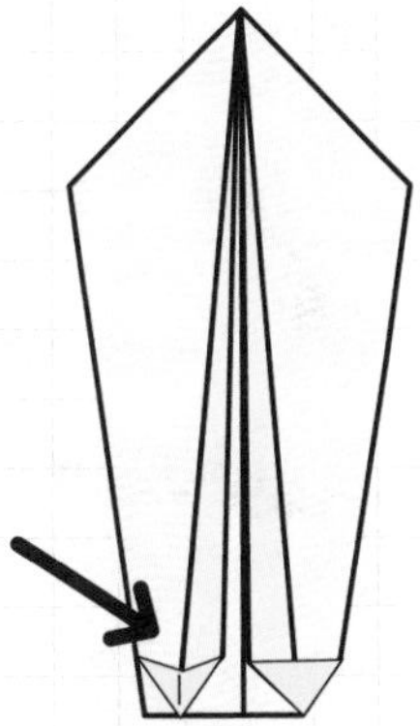

8 Repeat on the other side.

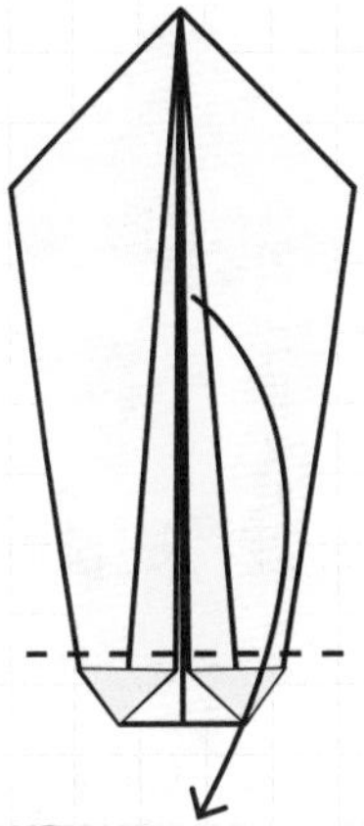

9 Fold the tip down.

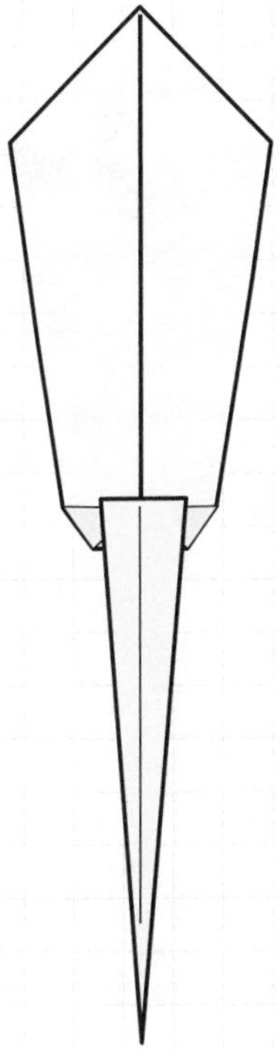

Find the Math!

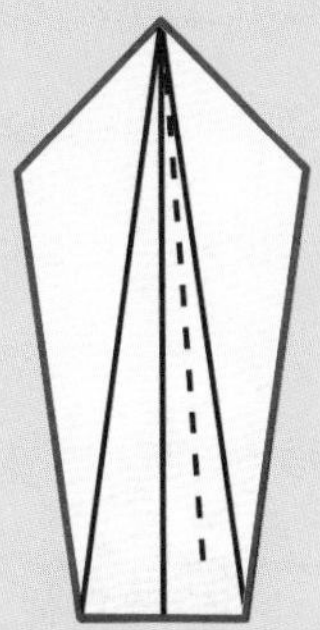

This picture shows step 6 of making a Catapult. What's the name of the shape outlined in red?

ANSWER ON P. 103

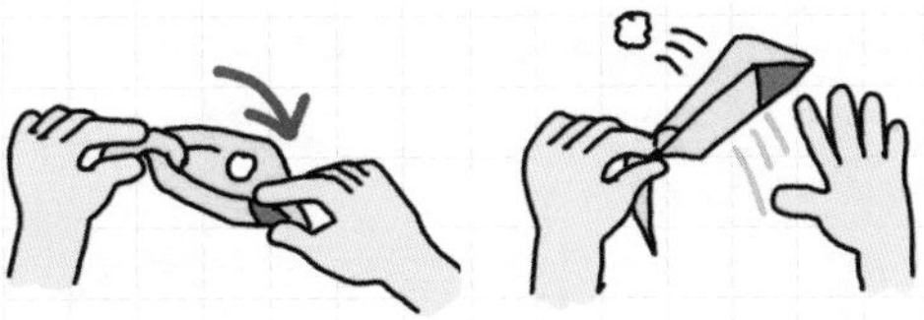

10 Holding the thin, pointed handle, load the wide launcher with a crumpled paper ball. Raise the catapult up in front of you and use your other hand to pull the launcher back. Then, let go!

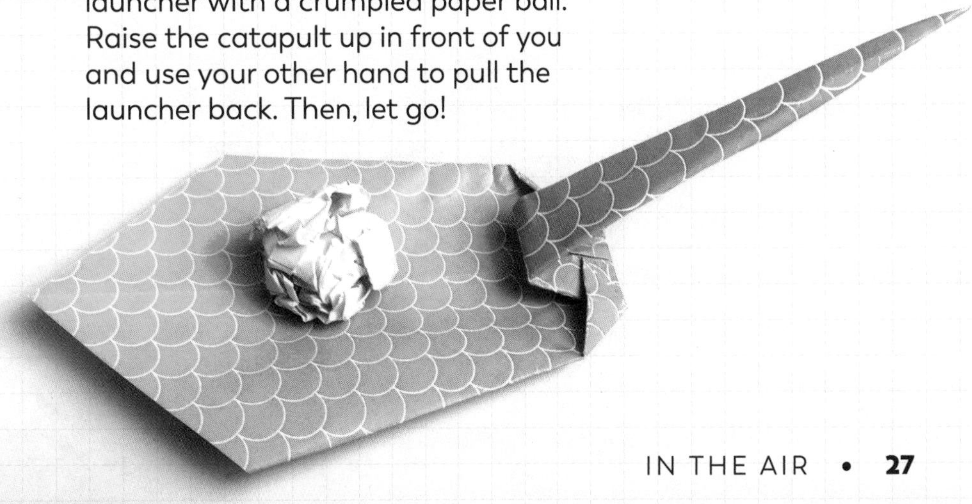

Make It Move

These paper creations come to life! Use fractions and angles to make flapping wings and yapping mouths.

45°
90°

Flapping Bird

Remember how symmetry can help things fly? Almost every animal's body has a special kind called **bilateral symmetry,** which means if you draw an imaginary line dividing them straight down the center, they're the same on both sides. Just like this bird—from the point of its beak to the tip of its tail, it's the same shape on the left as it is on the right.

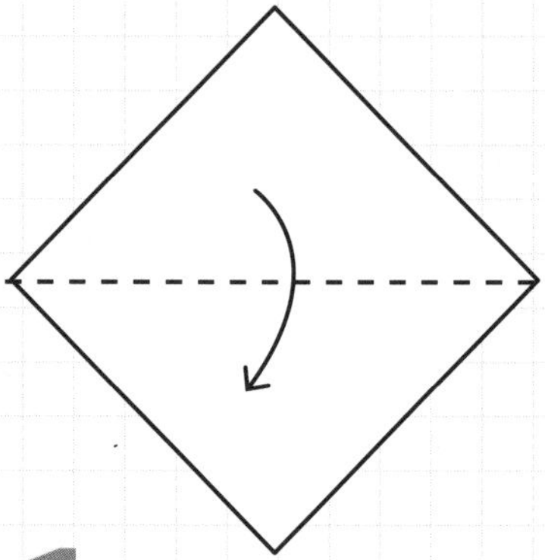

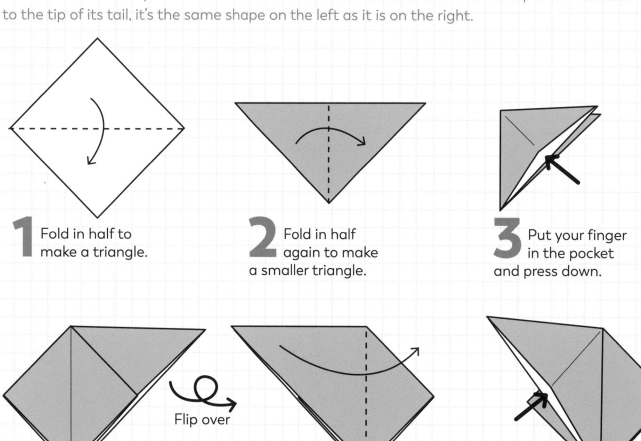

1 Fold in half to make a triangle.

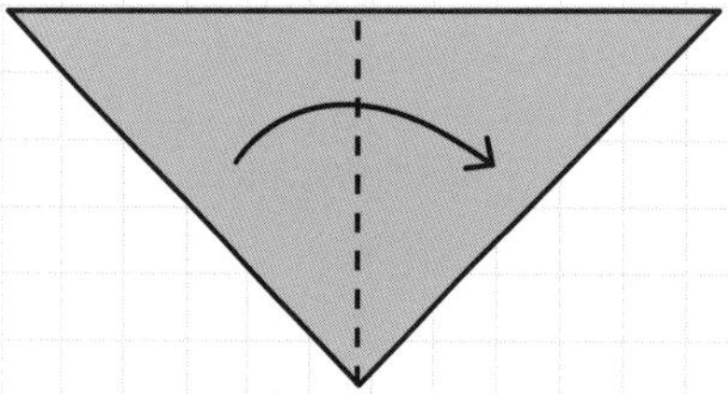

2 Fold in half again to make a smaller triangle.

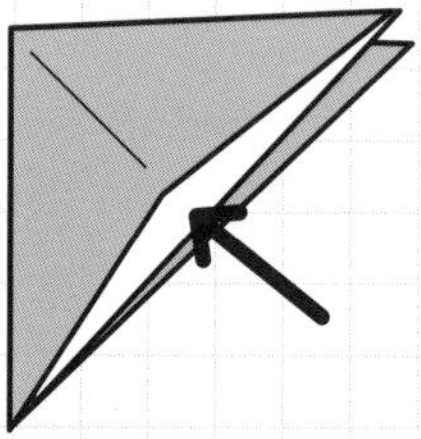

3 Put your finger in the pocket and press down.

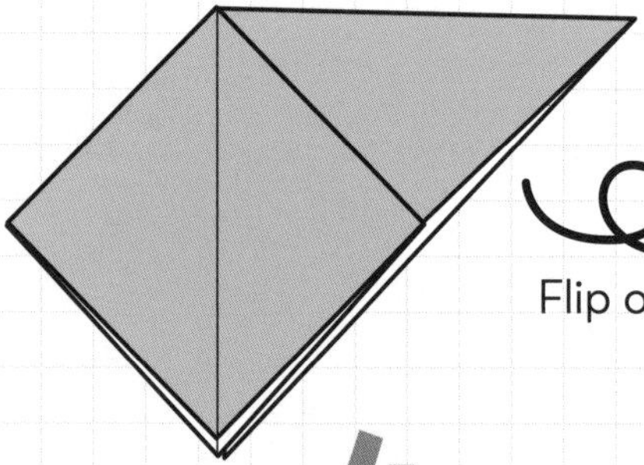

Flip over

4

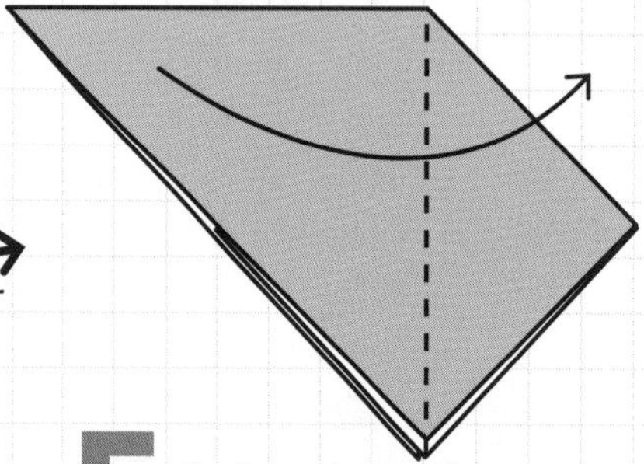

5 Swing the point to the opposite side, then back to the center.

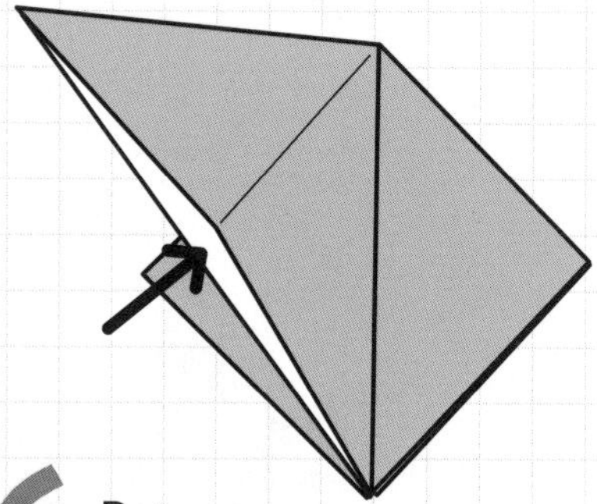

6 Put your finger in the other pocket and press down.

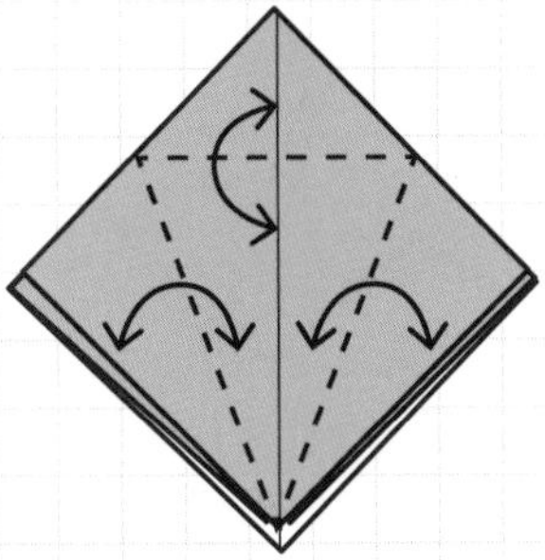

7 Fold and unfold.

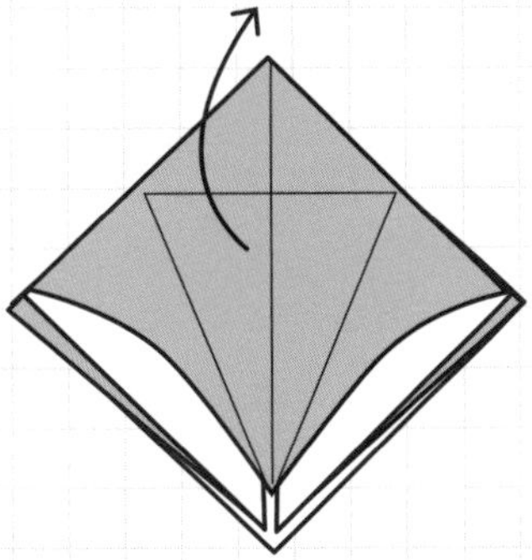

8 Open the top layer and fold up using the creases you just made.

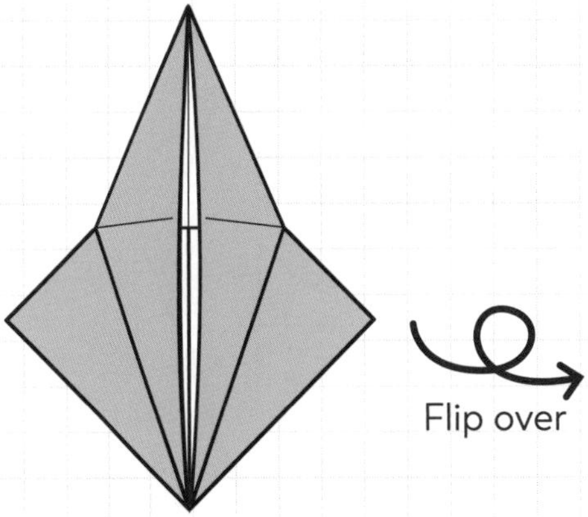

9 Press down.

Find the Math!

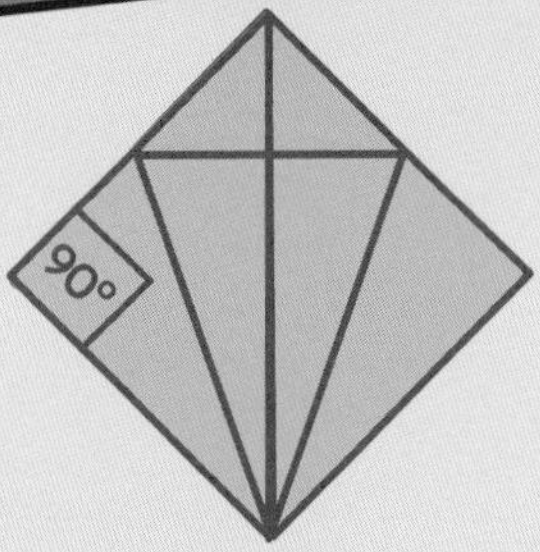

This picture shows step 7 of making a Flapping Bird. All of the triangles shown here are the same kind, and they all have a 90° angle in one corner. What type of triangle are they?

ANSWER ON P. 103

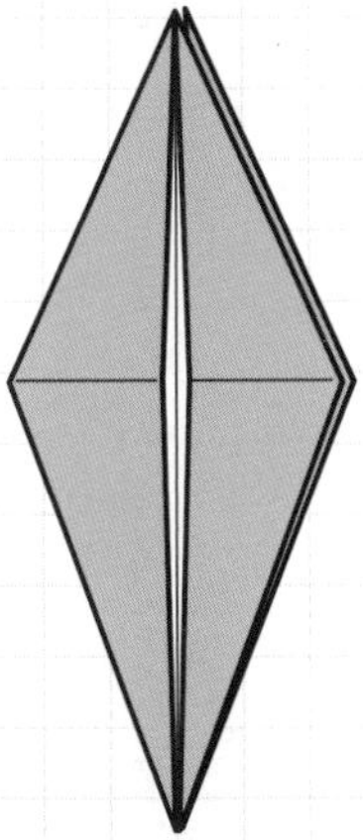

10 Repeat steps 8 and 9 on the other side.

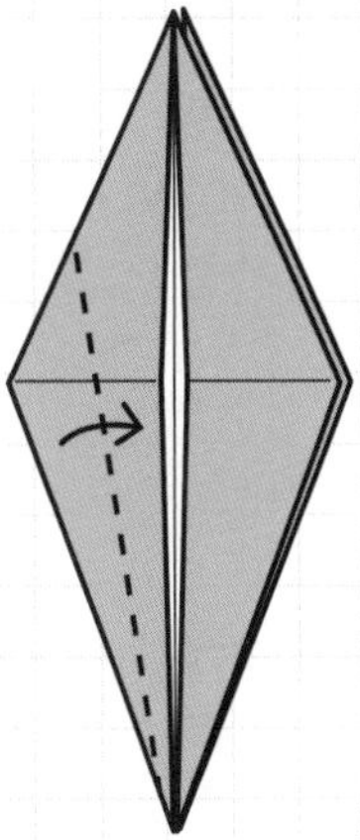

11 Fold the left flap in half towards the center. Repeat on the other side.

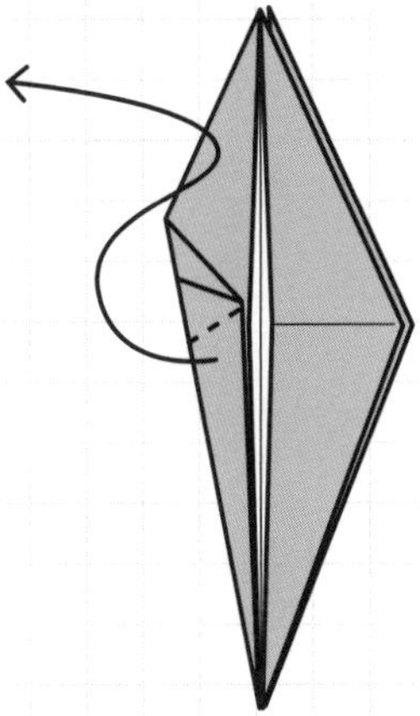

12 Fold the bottom left section inside and away from the center.

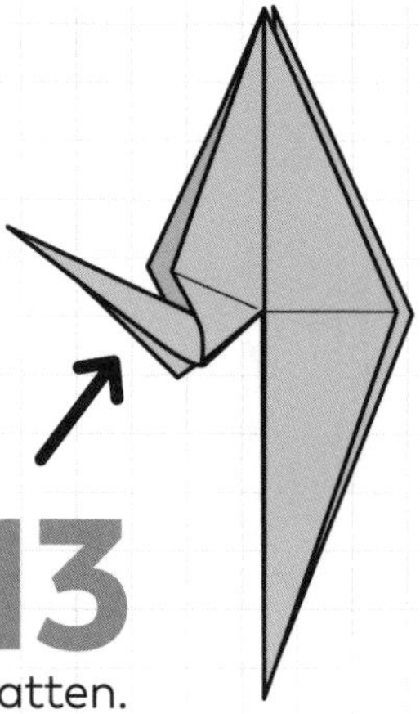

13 Flatten.

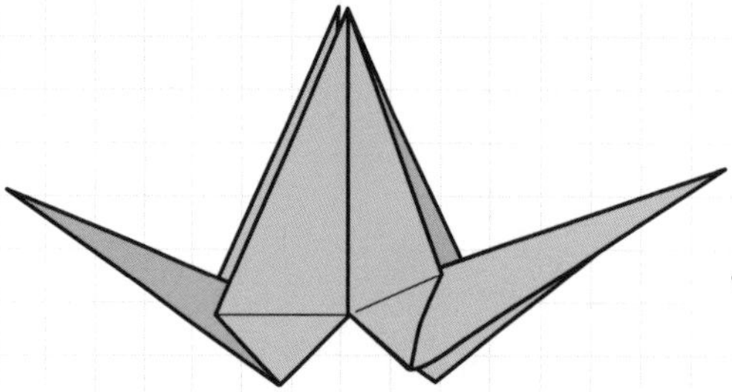

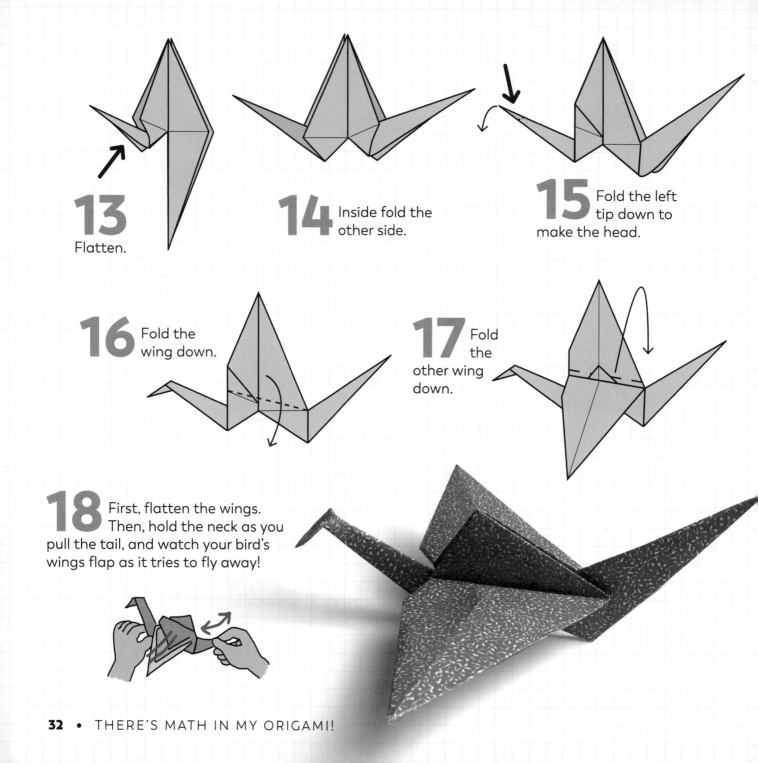

14 Inside fold the other side.

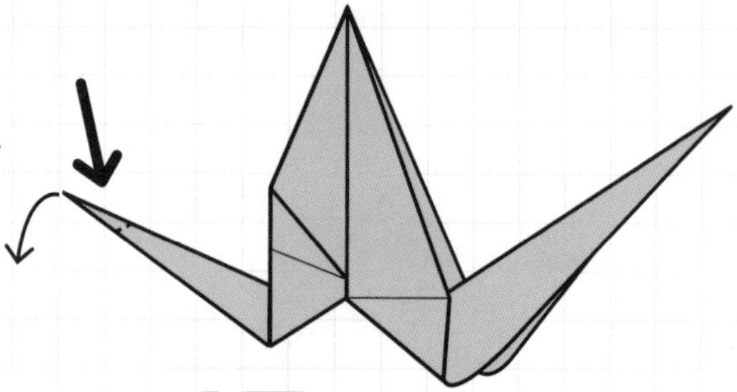

15 Fold the left tip down to make the head.

16 Fold the wing down.

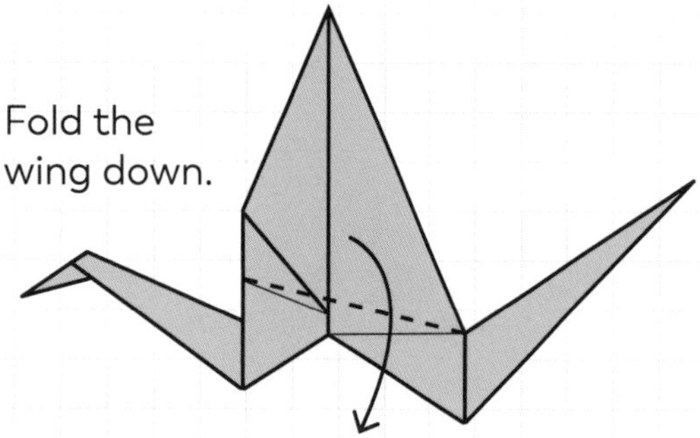

17 Fold the other wing down.

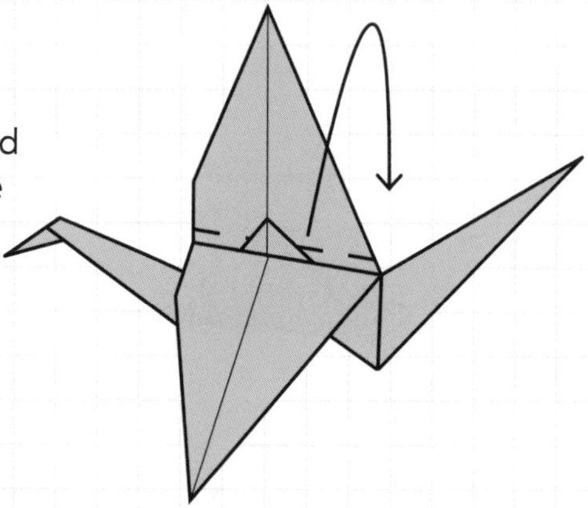

18 First, flatten the wings. Then, hold the neck as you pull the tail, and watch your bird's wings flap as it tries to fly away!

Fluttering Bird

Just like this piece of paper transforms into a bird that can fly, shapes can be transformed to change how they look. One kind of **transformation** is called **dilation**—meaning the shape is resized to get bigger or smaller. Steps 2 and 3 show how this works. The square in step 2 is made of 2 big triangles. The triangle in step 3 is also made of 2 triangles that are the same shape as, but smaller than, the ones in step 2. That's dilation!

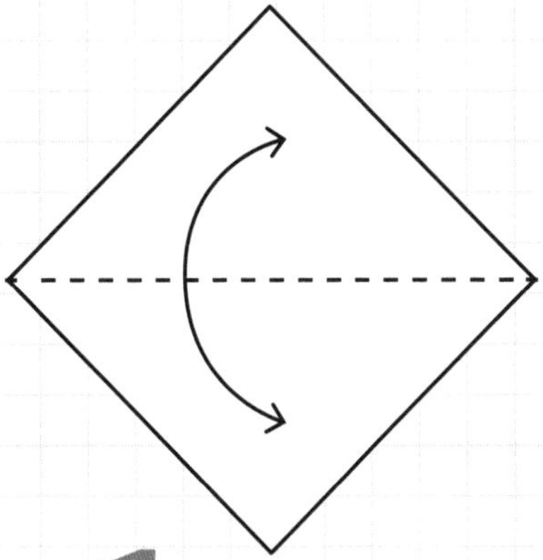

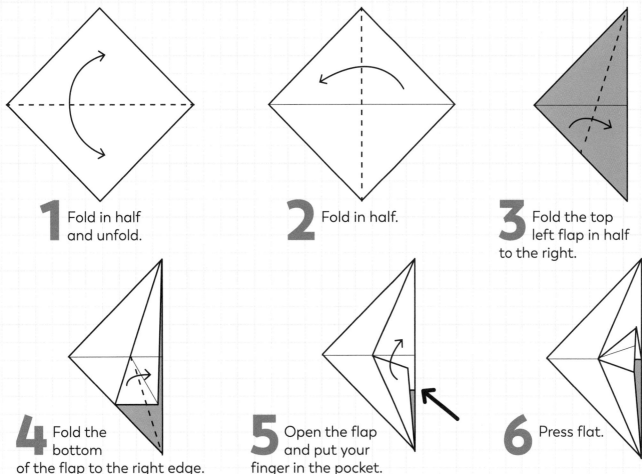

1 Fold in half and unfold.

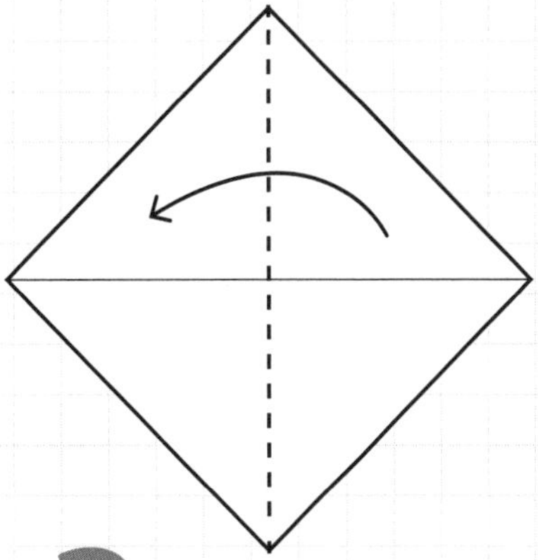

2 Fold in half.

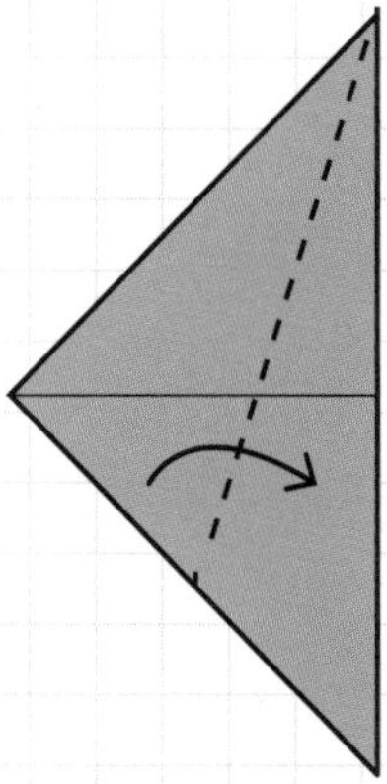

3 Fold the top left flap in half to the right.

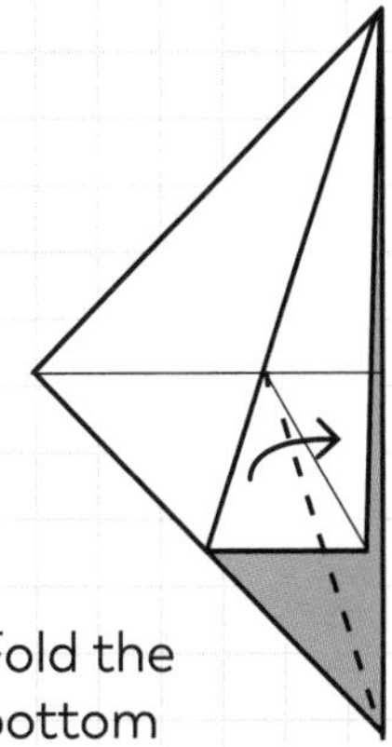

4 Fold the bottom of the flap to the right edge.

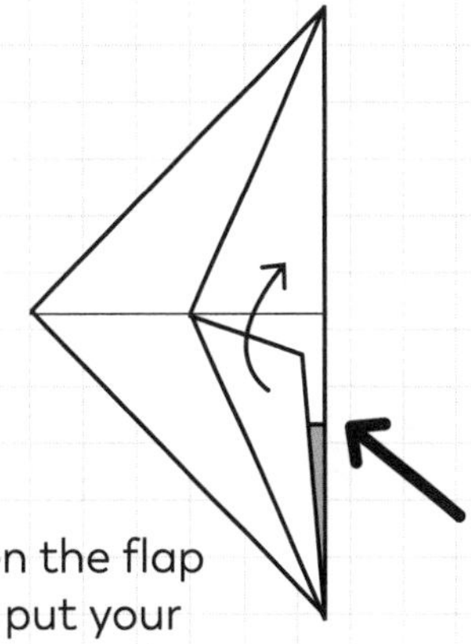

5 Open the flap and put your finger in the pocket.

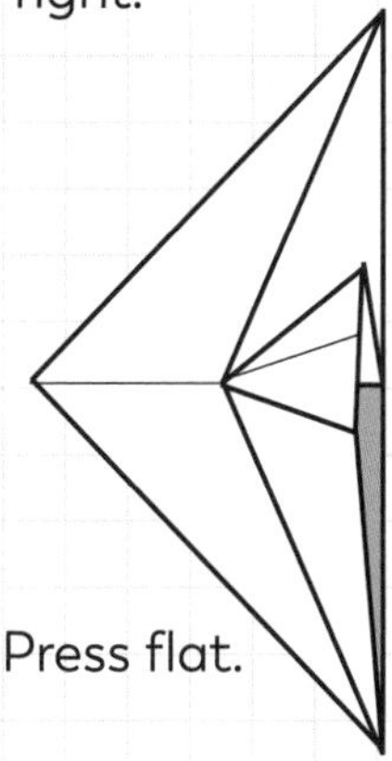

6 Press flat.

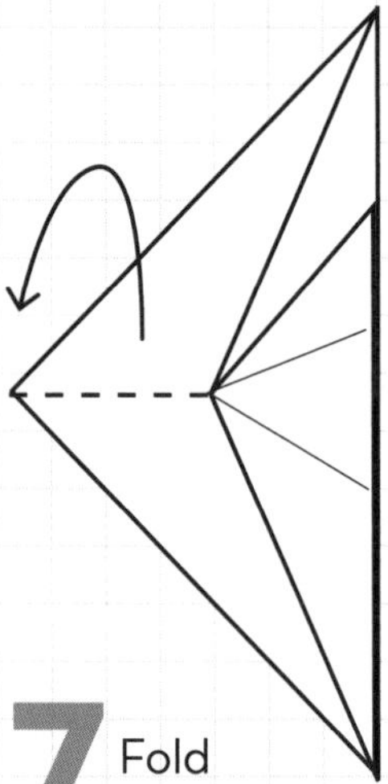

7 Fold back.

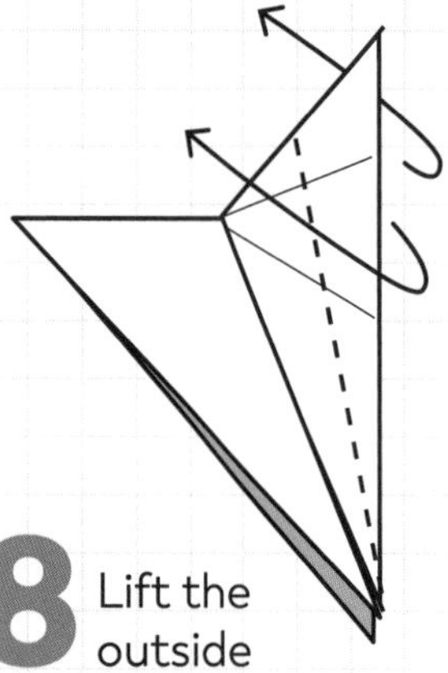

8 Lift the outside of the flap and fold it inside out on both sides.

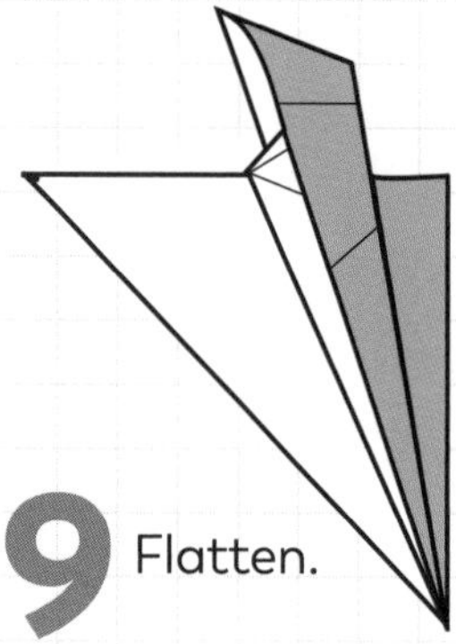

9 Flatten.

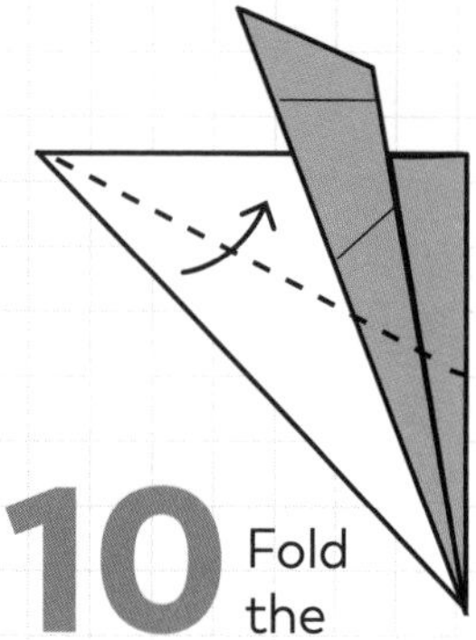

10 Fold the top layer up.

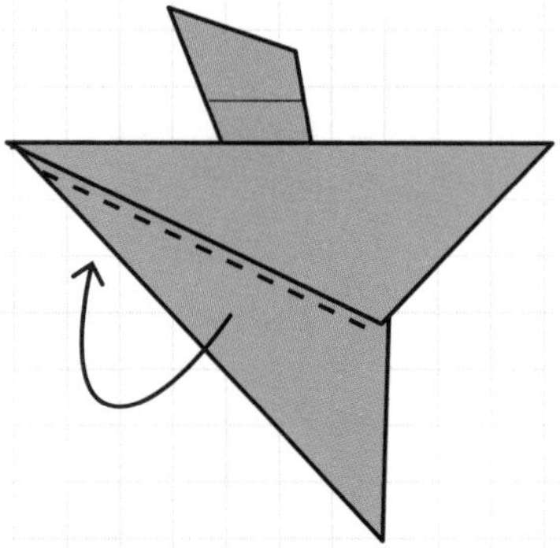

11 Fold the lower wing behind and up.

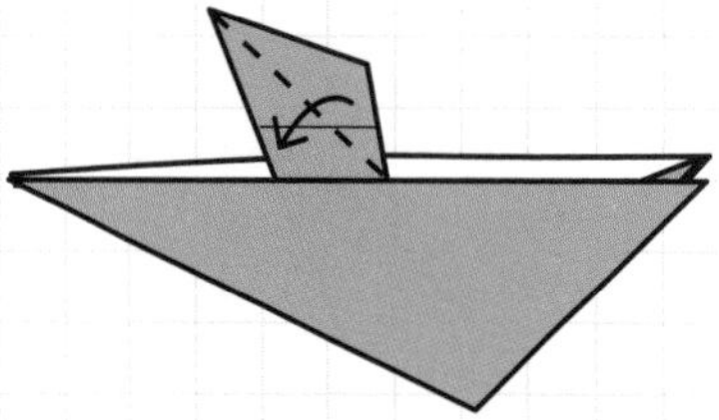

12 Fold the right corner down.

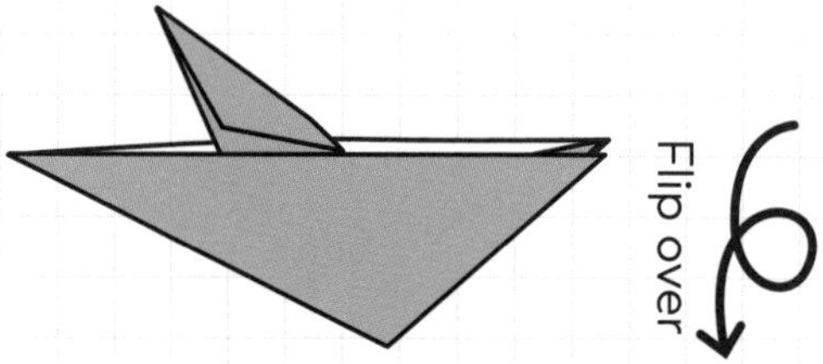

13 Turn upside down.

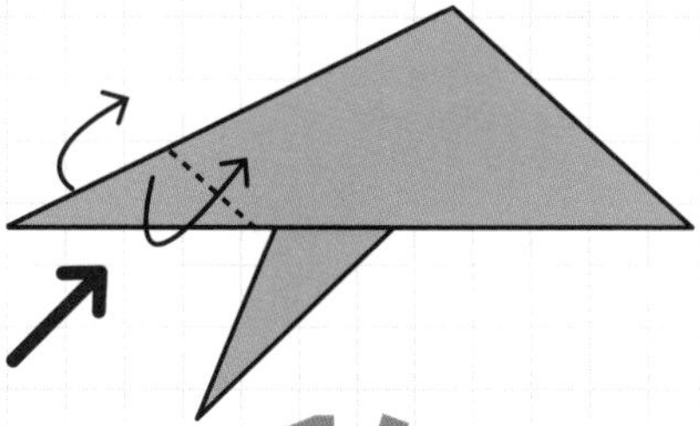

14 Fold up and to the right.

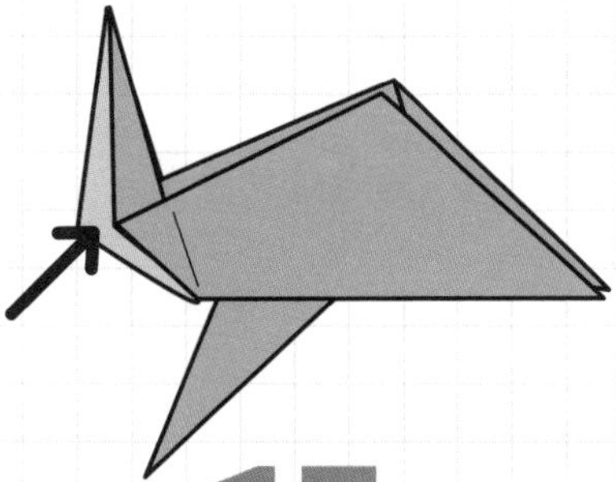

15 Fold in.

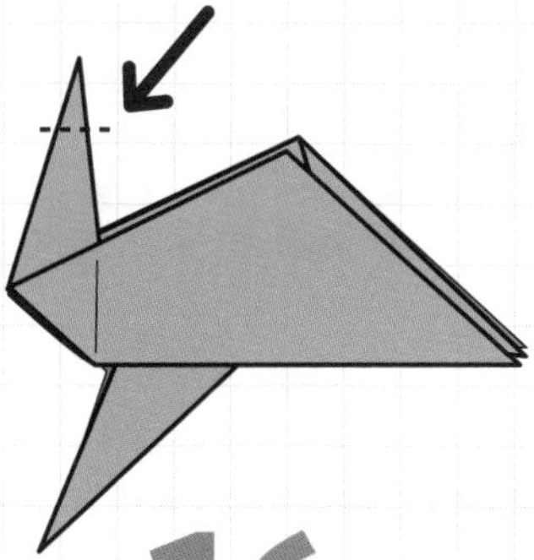

16 Fold down and back.

17 Fold in.

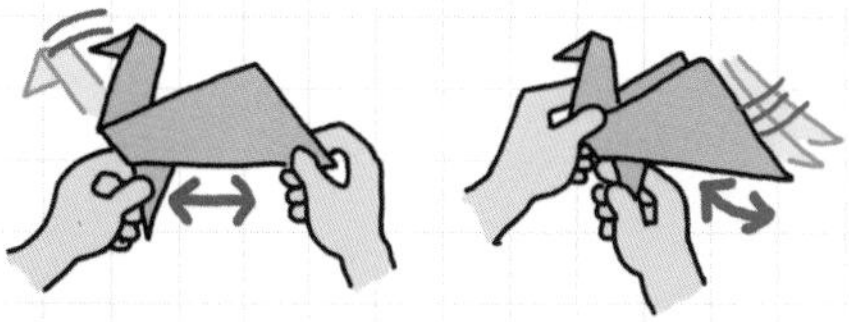

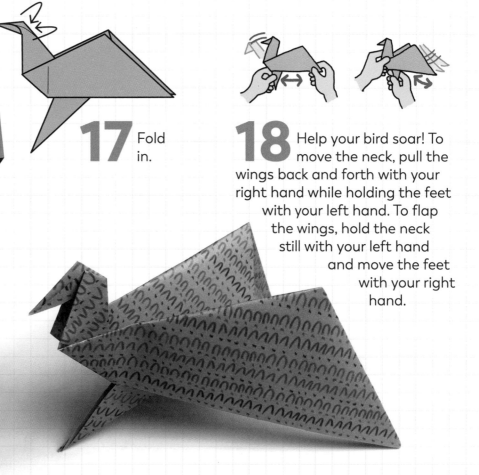

18 Help your bird soar! To move the neck, pull the wings back and forth with your right hand while holding the feet with your left hand. To flap the wings, hold the neck still with your left hand and move the feet with your right hand.

Find the Math!

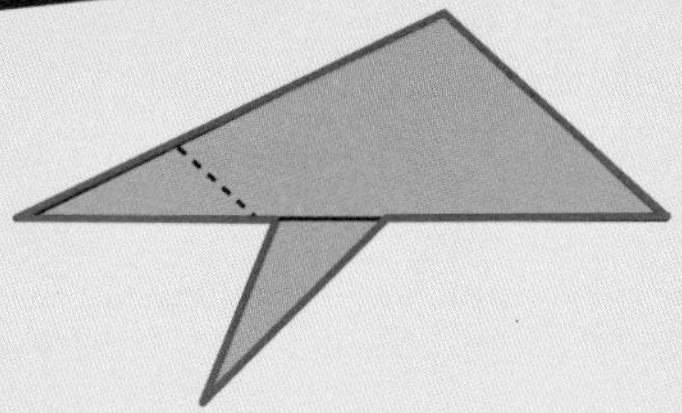

This picture shows step 14 of making a Fluttering Bird. Count the number of sides on the shape outlined in red. What do we call a shape with this many sides?

1. Hexagon
2. Octagon

ANSWER ON P. 103

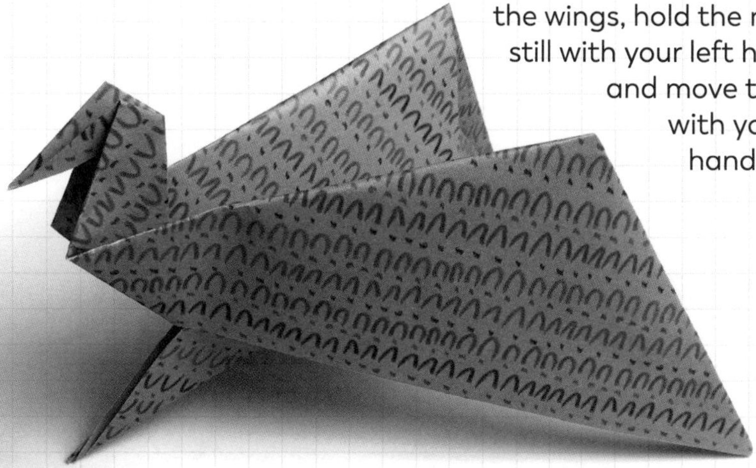

Roaring Dinosaur ★★★★★

This dinosaur has another talent besides roaring—it can teach us a new idea about how lines are related to each other. Take a look at step 5. In the middle of the triangle, the dotted line meets the solid line in a cross, making 90° angles on each side. When one line connects with another to create this shape, we call them **perpendicular** lines. Or, as the dino might say, PERPENDICULARRRR!

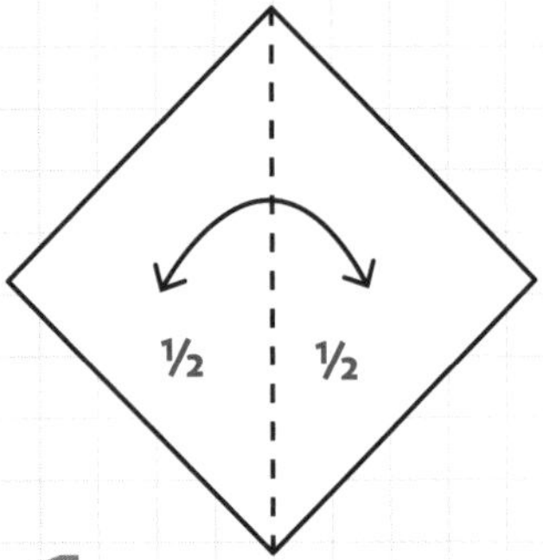

1 Fold in half and unfold.

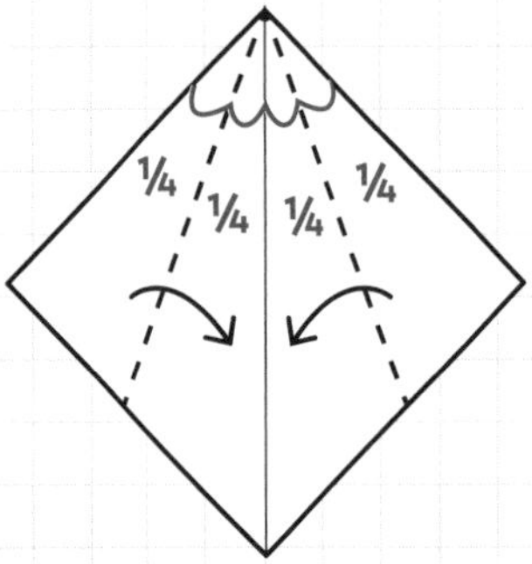

2 Make quarter folds so the edges meet at the center crease.

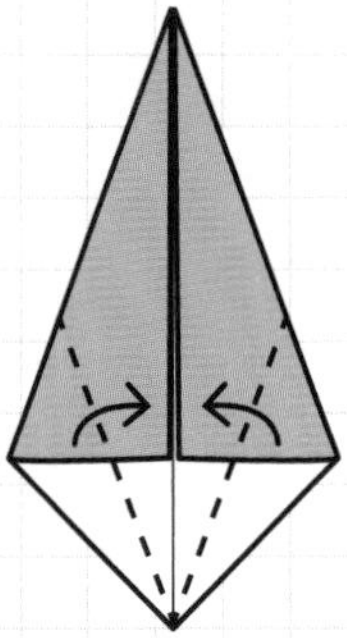

3 Fold the left and right corners to the center crease.

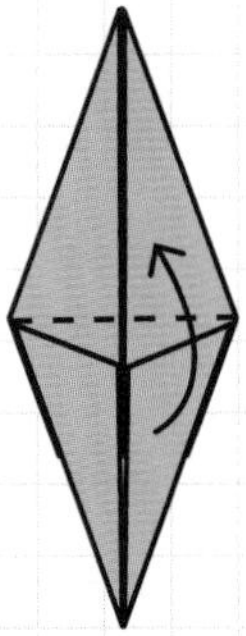

4 Fold in half up.

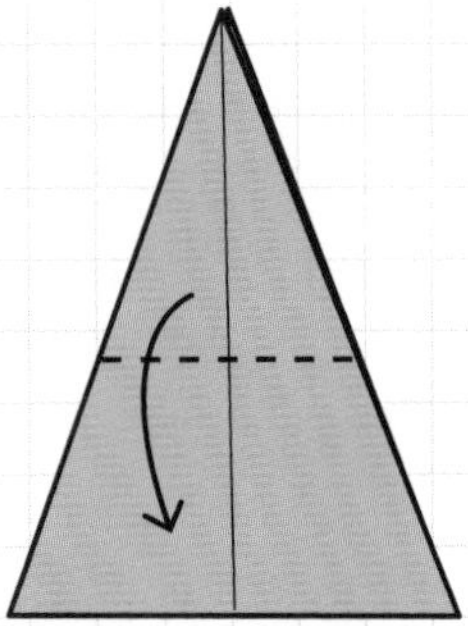

5 Fold the top point down.

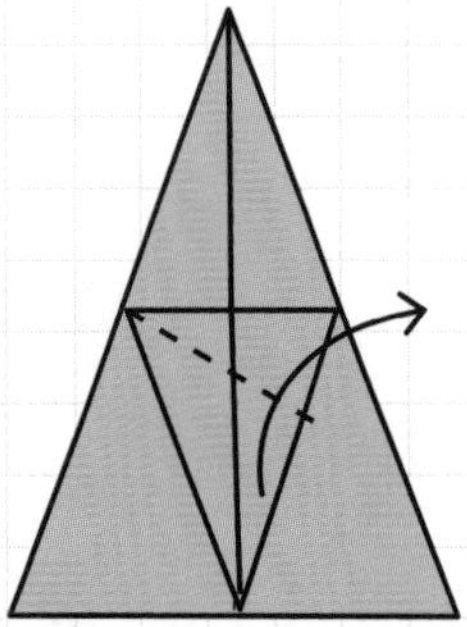

6 Fold the bottom point up.

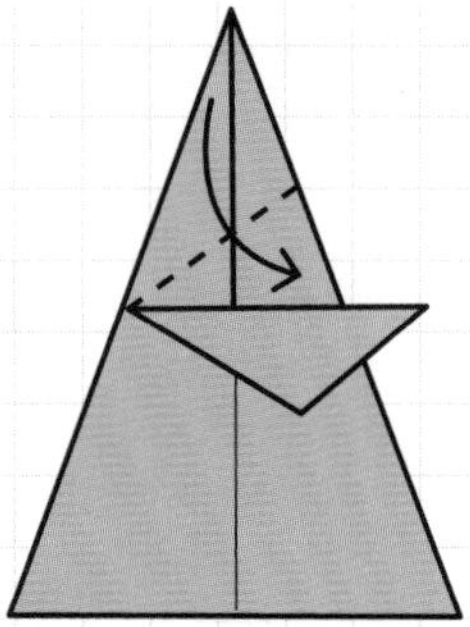

7 Fold the top point down to meet the bottom point.

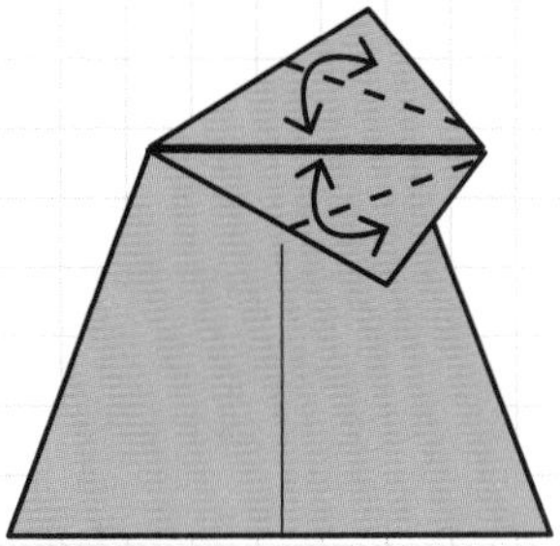

8 Fold and unfold.

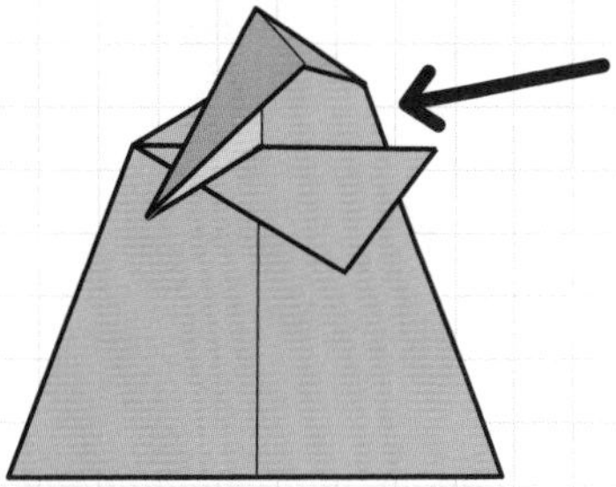

9 Lift the top flap and put your finger in the pocket, then press down.

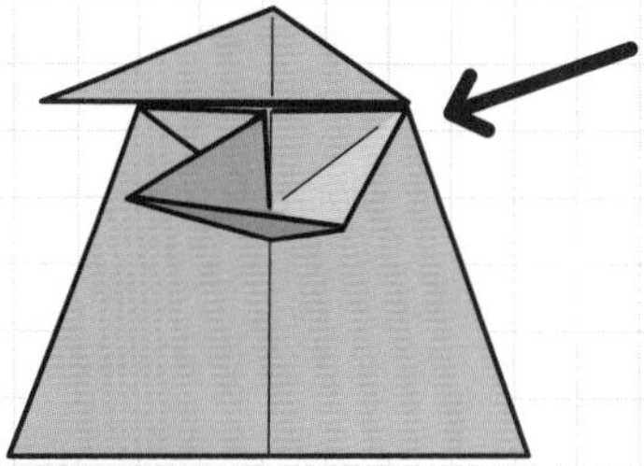

10 Lift and press the bottom flap.

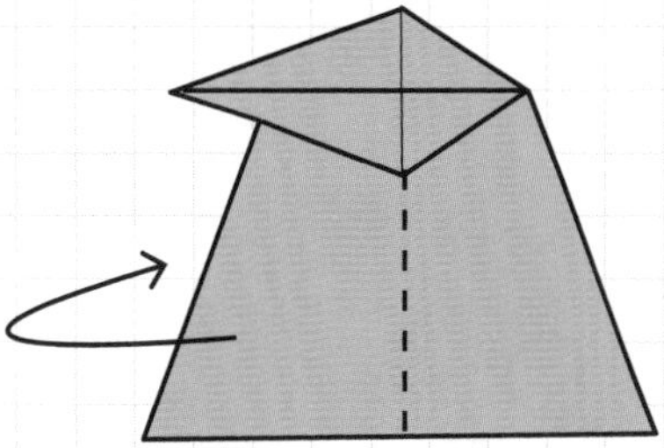

11 Fold back. Add eyes to get your ferocious dino ready to roar!

Find the Math!

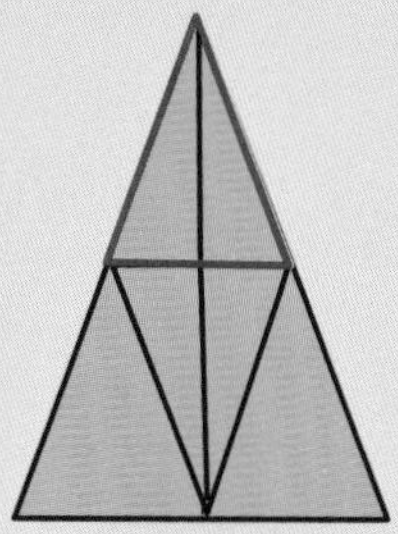

This picture shows step 6 of making the Roaring Dinosaur. Are there any other triangles that are the same size and shape as the triangle outlined in red?

ANSWER ON P. 103

12 Hold the dinosaur at the points marked with ★ (on both the front and back). Move these corners back and forth with each hand to make it roar.

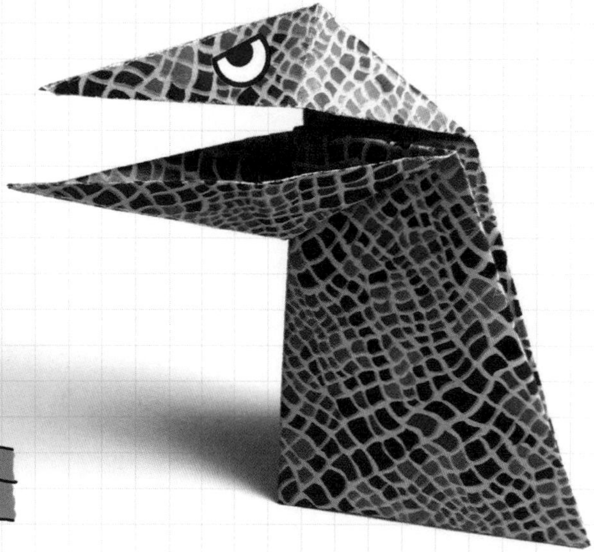

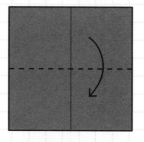

Hungry Raven

★★★★★

We can describe shapes as either **convex** or **concave.** Let's look at step 3 to see what these words mean. A shape is convex when all of its points go outward from the middle of the shape—like the gray triangles on the edges. When some of a shape's points "cave" inward, like the pink star shape in the middle, that shape is called concave. Now, you can figure out whether the Hungry Raven's pointy beak is convex or concave.

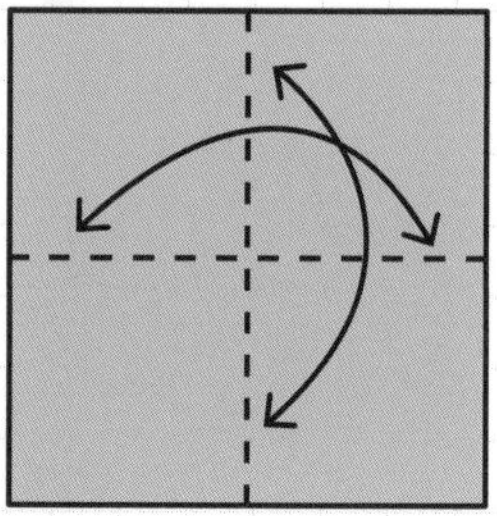

1 Fold and unfold.

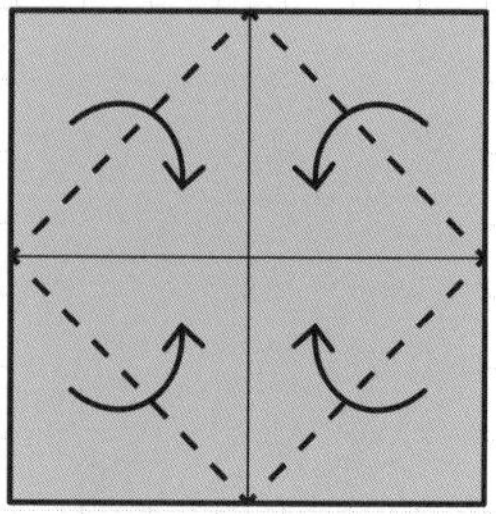

2 Fold the corners to the center.

3

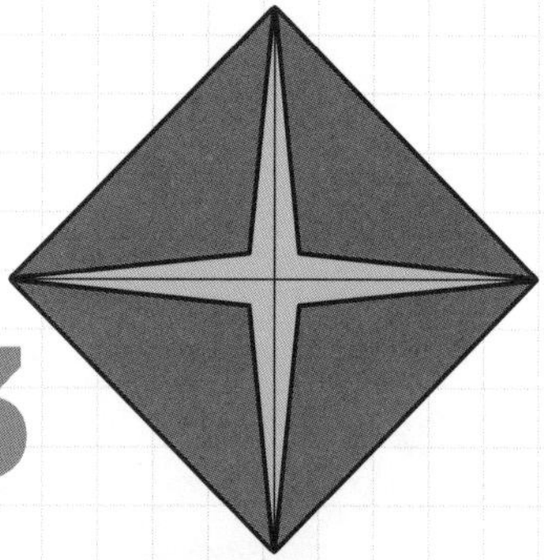

Flip over

4 Fold the corners to the center.

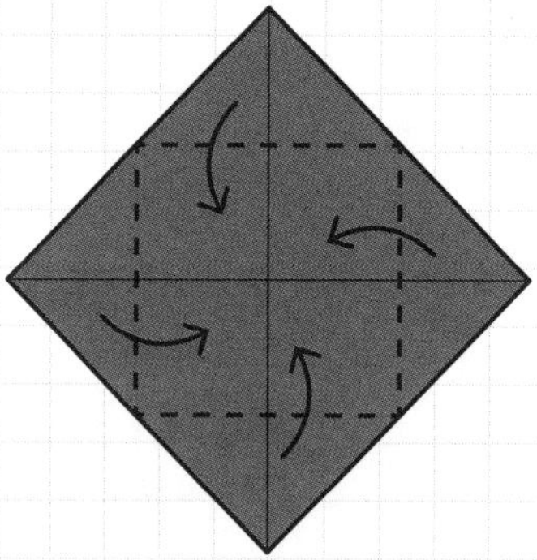

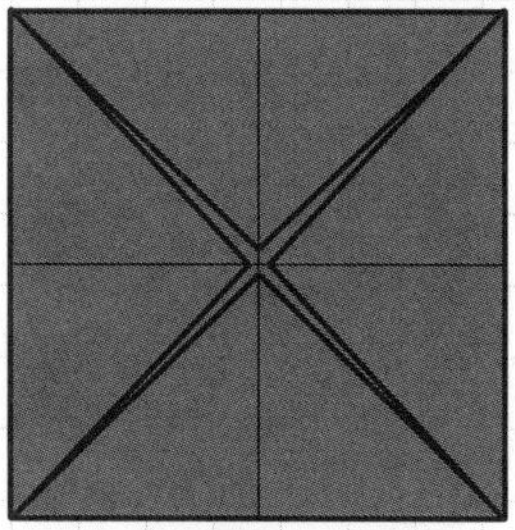

5

Flip over

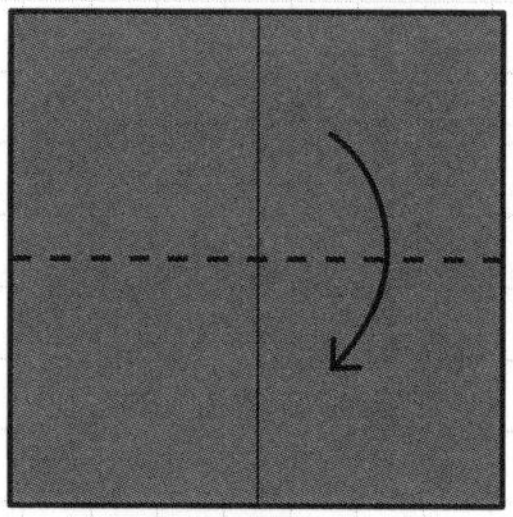

6 Fold in half.

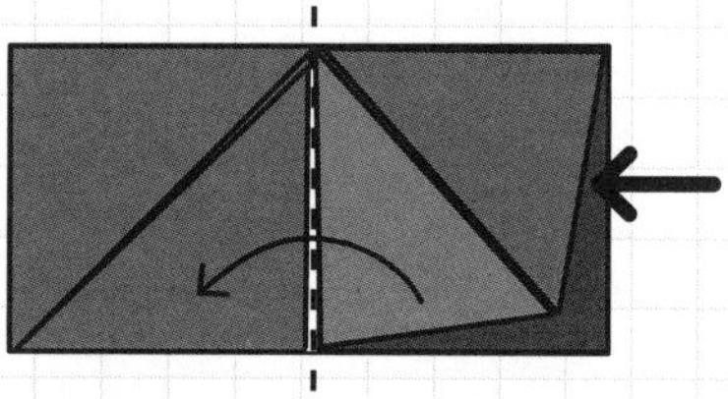

7 Swing the right edge to the center and put your finger in the pocket.

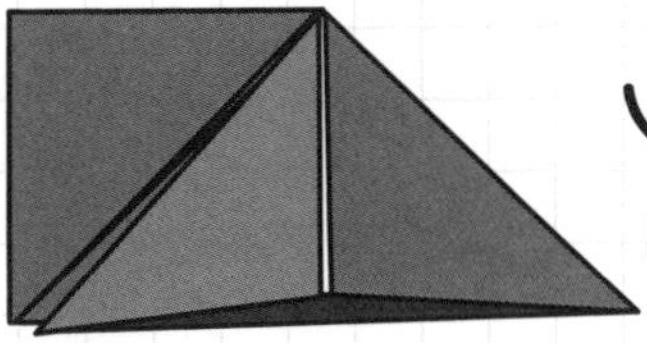

Flip over

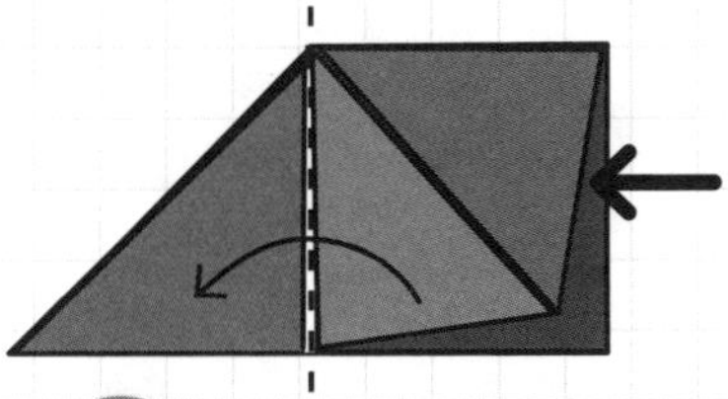

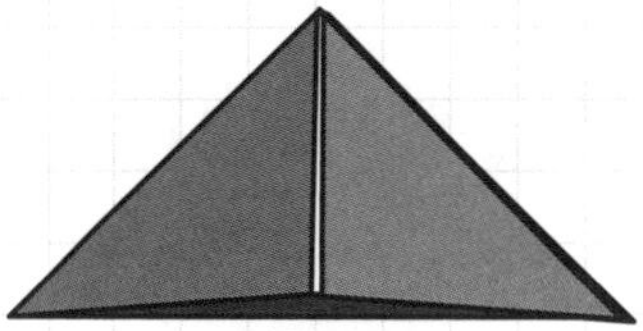

8 Flatten into a triangle.

9 Repeat steps 7 and 8.

10

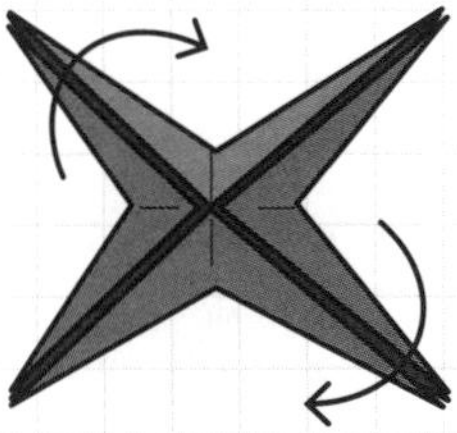

11 Swing the points out to make an X.

12 Turn the shape over and pull out one of the inside flaps. Add eyes and get ready for your raven to eat!

Find the Math!

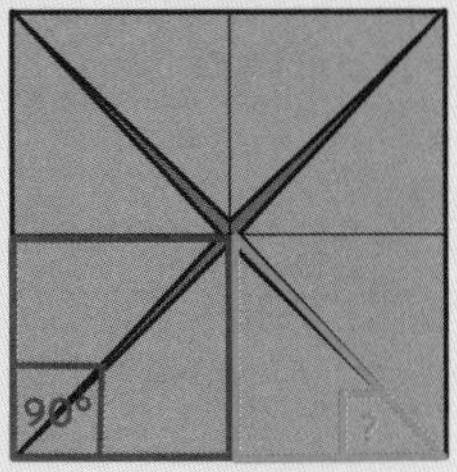

This picture shows step 5 of making a Hungry Raven. If the square corner outlined in red makes a 90° angle, what angle is made by the triangle corner outlined in blue? (Hint: ? + ? = 90)

ANSWER ON P. 103

13 Hold your raven at the end of the wings. Push the wings together to open the raven's mouth, and pull them apart to close the raven's mouth.

Croaking Toad ★★★★★

Just like you can keep cutting a piece of paper in half again and again until it's the teeniest tiniest square, we can use fractions to take smaller and smaller pieces of a shape. Check out step 5. The long line through the middle of the rectangle splits it into 2 halves ($\frac{1}{2}$), and each of those 2 halves have 4 small squares inside them for a total of 8 ($\frac{1}{8}$). Some of those squares are split into even smaller triangles ($\frac{1}{16}$). We could keep going forever ... but let's start folding the Croaking Toad instead!

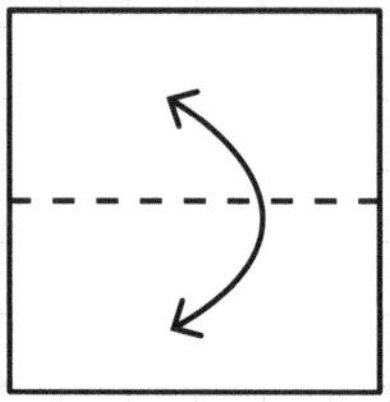

1 Fold in half and unfold.

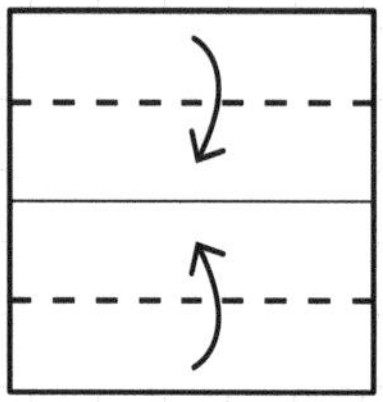

2 Fold the top and bottom edges to the center crease.

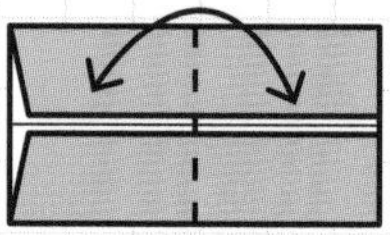

3 Fold in half and unfold.

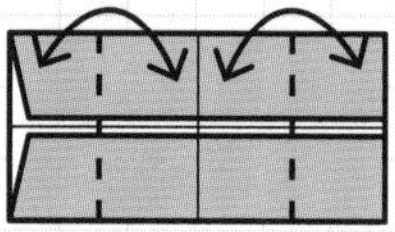

4 Fold and unfold.

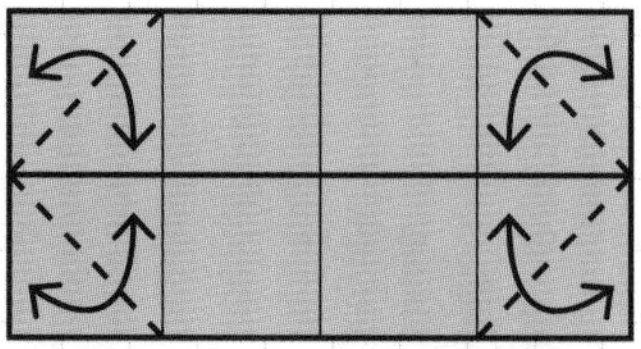

5 Fold and unfold all 4 corners.

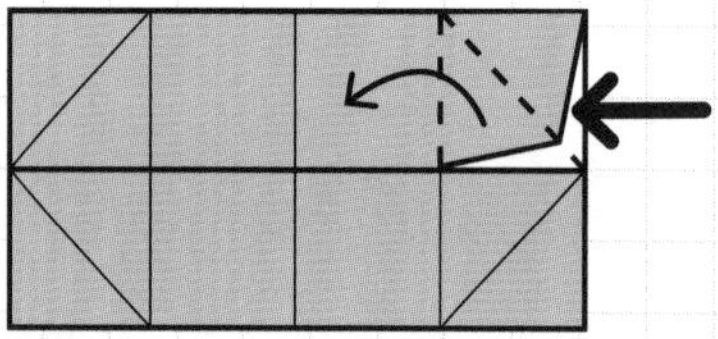

6 Lift and put your finger in the pocket.

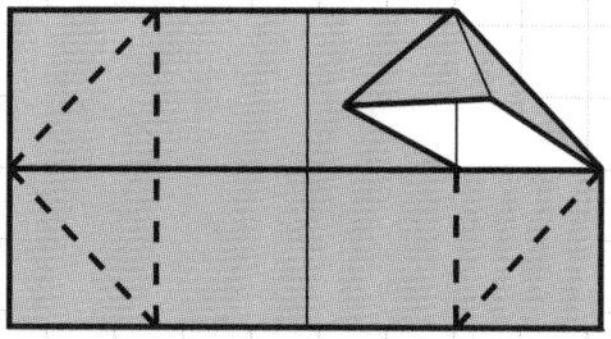

7 Press down to make a triangle. Repeat on the other 3 corners.

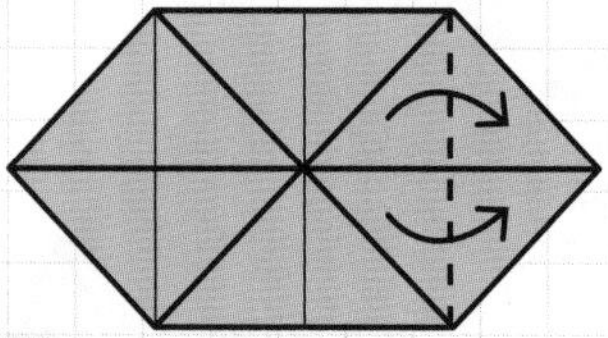

8 Fold the 2 right flaps to the right.

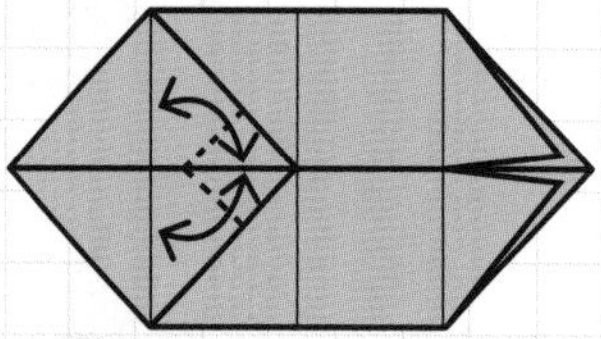

9 Fold the left tips and unfold.

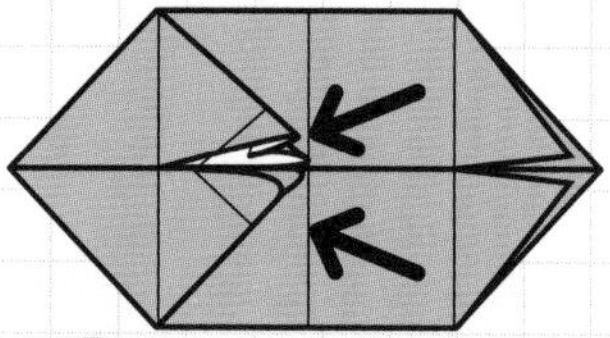

10 Lift the flaps and tuck the tips inside the pockets.

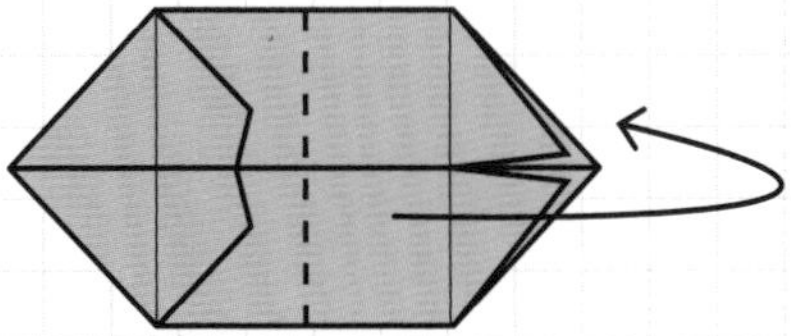

11 Fold back in half.

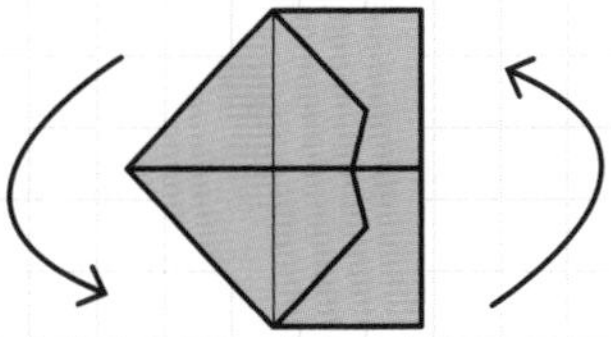

12 Turn counterclockwise.

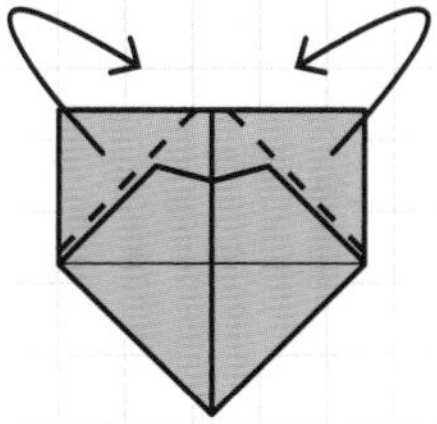

13 Fold back each corner.

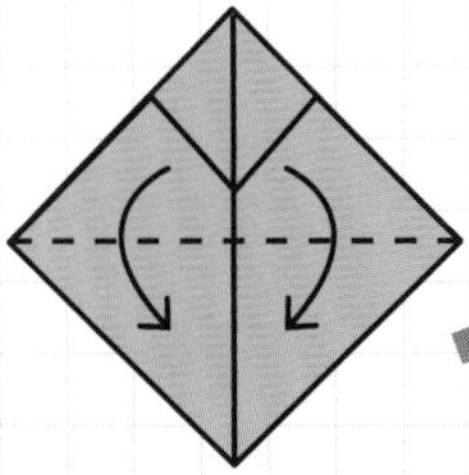

14 Lift both flaps so they stand upright at 90° angles.

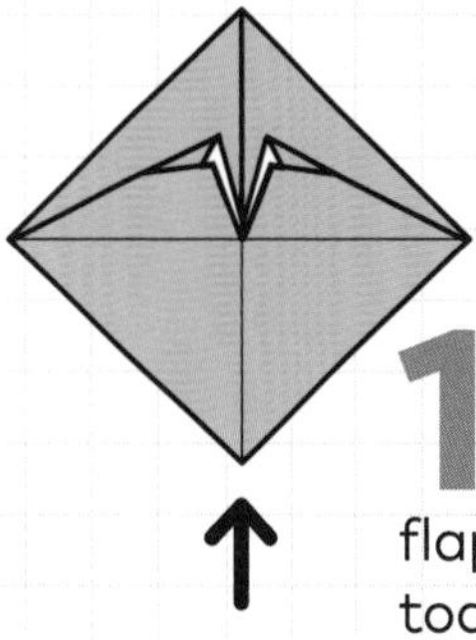

15 Add eyes. Lift the flap to open your toad's mouth and say hello to your new friend!

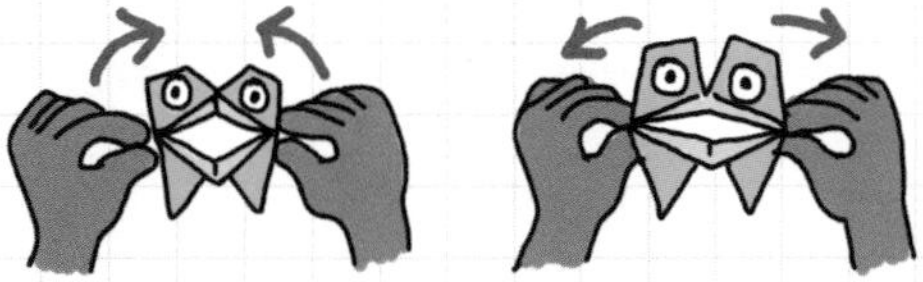

16 Pinch the sides of the toad's mouth. Push the sides together to open the toad's mouth and make it croak, and pull the sides apart to close its mouth.

Find the Math!

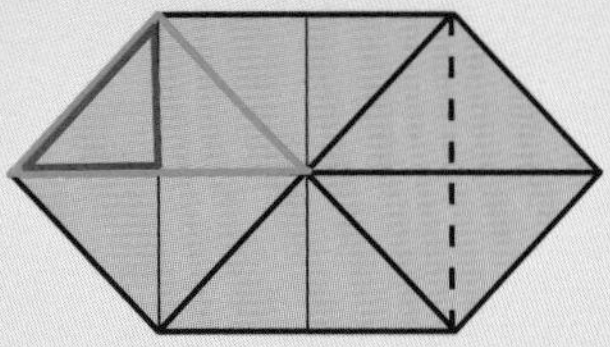

This picture shows step 8 of making a Croaking Toad: 2 of the triangles outlined in red make 1 of the triangles outlined in blue. How many of the triangles outlined in red would it take to cover the whole piece of origami paper?

ANSWER ON P. 103

Beating Heart ★★★★★

Fractions are helpful for dividing things up equally. Look at the paper in step 4—it's divided into 8 equal sections, meaning each square is ⅛ (or one eighth) of the whole paper. If it were a chocolate bar, you could give a piece to 8 friends and they'd all get to eat the same amount. We ♥ sharing!

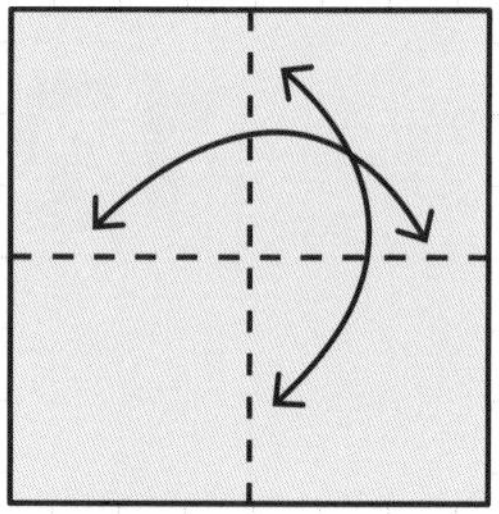

1 Fold and unfold.

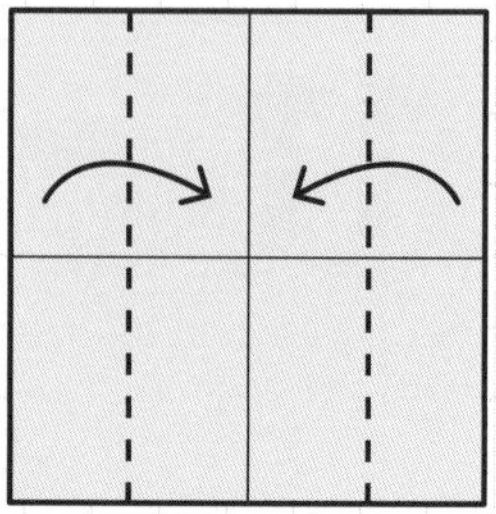

2 Fold the edges in to the center crease.

3 Fold and unfold.

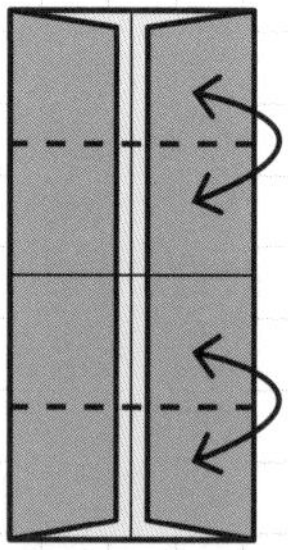

4

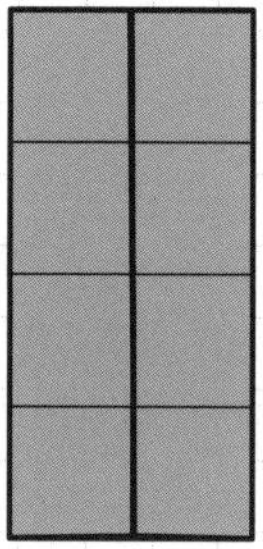

Flip over

5 Fold the top edge one third of the way down.

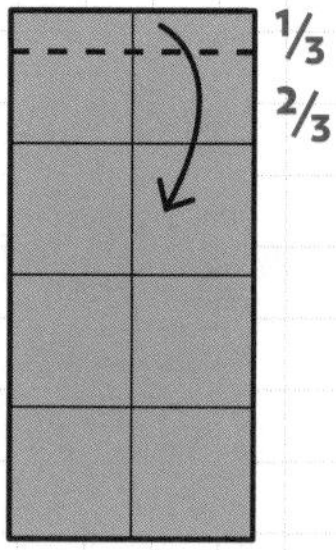

⅓
⅔

6 Lift the top left flap. Put your finger in the pocket and press down.

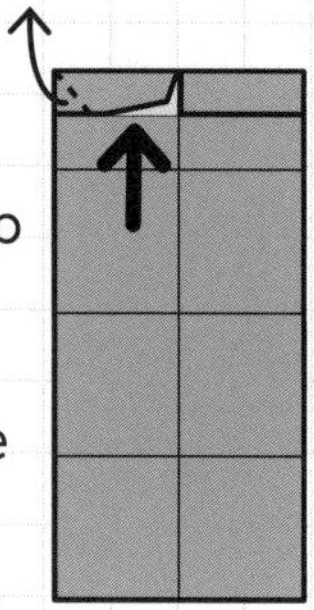

7 Repeat on the other side.

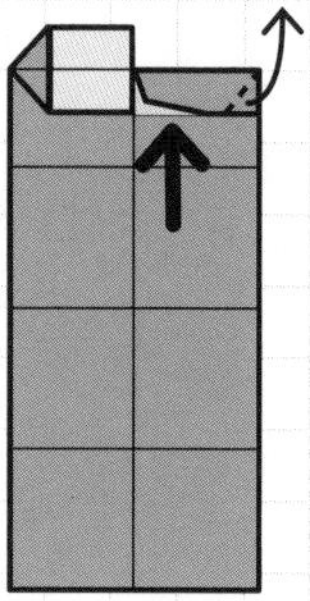

8 Fold the inside corners down.

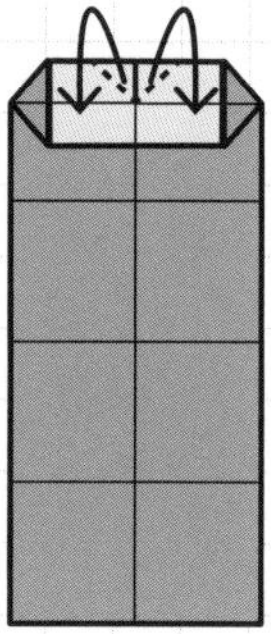

9 Fold in half up.

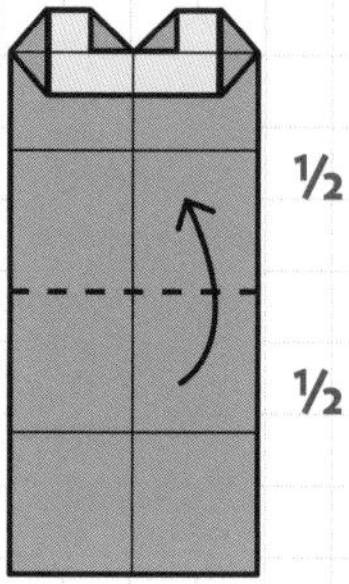

½
½

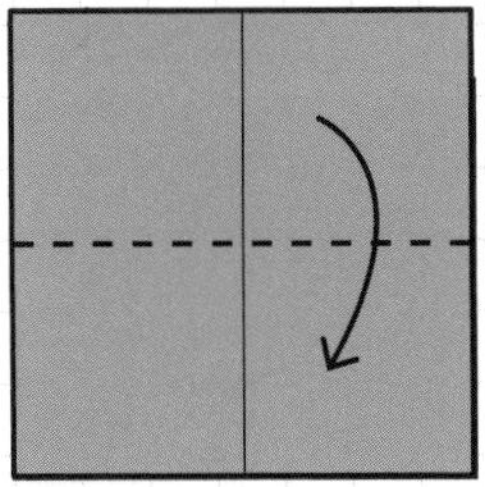

10 Fold the top flap down.

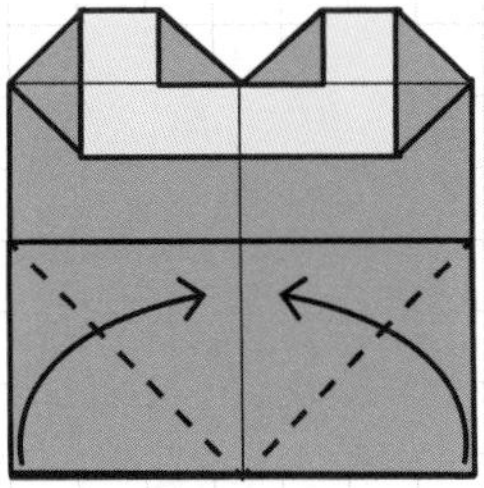

11 Fold the corners to the center.

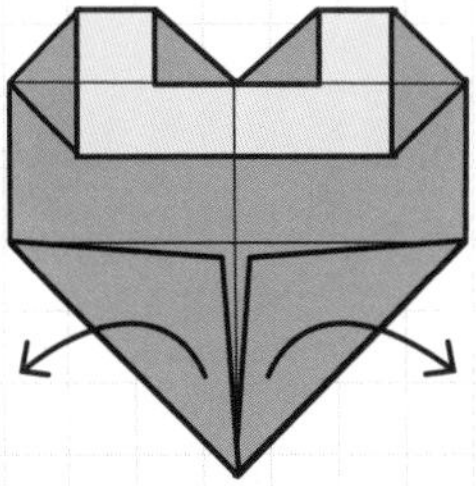

12 Lift both outer flaps so they stand up at 90° angles.

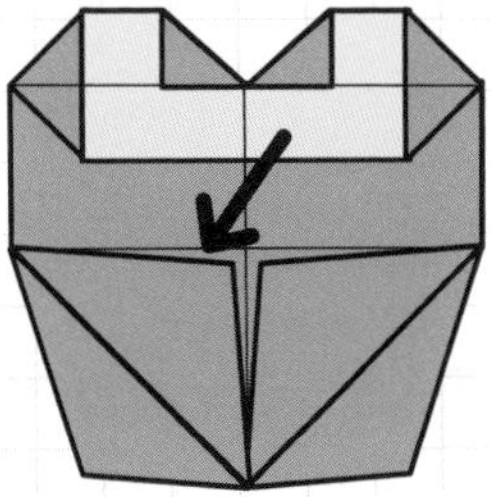

13 Lift the inner flap and put your finger in the pocket to push the flap out, making the pocket bulge outward.

Flip over

Find the Math!

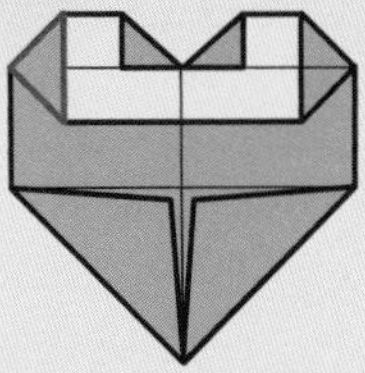

This picture shows step 12 of making a Beating Heart. Are there any other triangles that are the same shape as the triangle outlined in red? (It's OK if the other triangles are a different size as long as they're the same shape.)

ANSWER ON P. 104

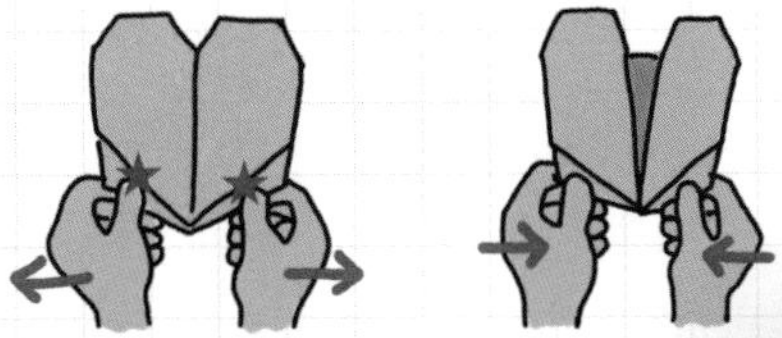

14 Hold the bottom of the heart in both hands where you see the ★ mark in the picture. Make the heart beat by moving your hands apart and back together again.

Jumping Frog

There are lots of ways to talk about fractions—we can say "one fourth" or "¼" or "a quarter" to mean the same thing. We can also say that the whole shape is a certain number of times the fractional part, like how the sheet of paper in step 1 is 2 times bigger than each of the rectangles made by the dotted line. Did you know that some frogs can jump a distance that's 20 times their body length? Let's see if the Jumping Frog is up for the challenge.

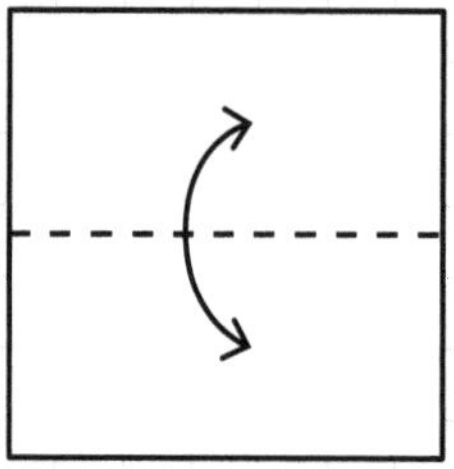

1 Fold in half and unfold.

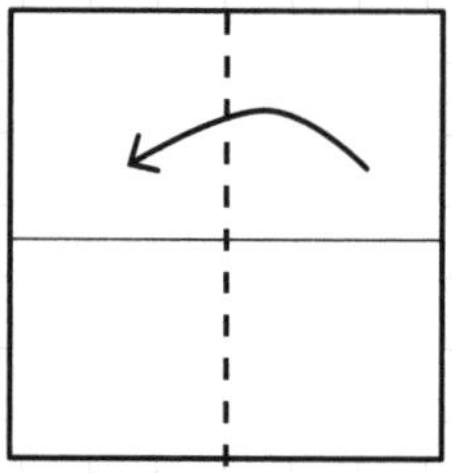

2 Fold in half to the left.

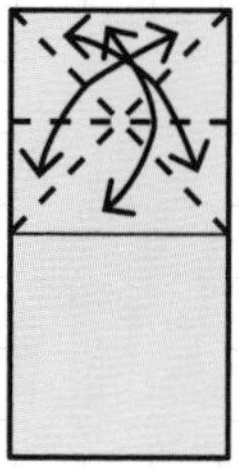

3 Fold and unfold.

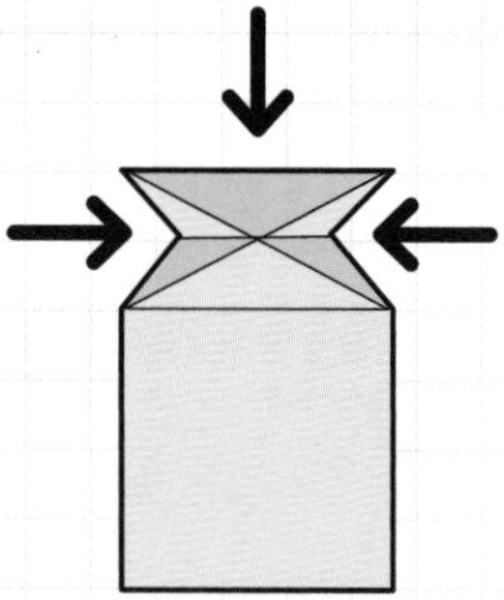

4 Fold the points marked with the arrows in and down so they're tucked under the top part of the square to form a triangle.

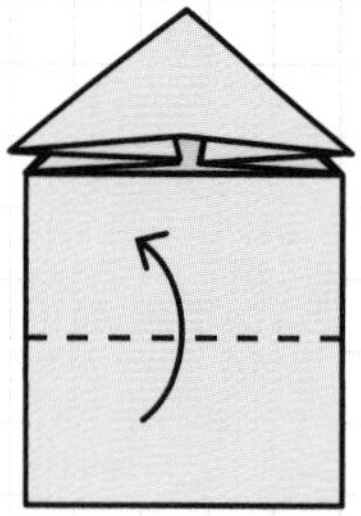

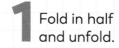

5 Fold the bottom edge up.

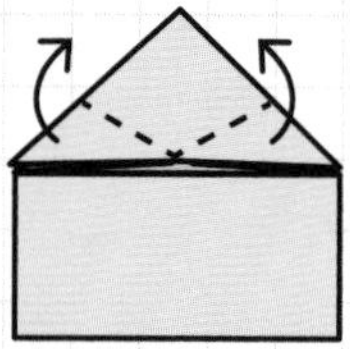

6 Fold the top points up.

7 Fold the left and right edges to meet in the center.

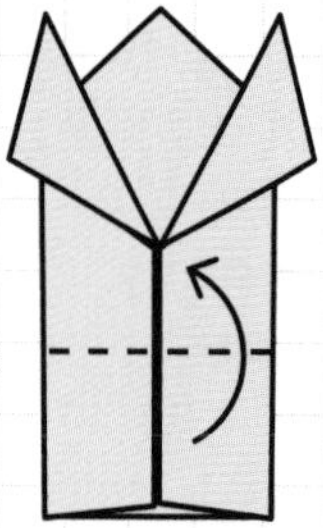

8 Fold the bottom edges up.

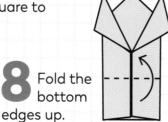

9 Fold and unfold the corners down.

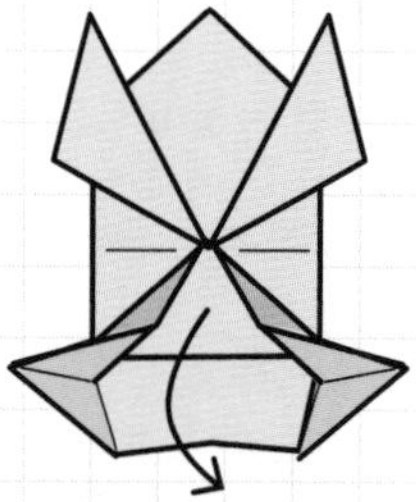

10 Unfold the bottom edge and spread the flaps.

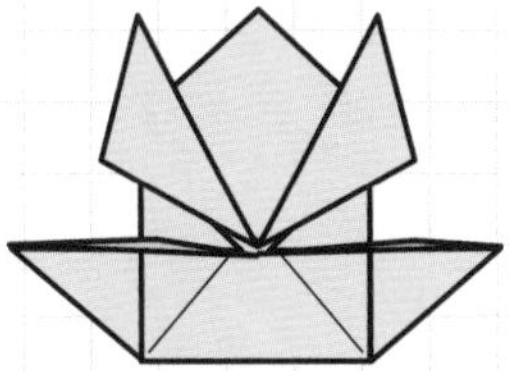

11 Flatten the flaps to the sides to form 2 points.

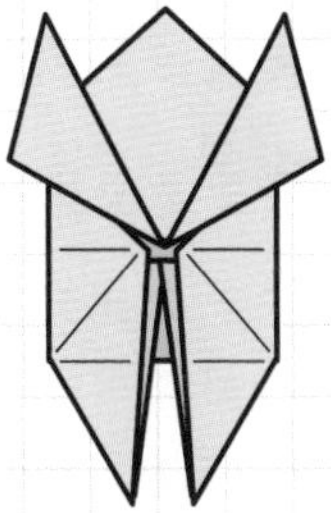

12 Fold the points down.

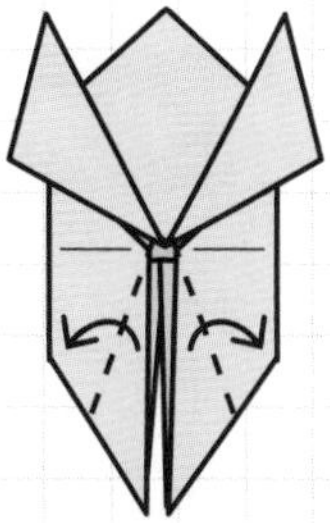

13 Fold the inner edges toward the outside edges.

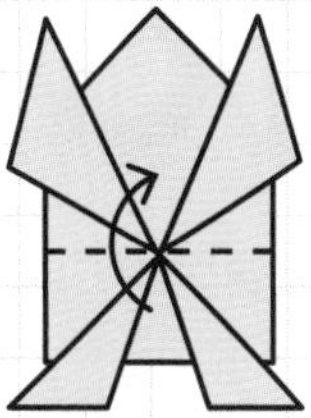

14 Fold the bottom up in half.

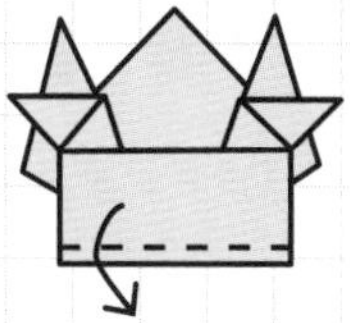

15 Fold the bottom up in half again to make a zigzag.

16

Flip over

17 Flip over and add eyes.

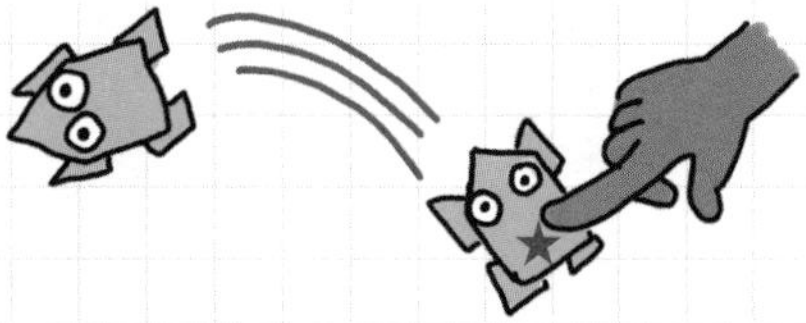

18 Press on the ★ and flick your finger down from the edge to see the frog leap forward!

Find the Math!

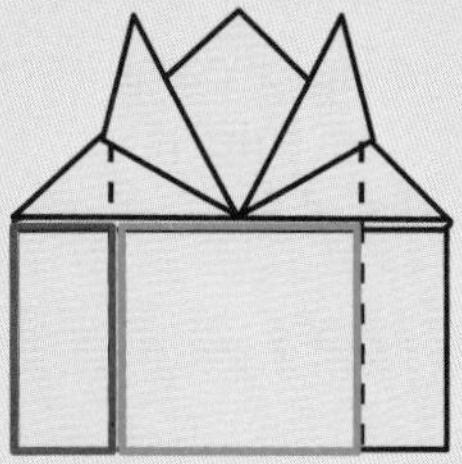

This picture shows step 7 of making a Jumping Frog. How many of the rectangles outlined in red could fit inside the square outlined in blue?

ANSWER ON P. 104

Hopping Crow

Have you ever noticed that shapes have other, smaller shapes hiding inside them? The gray area of the paper in step 3 could be just one large triangle. But look closer . . . this big shape can also be chopped up into 2 smaller triangles (along the white line down the middle) or a triangle sitting on top of a quadrilateral (along the dotted line). See what other secret shapes you can spot while making the Hopping Crow.

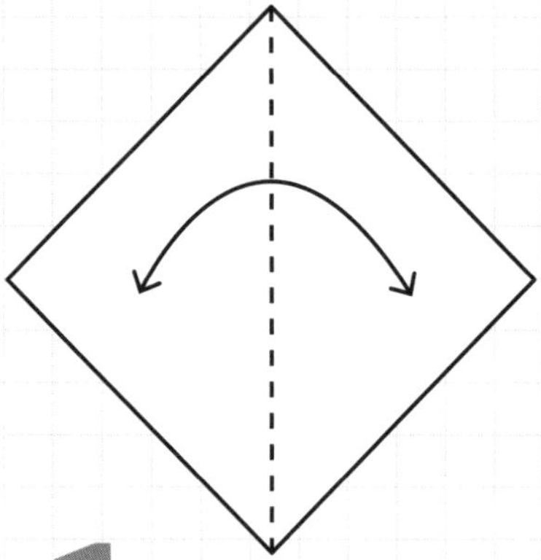

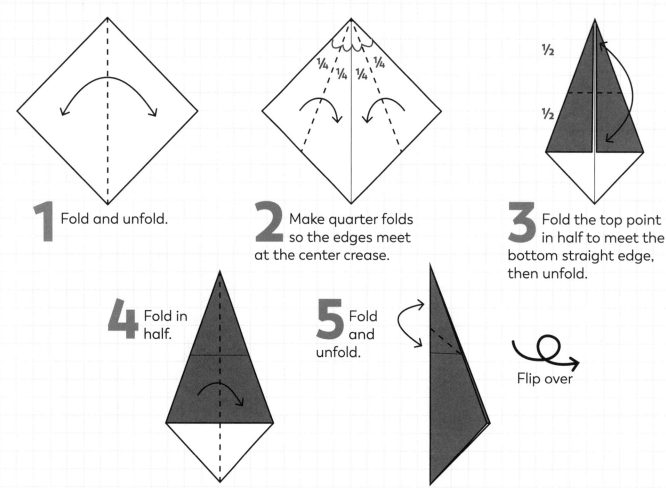

1 Fold and unfold.

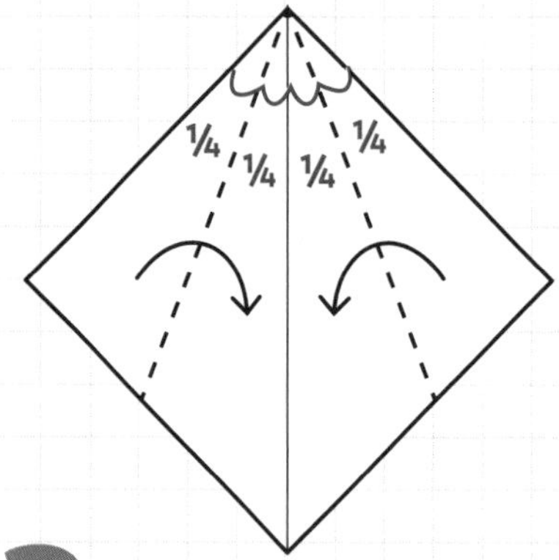

2 Make quarter folds so the edges meet at the center crease.

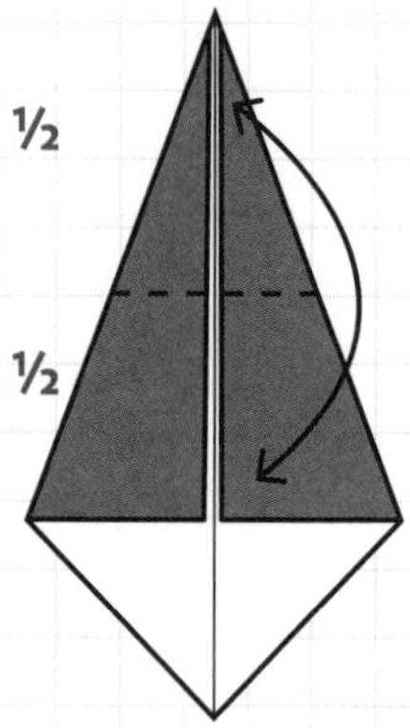

3 Fold the top point in half to meet the bottom straight edge, then unfold.

4 Fold in half.

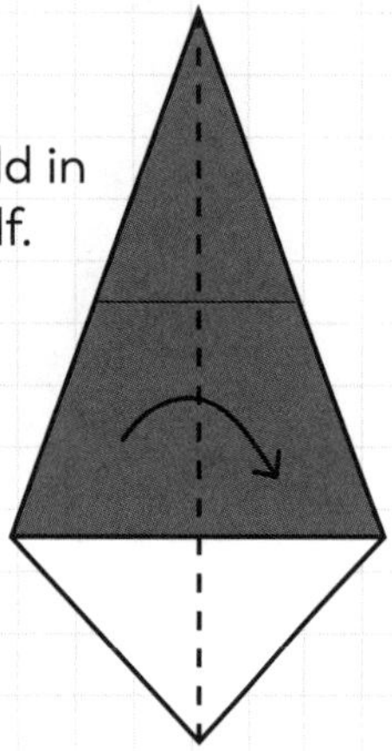

5 Fold and unfold.

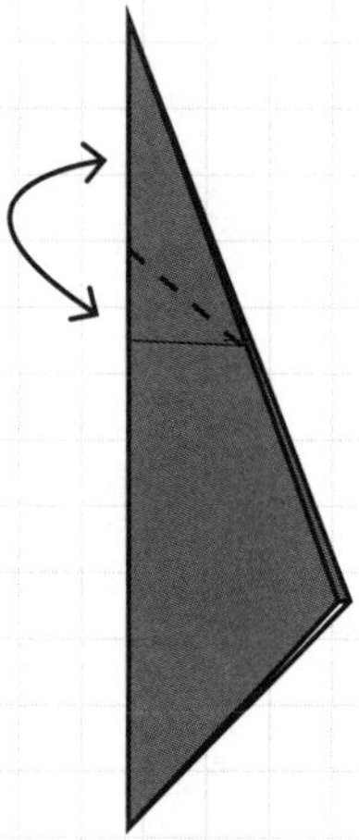

Flip over

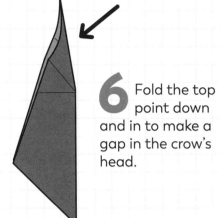

6 Fold the top point down and in to make a gap in the crow's head.

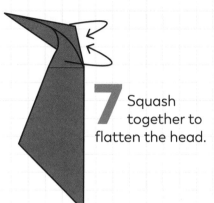

7 Squash together to flatten the head.

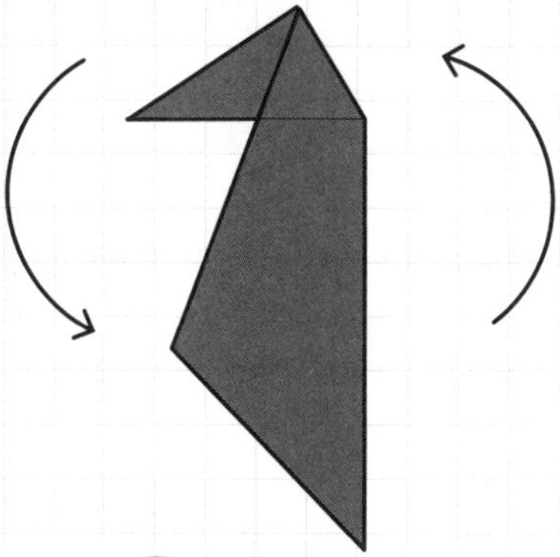

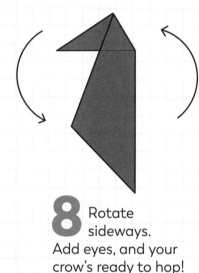

8 Rotate sideways. Add eyes, and your crow's ready to hop!

Find the Math!

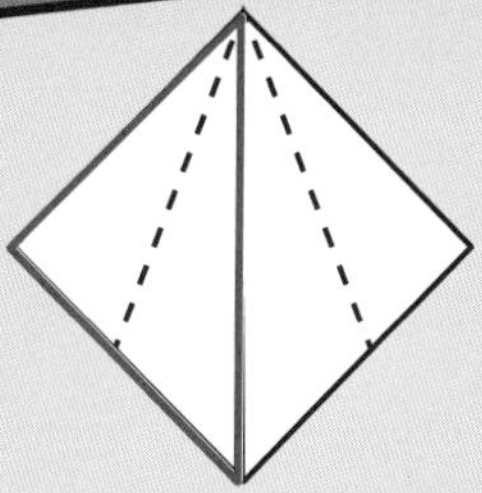

This picture shows step 2 of making a Hopping Crow. Look at the shape outlined in red—it's made up of 2 triangles that are each ¼ of the total piece of origami paper. If you add those quarters together, what fraction of the origami paper do you get?

ANSWER ON P. 104

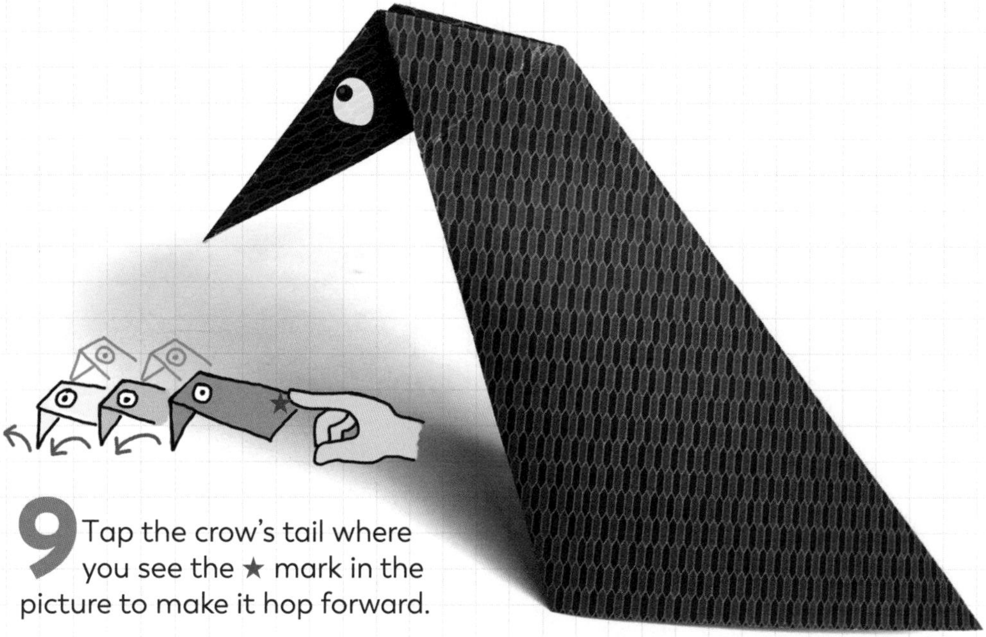

9 Tap the crow's tail where you see the ★ mark in the picture to make it hop forward.

Creeping Mouse

We already know about 90° (or right) angles, like the ones that make all 4 corners of the square in step 1. But there are also 2 other kinds of angles, and we can find 1 of them in the Creeping Mouse's tail. **Acute angles** measure less than 90°, meaning they're narrower—look how tiny the tip of the mouse's tail is compared to a square's corner. You can remember acute angles' name because they're so small and cute!

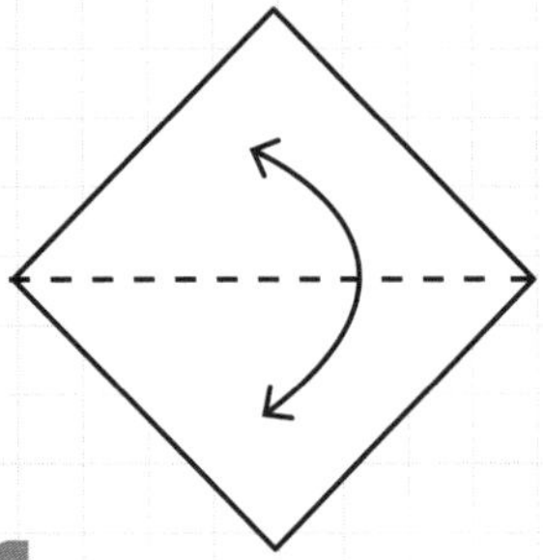

1 Fold in half and unfold.

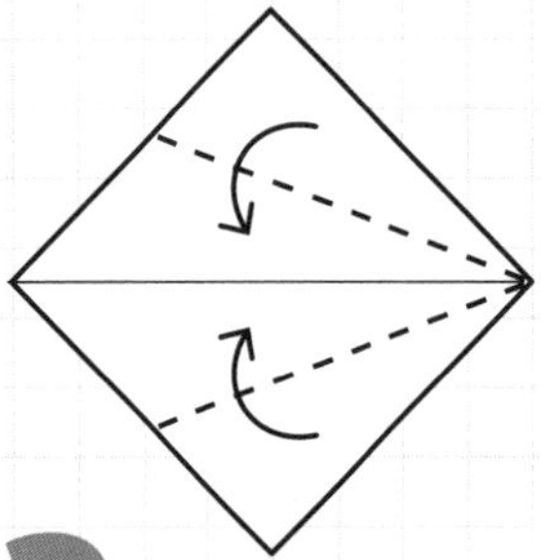

2 Fold the top and bottom corners to the center crease.

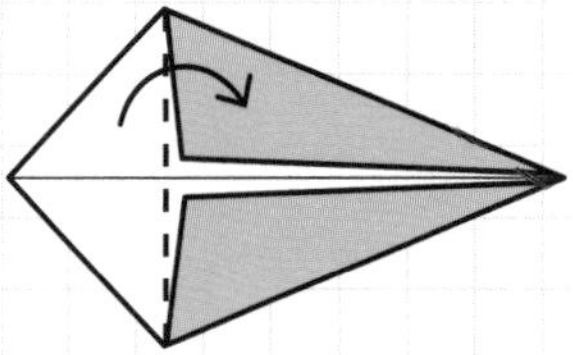

3 Fold the left point in.

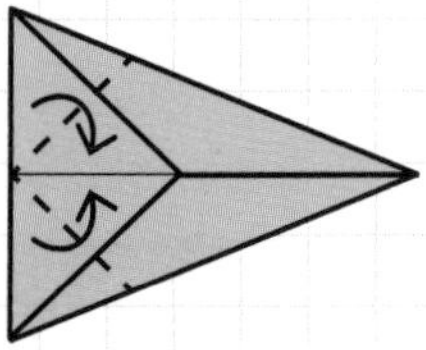

4 Fold the top and bottom corners to the center.

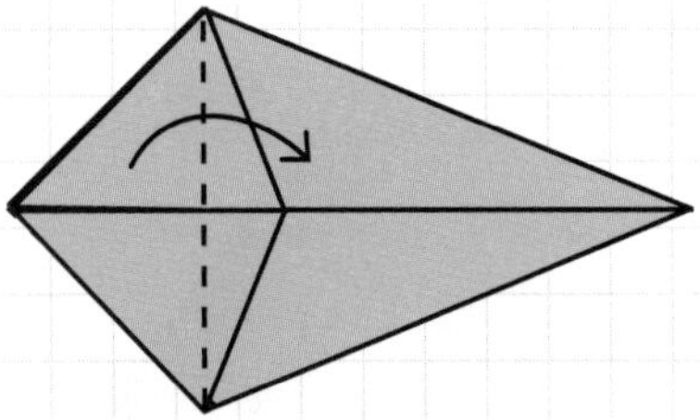

5 Fold the left point in.

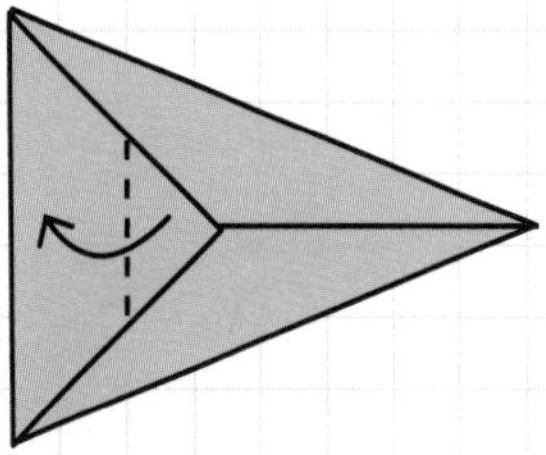

6 Fold the point to the left.

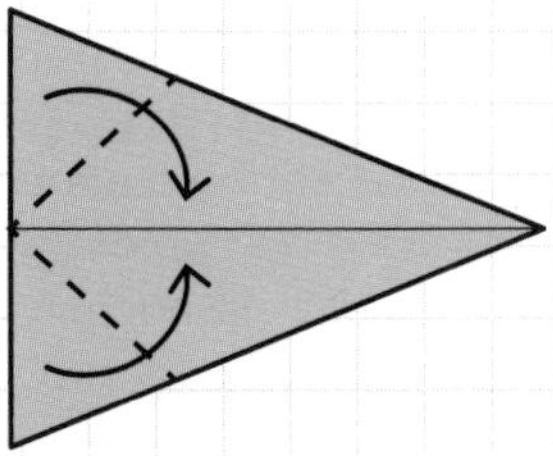

7 Fold the corners to the center.

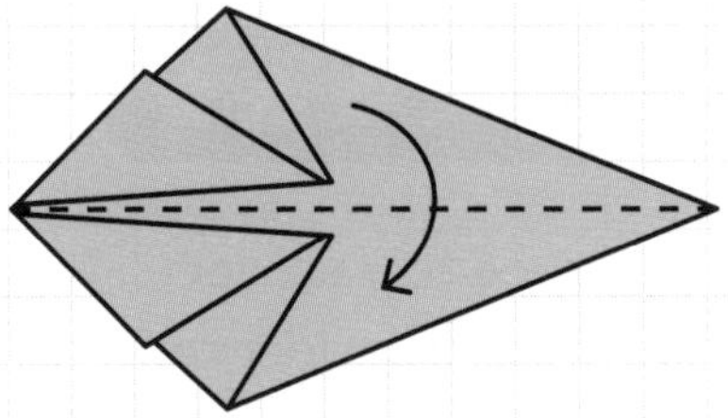

8 Fold in half down.

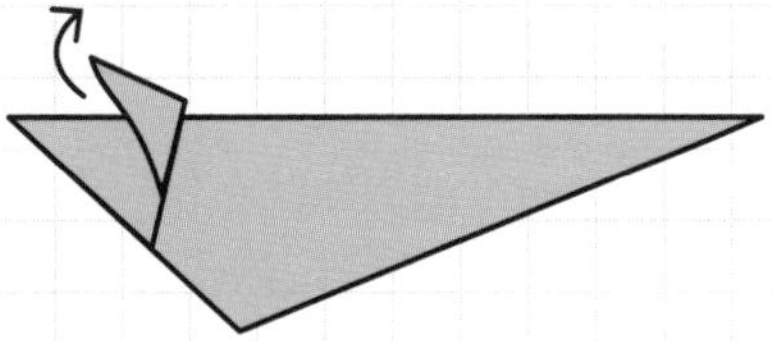

9 Push the ears up.

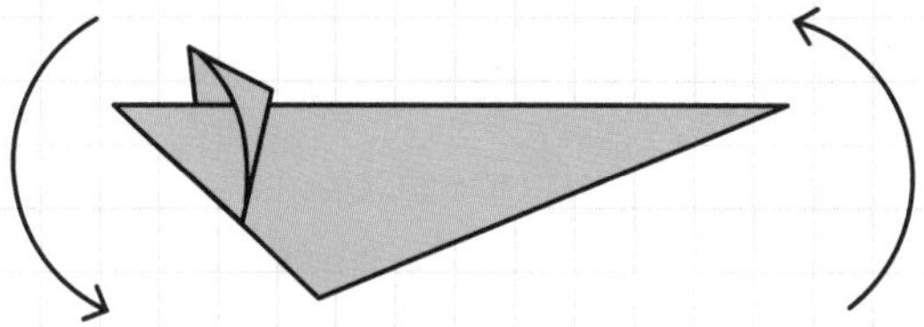

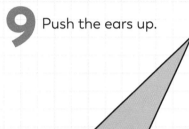

10 Rotate so the mouse can stand on its bottom edges.

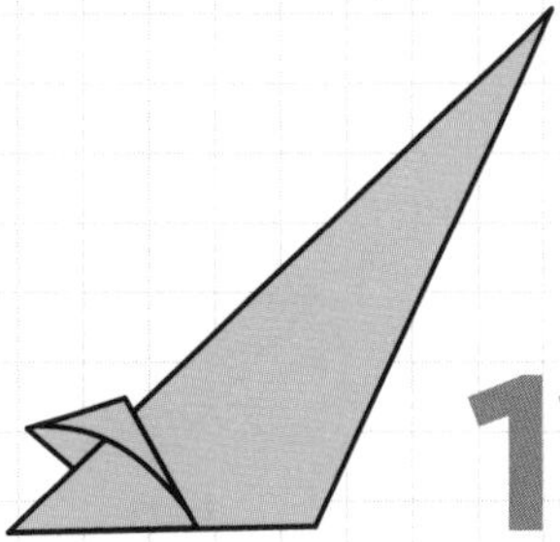

11 Add eyes, a nose, and whiskers.

Find the Math!

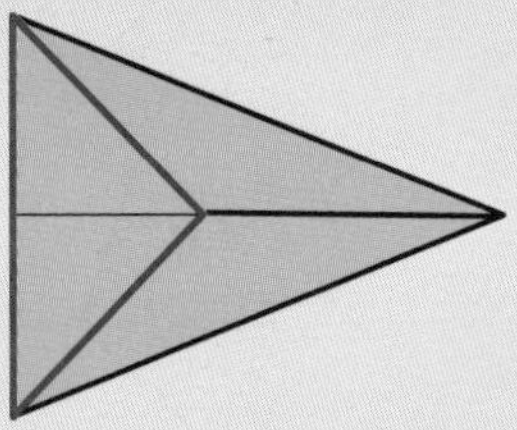

This picture shows step 6 of making a Creeping Mouse. What kind of triangle is the one outlined in red? (Hint: Look at the kinds of angles this triangle has.)

1. Isosceles triangle
2. Isosceles right triangle

ANSWER ON P. 104

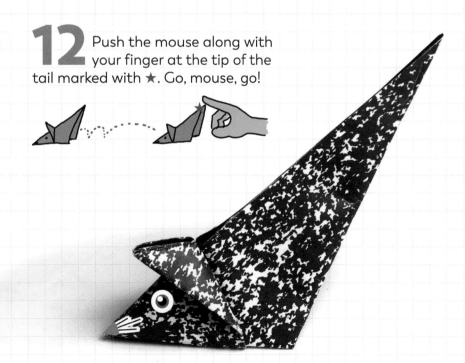

12 Push the mouse along with your finger at the tip of the tail marked with ★. Go, mouse, go!

Fighting Sumo Wrestler

We just learned about acute angles with the Creeping Mouse (p. 48), so now it's time to discover another kind of angle: **obtuse angles.** This kind of angle measures more than 90°, so it's wider than a square's right angles. You can see some obtuse angles in step 6, at the parts of the green paper that are closest to the center. Look out for other obtuse angles as you fold the Fighting Sumo Wrestler!

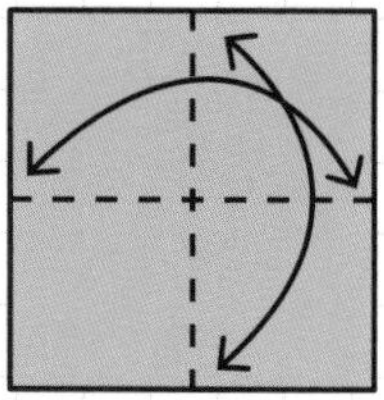

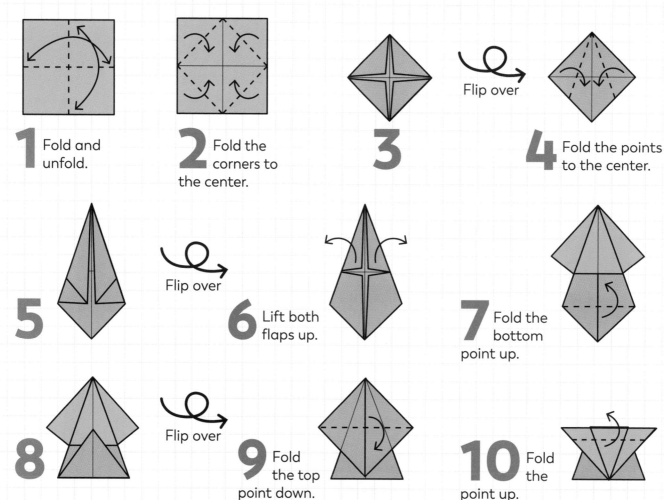

1 Fold and unfold.

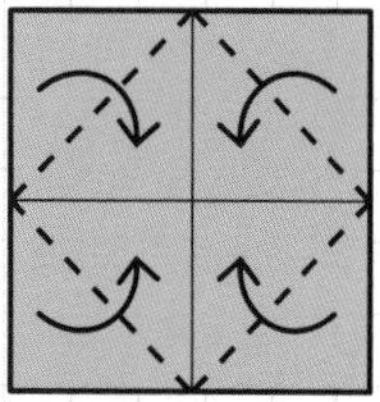

2 Fold the corners to the center.

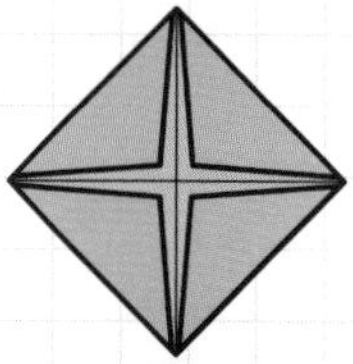

3

Flip over

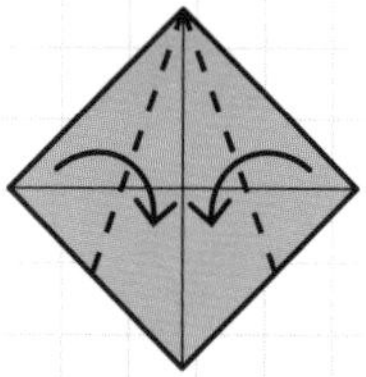

4 Fold the points to the center.

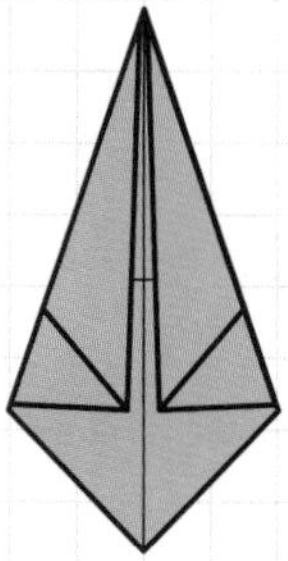

5

Flip over

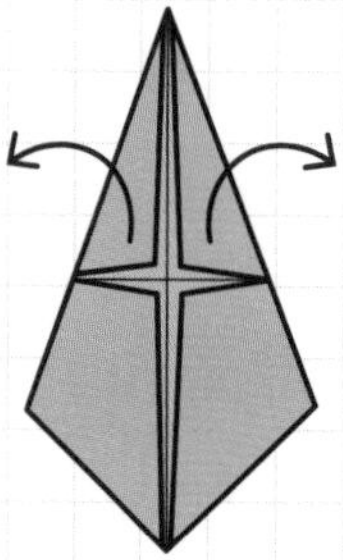

6 Lift both flaps up.

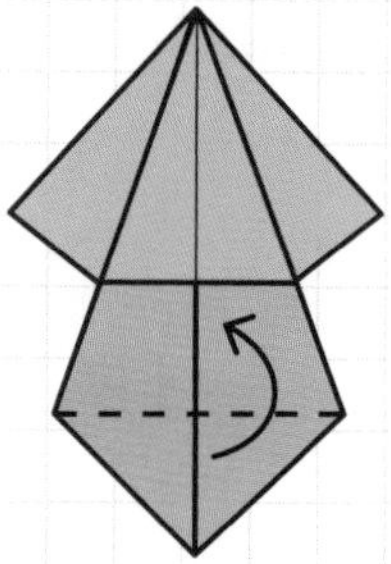

7 Fold the bottom point up.

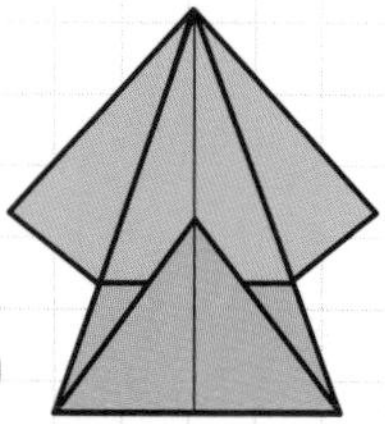

8

Flip over

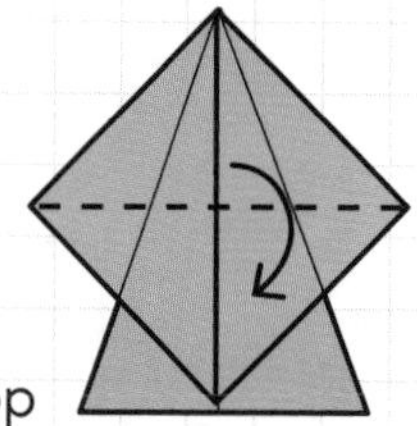

9 Fold the top point down.

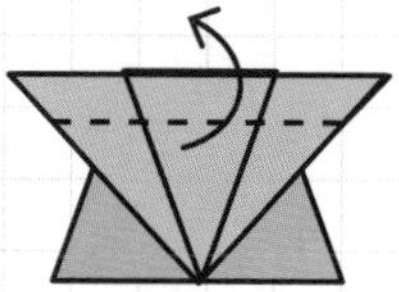

10 Fold the point up.

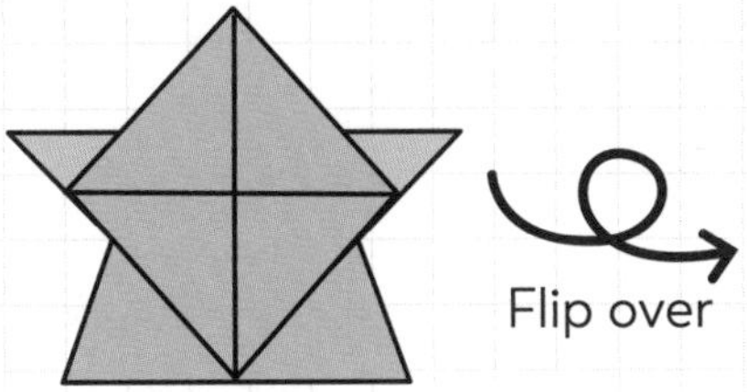

11

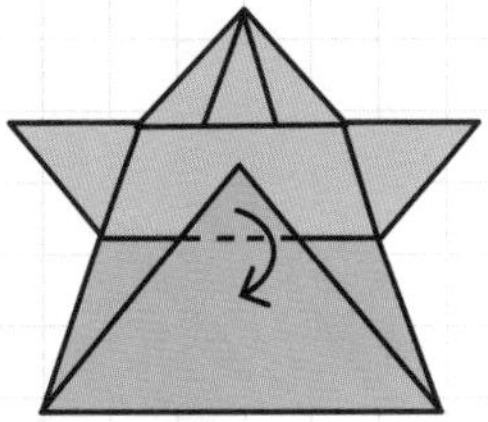

12 Fold down.

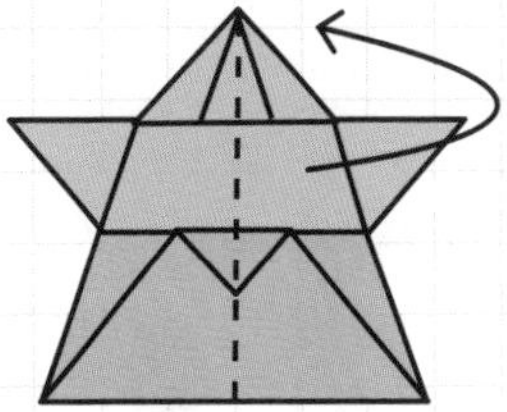

13 Fold in half to the back.

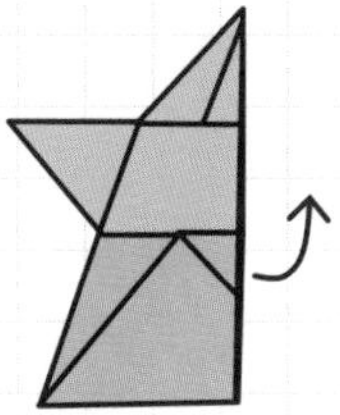

14 Pinch the small flap and pull up gently.

15 Spread the bottom corners apart a little.

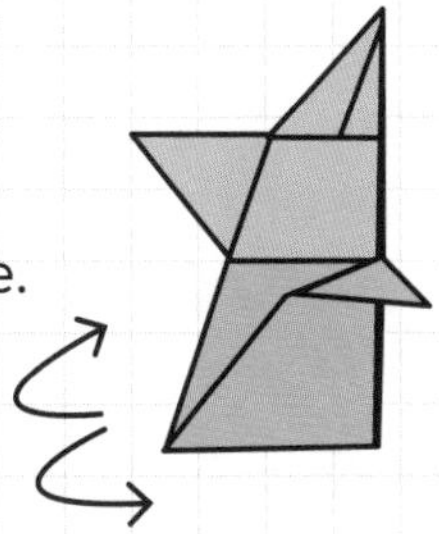

Find the Math!

This picture shows step 14 of making a Fighting Sumo Wrestler. Are there any other shapes that are congruent to the triangle outlined in red? What about similar?

ANSWER ON P. 104

16 Make a sumo wrestling ring and have a match! To make the ring, you'll need a box lid (like a shoebox or gift box lid) and something to draw with (like crayons or markers). Draw the ring on the box and place two sumo wrestlers in the ring facing each other. To start the match, bang on the table. The wrestlers will move forward to fight each other as the table vibrates. The first sumo wrestler to fall down loses. Try having a tournament with your friends!

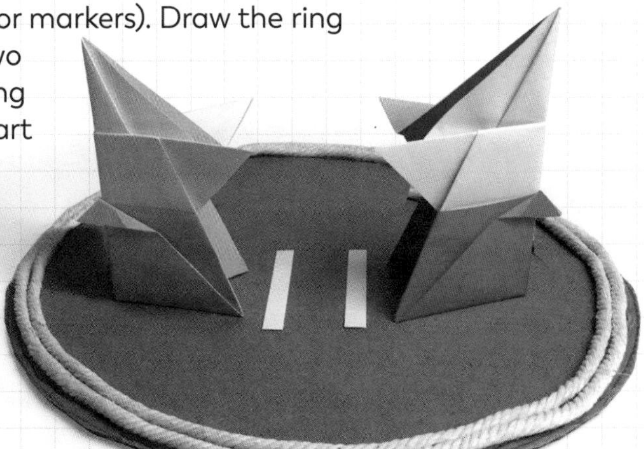

Animal Friends

You can use a single sheet of origami paper (and the power of lines and number operations) to make more than 1 friendly creature at a time. 2, 4, 6 and more—that's a lot of animals!

5
6
4
3
2
1

Grasshoppers ★☆☆☆☆

Not every way we can divide a shape cuts it into equal pieces. For example, take a look at step 4 and the triangles that are cut by the dotted line. The piece of the triangle on one side of the line isn't the same size as the piece on the other—each is being split into $\frac{1}{3}$ and $\frac{2}{3}$. Watch for other steps where a shape gets sliced up into unequal sections while you're folding this mama and baby grasshopper.

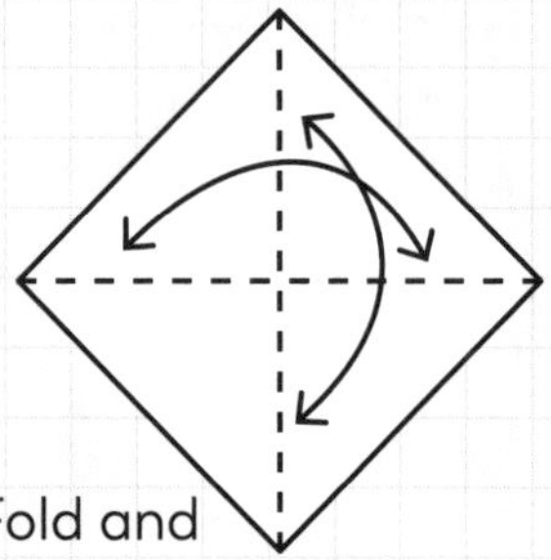

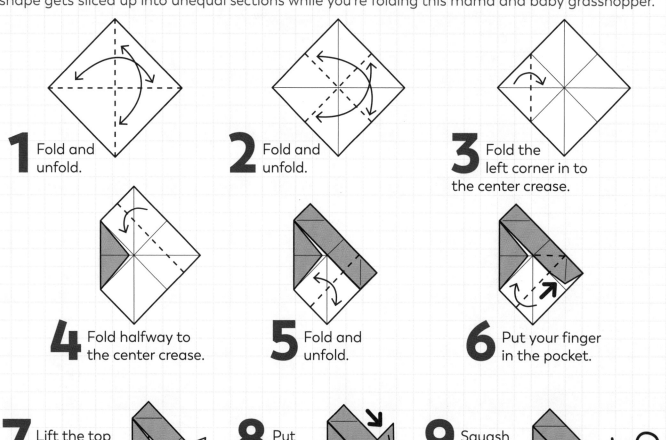

1 Fold and unfold.

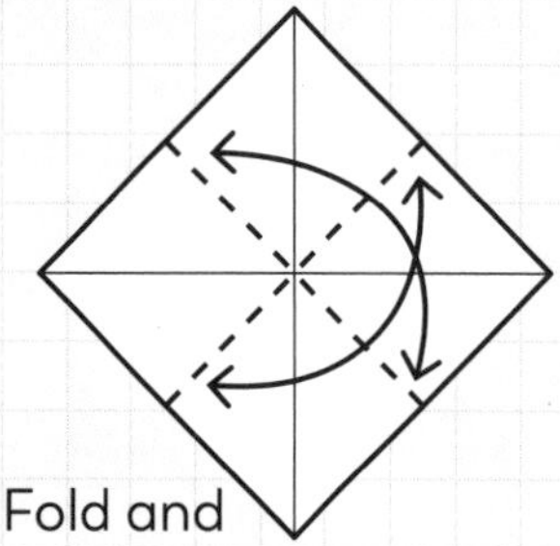

2 Fold and unfold.

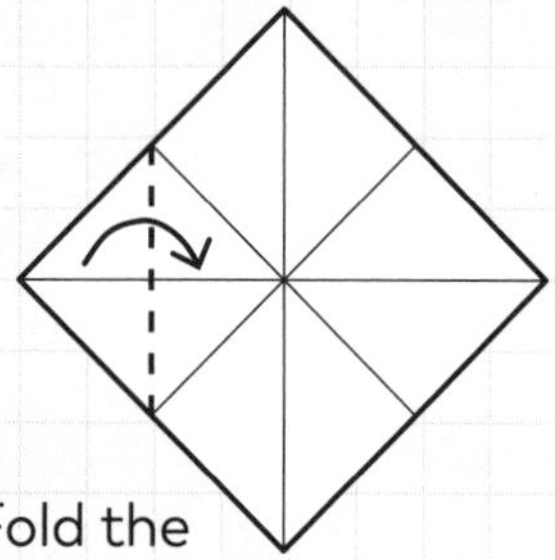

3 Fold the left corner in to the center crease.

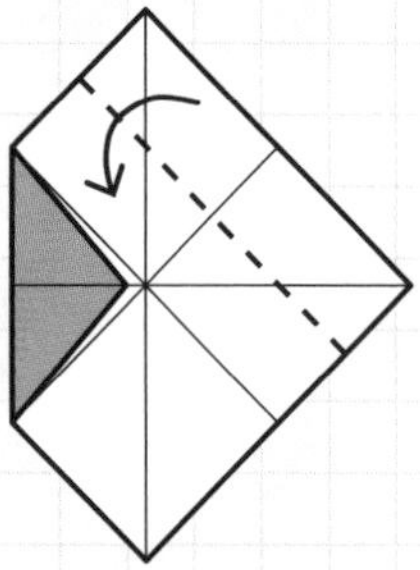

4 Fold halfway to the center crease.

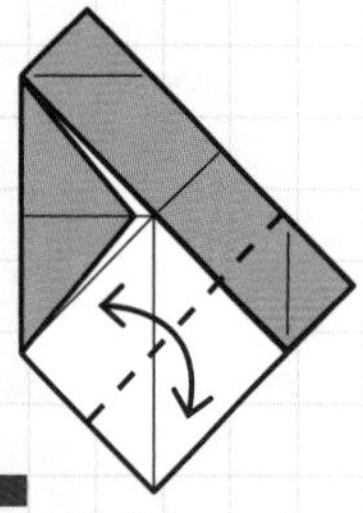

5 Fold and unfold.

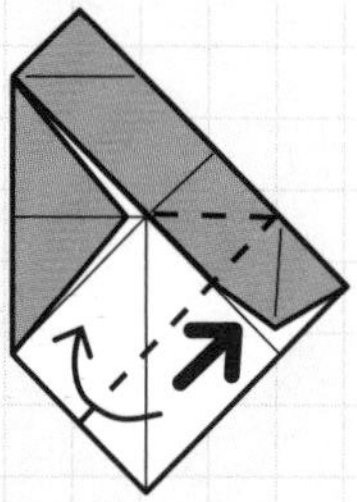

6 Put your finger in the pocket.

7 Lift the top of the flap while folding in and press down.

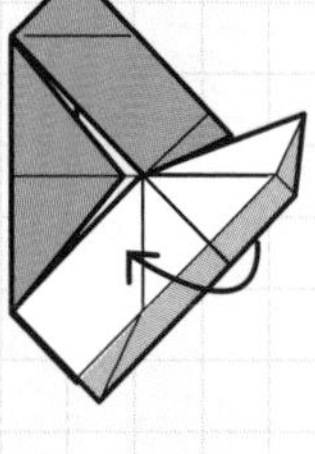

8 Put your finger in the pocket.

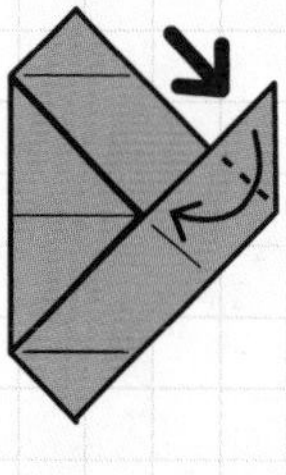

9 Squash to make a square.

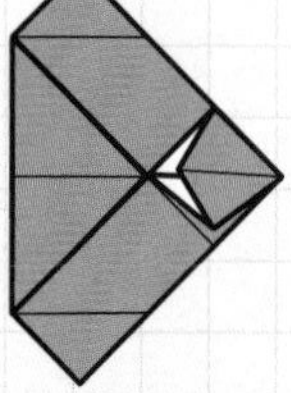

Flip over

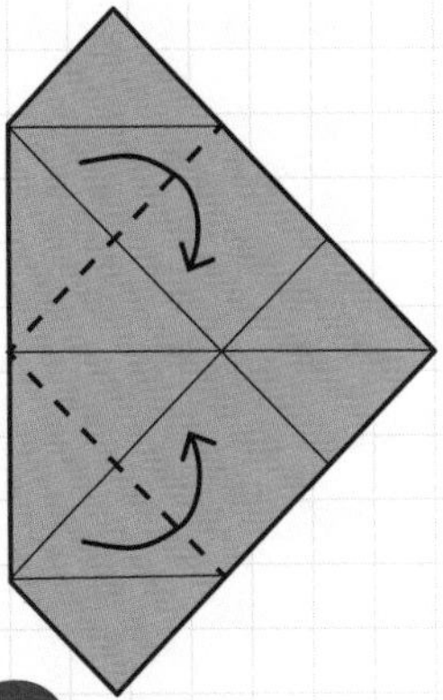

10 Fold the top and bottom in to make a square.

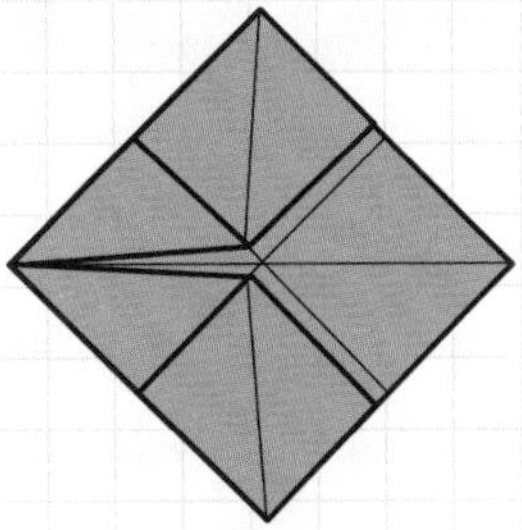

11

Flip over

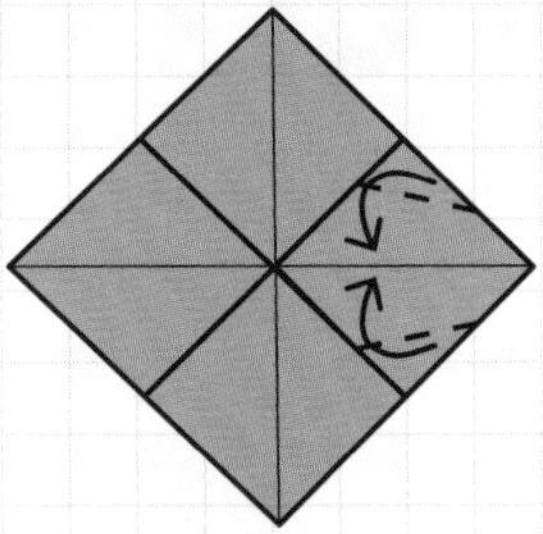

12 Fold in.

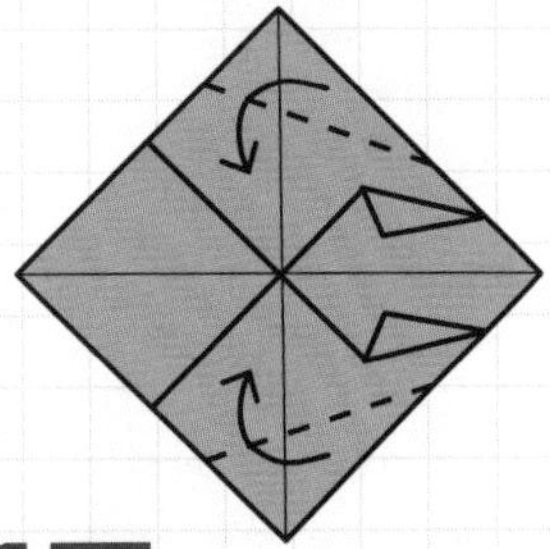

13 Fold the top and bottom points in.

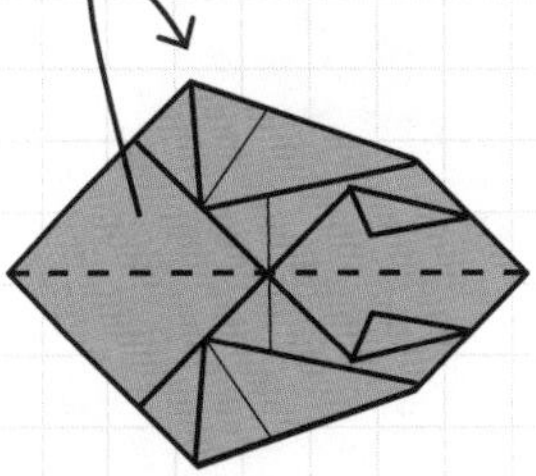

14 Fold the top behind the bottom. Add eyes to bring your grasshoppers to life!

Find the Math!

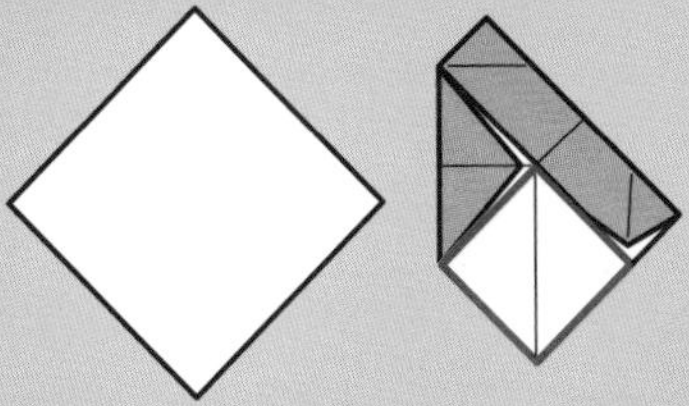

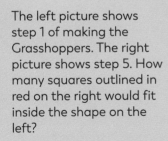

The left picture shows step 1 of making the Grasshoppers. The right picture shows step 5. How many squares outlined in red on the right would fit inside the shape on the left?

ANSWER ON P. 104

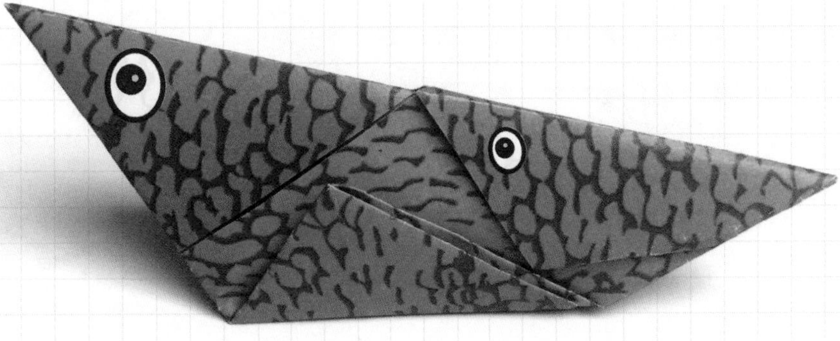

Bear and Cub

To make the Bear and Cub, you'll fold on lots of **diagonal** lines. When a line goes straight across, it's horizontal (like the dotted line in step 6), and when a line goes straight up-and-down, it's vertical (like the line down the middle of step 7). A diagonal line doesn't do either of these things—it slants sideways at an angle. Notice how many diagonal lines you see as you fold!

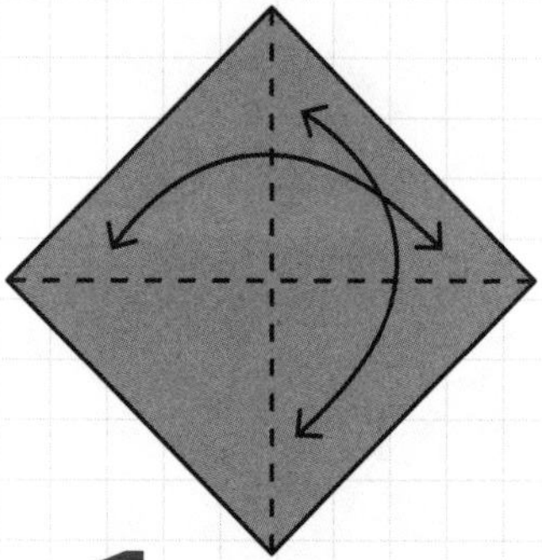

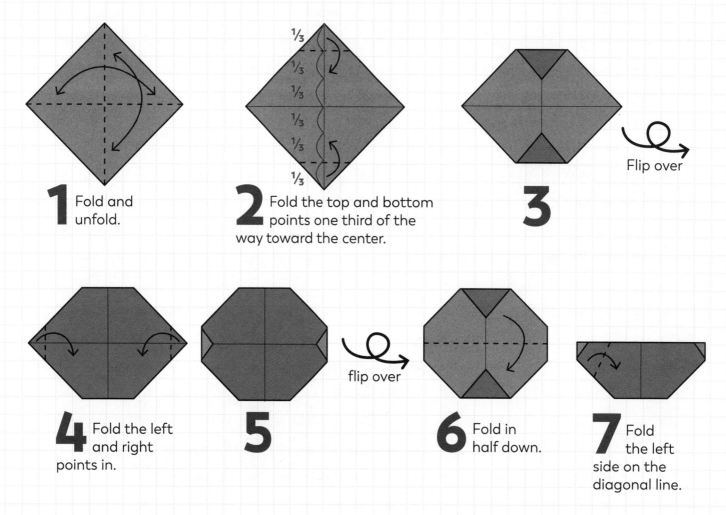

1 Fold and unfold.

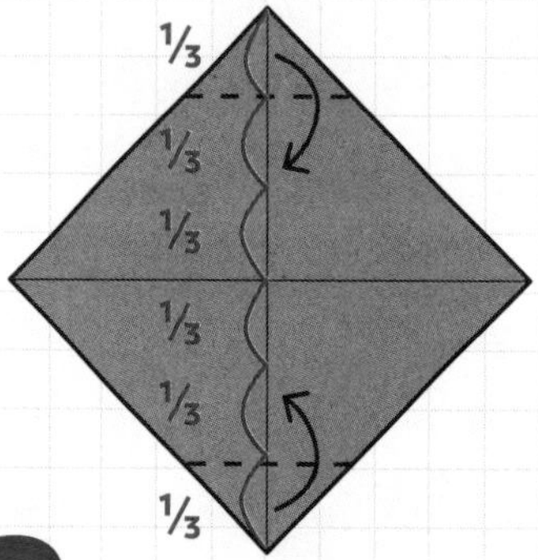

2 Fold the top and bottom points one third of the way toward the center.

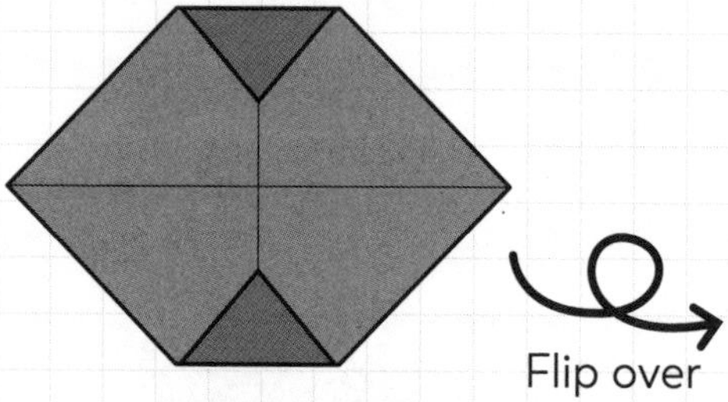

3

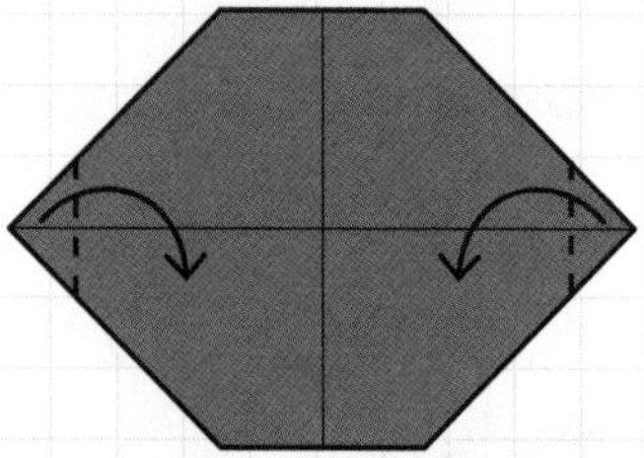

4 Fold the left and right points in.

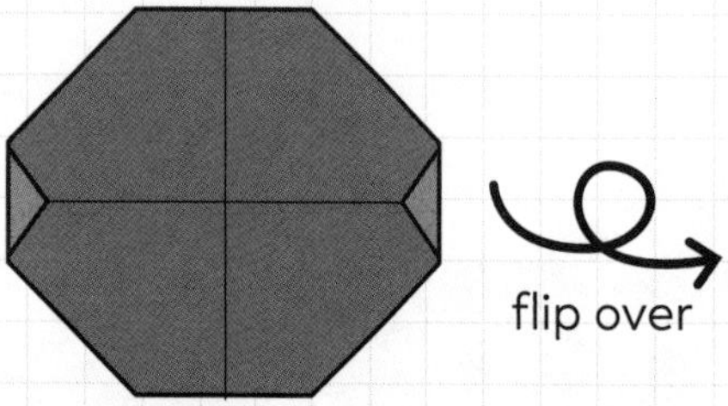

5

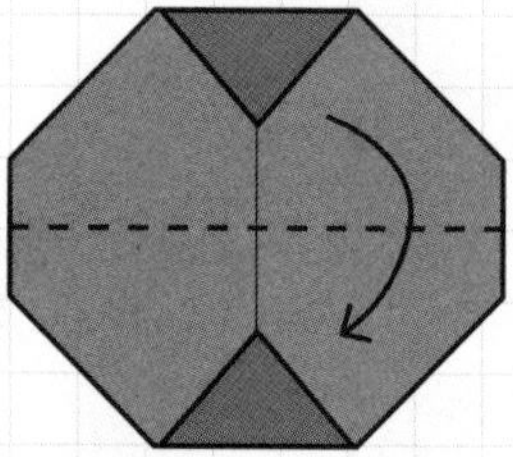

6 Fold in half down.

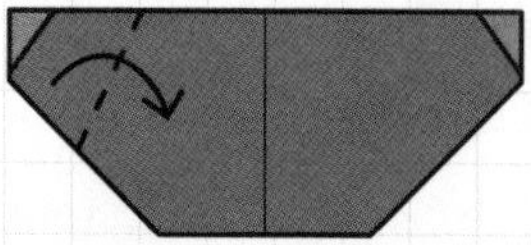

7 Fold the left side on the diagonal line.

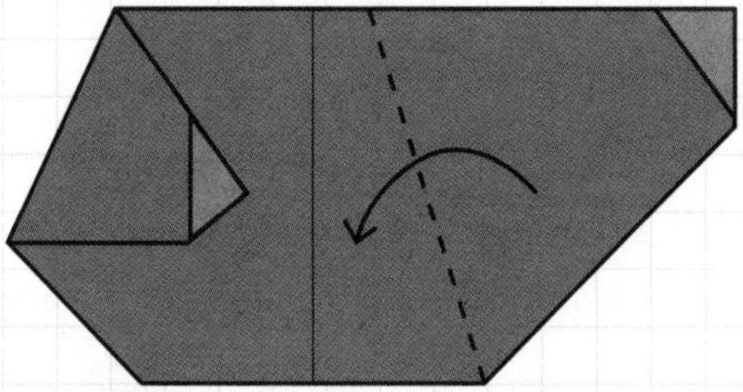

8 Fold the right side on the diagonal line.

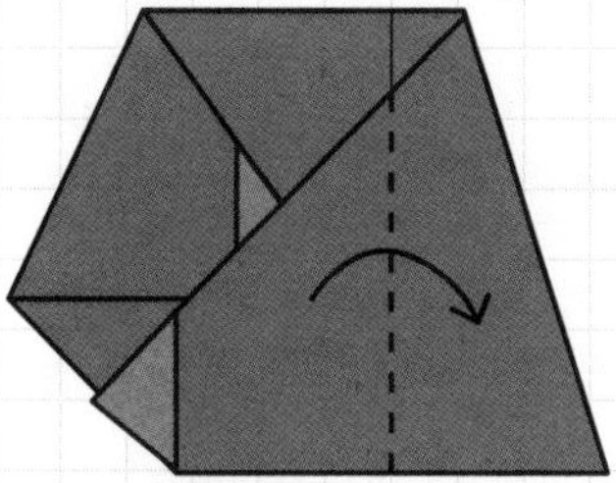

9 Fold to the right.

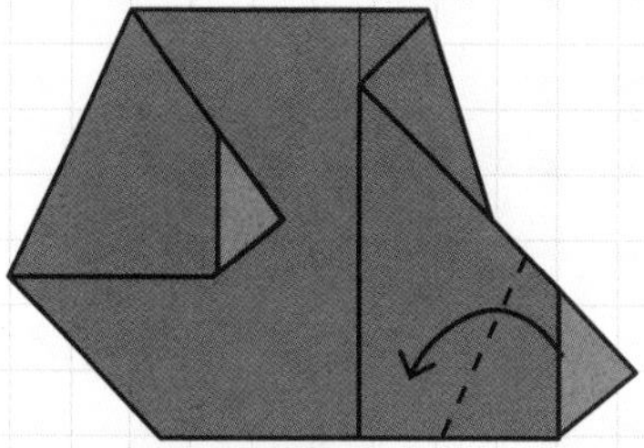

10 Fold the right side on the diagonal line.

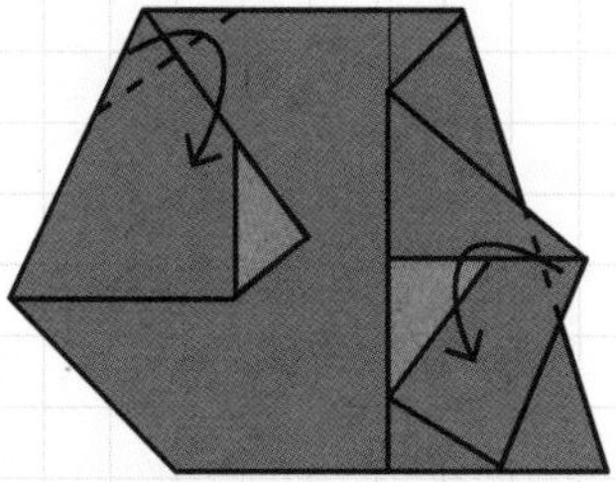

11 Fold down the top corner and fold in the right point.

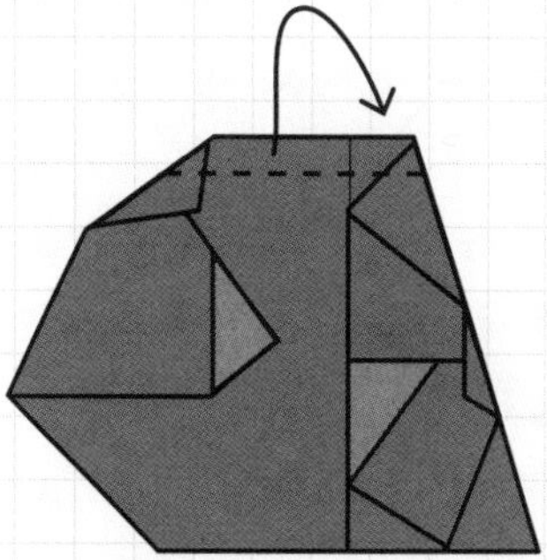

12 Fold back the top edge. Add eyes to finish your cuddly pair of bears!

Find the Math!

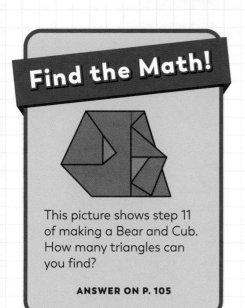

This picture shows step 11 of making a Bear and Cub. How many triangles can you find?

ANSWER ON P. 105

Penguin and Chick ★★★★★

We've talked about a couple of shapes so far, but we haven't introduced the **circle** yet. If you're wondering where the circles are hiding on these pages, look at the eyes of the finished Penguin and Chick. Circles are special because unlike other shapes, we can't describe them using their number of sides—circles have no straight sides at all because they're made up of a closed curving line.

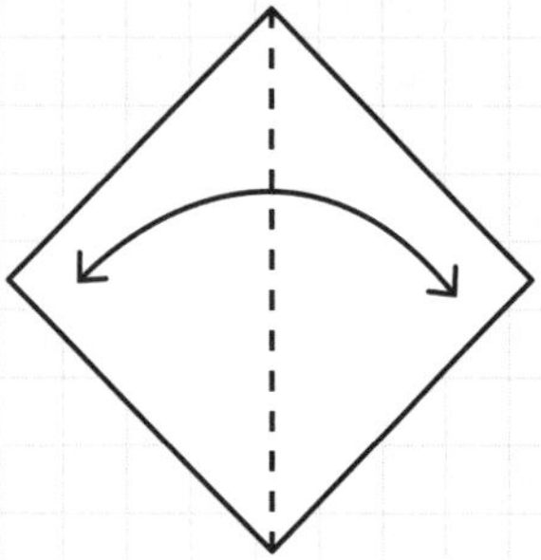

1 Fold in half and unfold.

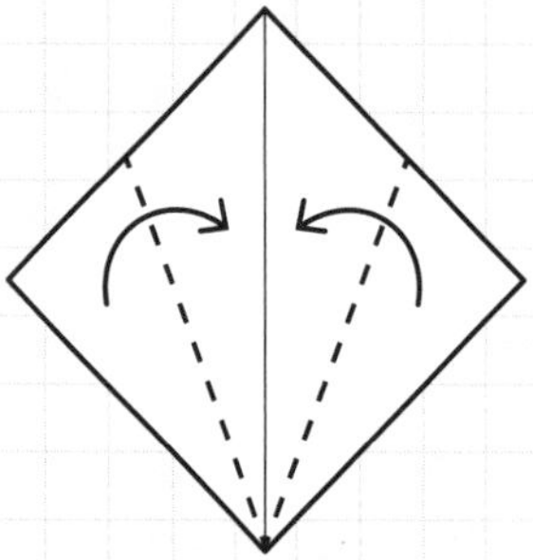

2 Fold the left and right points to the center crease.

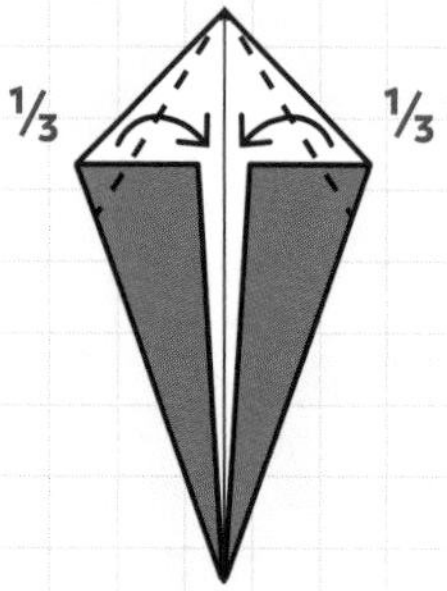

3 Fold the left and right points one third of the way to the center.

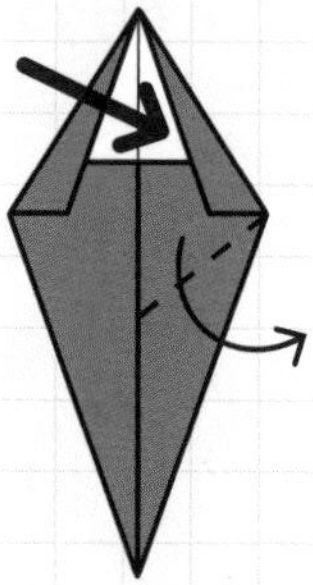

4 Lift the inside flap from underneath the triangle fold on the right side and bring it down and to the right. Fold the flap underneath itself, using the pocket on the inside as a guide.

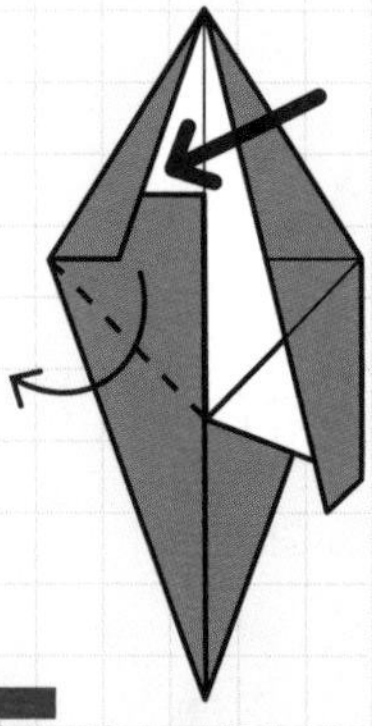

5 Repeat step 4 with the triangle fold on the left side.

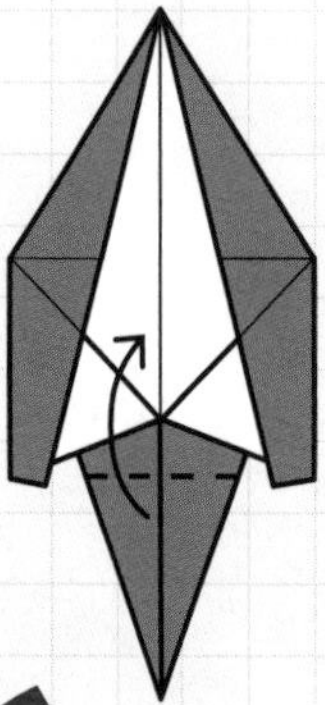

6 Fold the bottom point up.

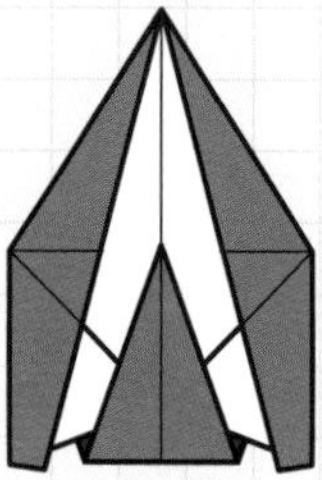

7

Flip over

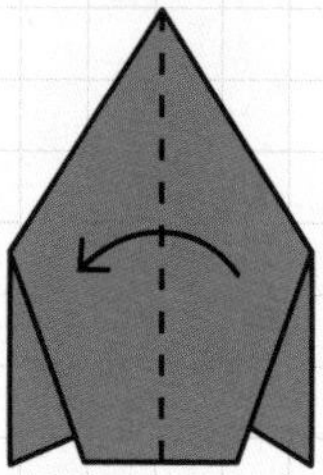

8 Fold to the left.

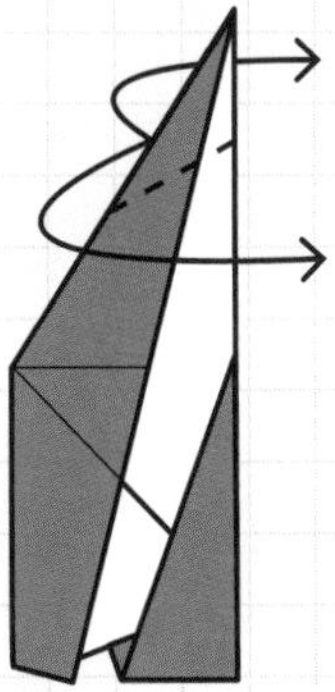

9 Turn the top point inside out and fold down to make the big penguin's beak.

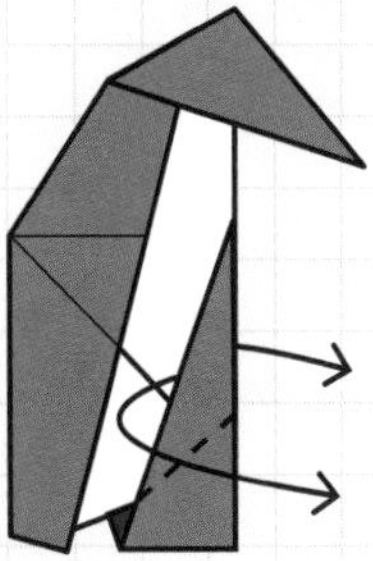

10 Turn the small point under the beak inside out and fold down to make the baby penguin's head.

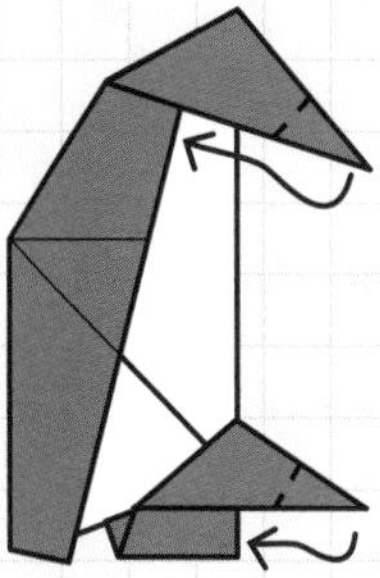

11 Fold in while separating the edges before pressing down.

Find the Math!

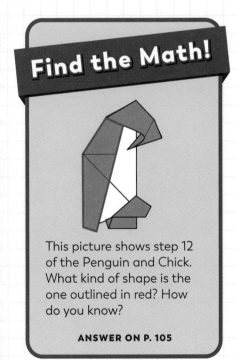

This picture shows step 12 of the Penguin and Chick. What kind of shape is the one outlined in red? How do you know?

ANSWER ON P. 105

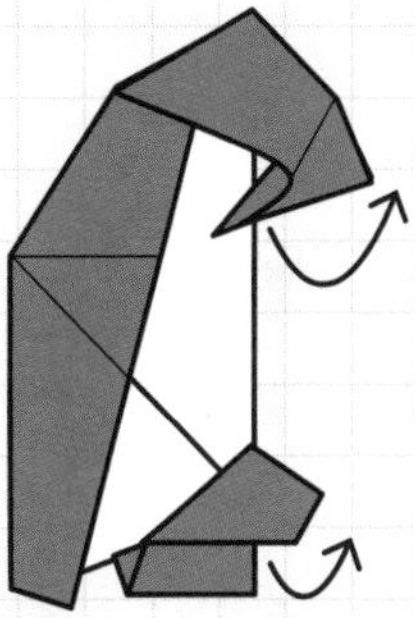

12 Pull the tip of the pointed flap out and pinch slightly to make the beak. Then, add eyes. Now these adorable penguins are ready to waddle into your heart!

Ladybugs

Some shapes can look almost exactly like each other but still not be congruent or similar. When the Ladybugs are finished, the big and little bugs seem like they could be the same, right? But if you look closer, you'll notice that the big ladybug's head is a different shape than the little ladybug's, and so is its back. Counting the number of sides is one helpful way to figure out if shapes are congruent or similar.

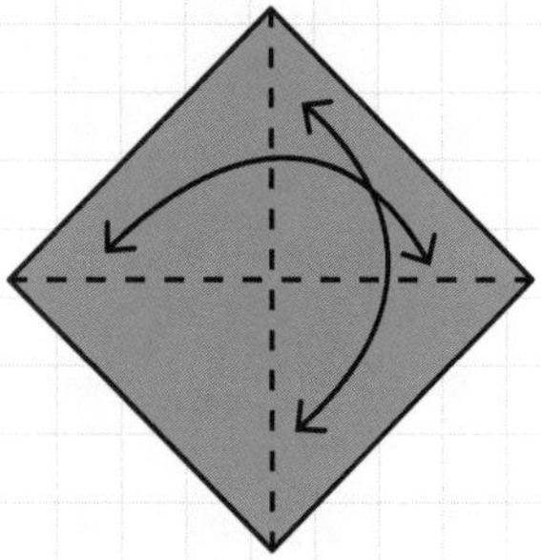

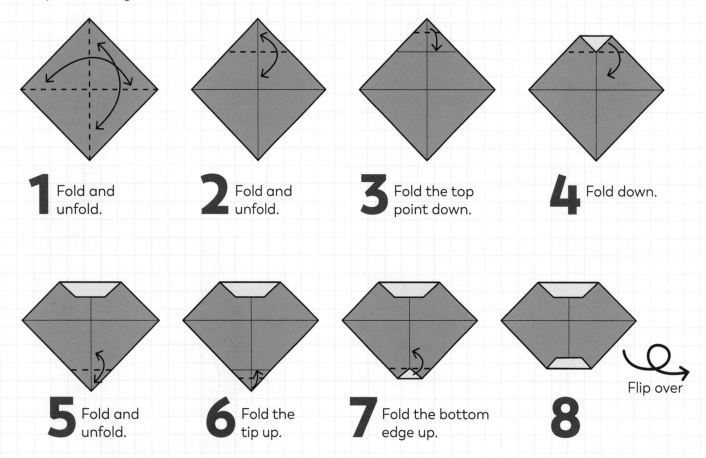

1 Fold and unfold.

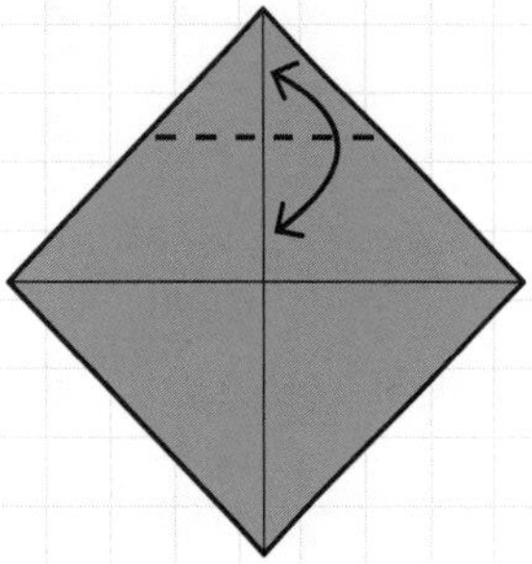

2 Fold and unfold.

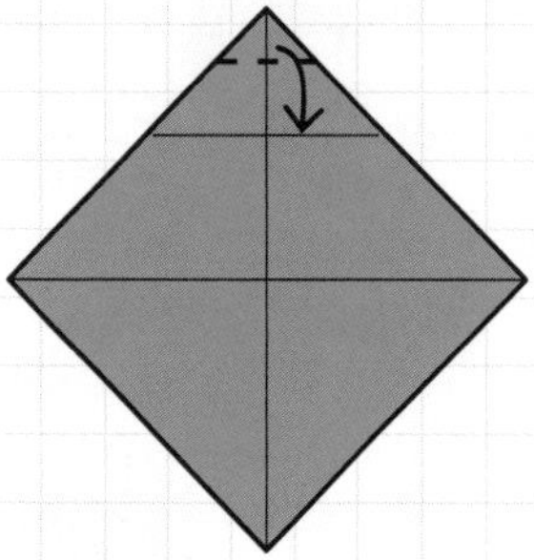

3 Fold the top point down.

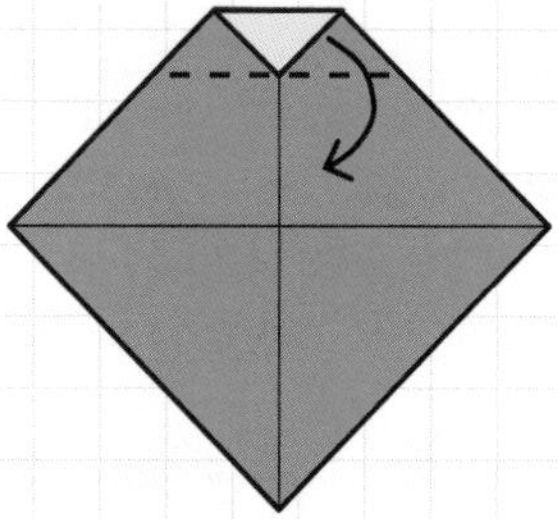

4 Fold down.

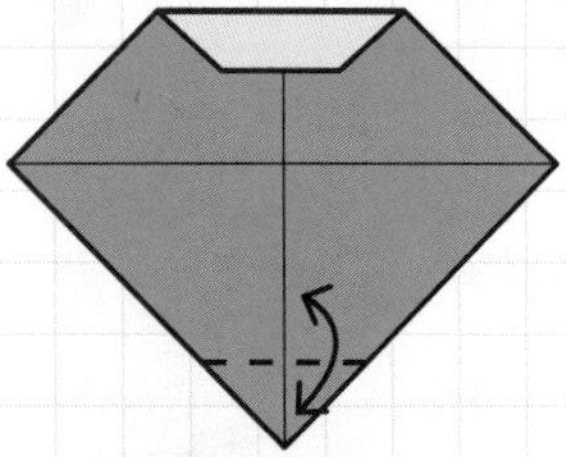

5 Fold and unfold.

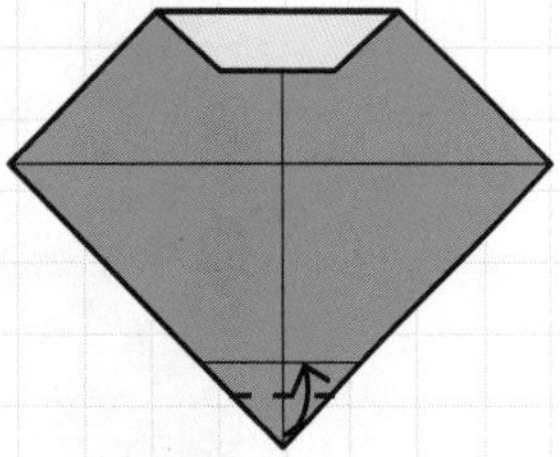

6 Fold the tip up.

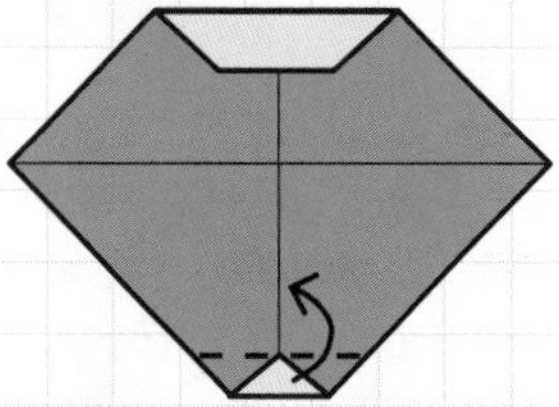

7 Fold the bottom edge up.

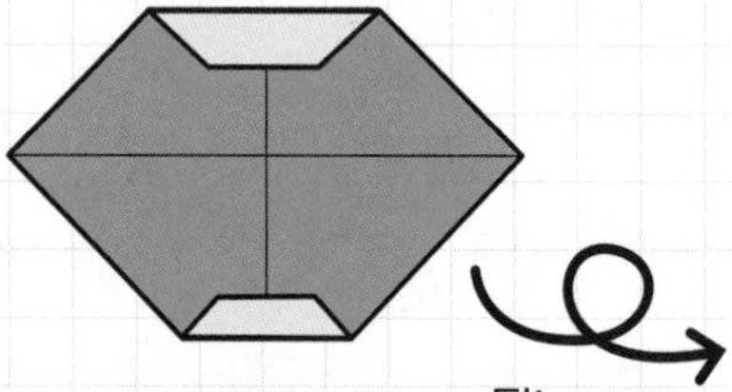

Flip over

8

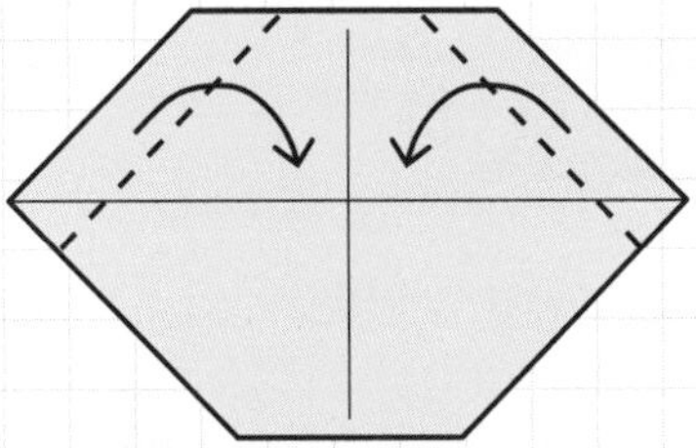

9 Fold the left and right edges in.

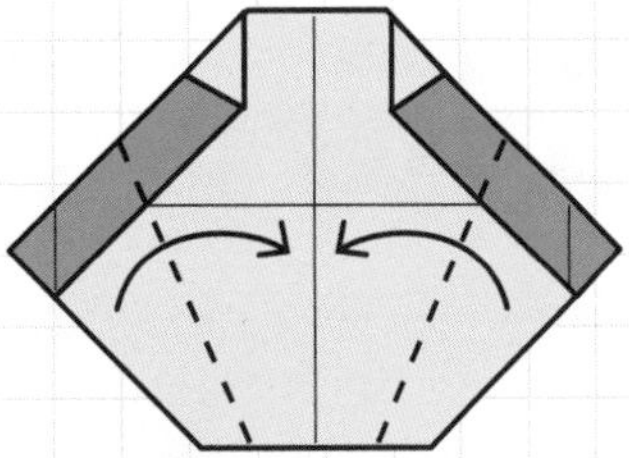

10 Fold to the center.

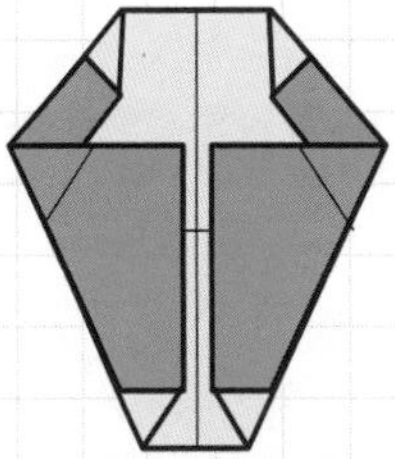

Flip over

11

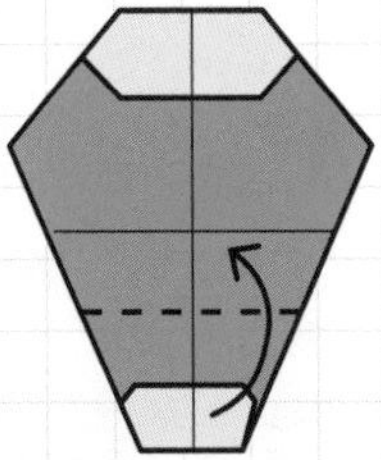

12 Fold up.

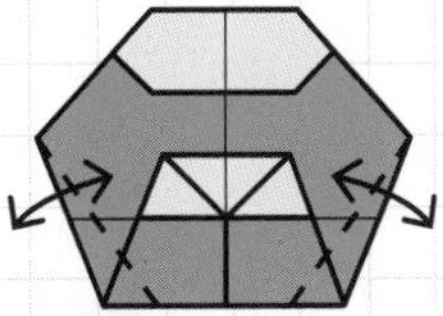

13 Fold and unfold.

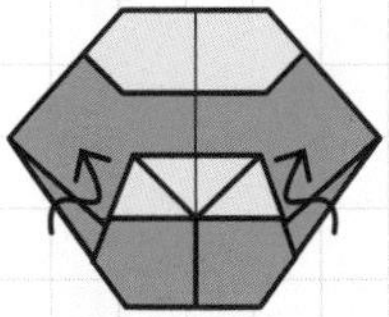

14 Fold in and tuck behind the front flap.

Find the Math!

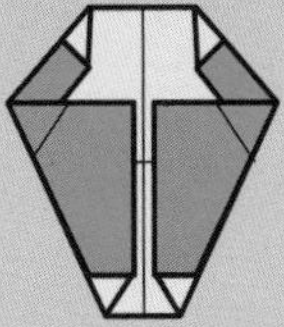

This picture shows step 11 of making the Ladybugs. What kind of symmetry does this shape have?

1. Reflection symmetry
2. Mirror symmetry

ANSWER ON P. 105

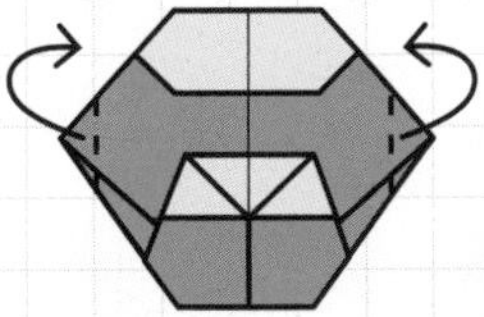

15 Fold back. Add eyes and black spots, and your adorable bug buddies are finished!

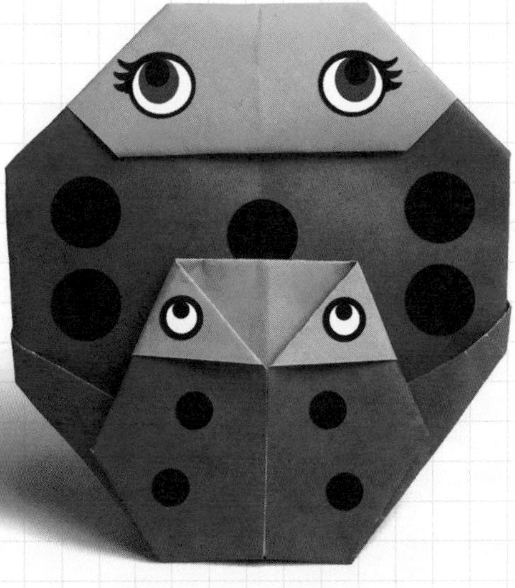

Tortoise and Hare

You can find a math secret hidden in the finished tortoise's shell. Where? Check out the overlapping hexagons you'll draw to create the shell's pattern. When a shape makes a pattern with itself like this—fitting together over and over with no gaps in between—that shape is able to **tessellate.** Not every shape can do this, so try to find shapes that wouldn't be able to make a complete pattern as you fold this tessellating tortoise and its hare friend.

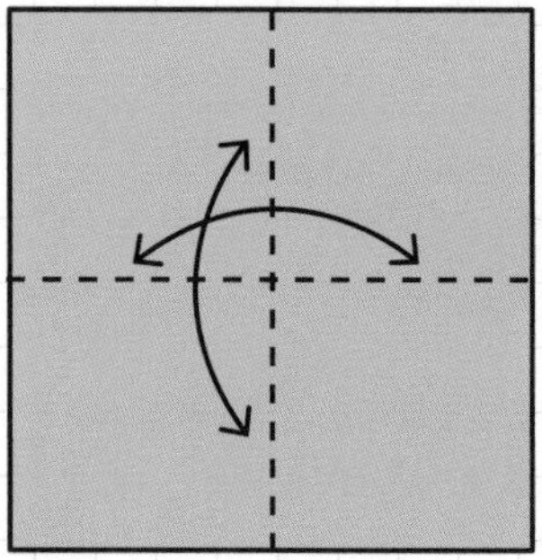

1 Fold and unfold.

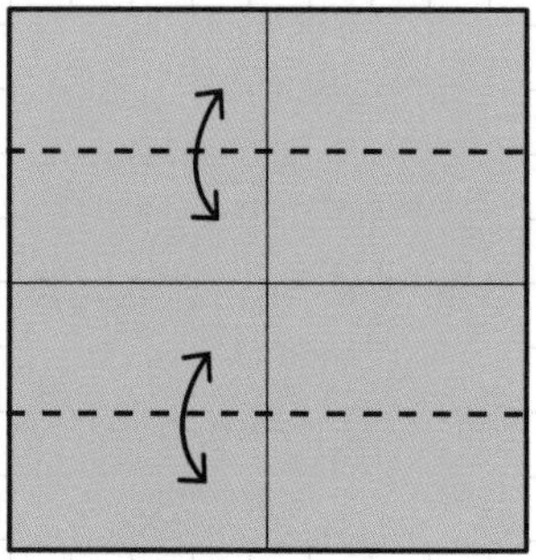

2 Fold and unfold.

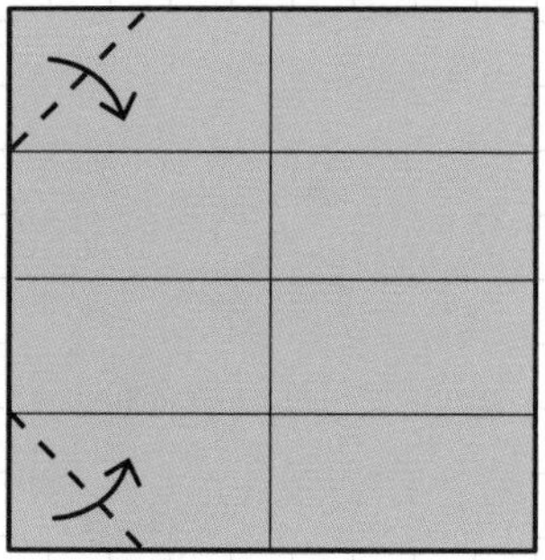

3 Fold the corners in.

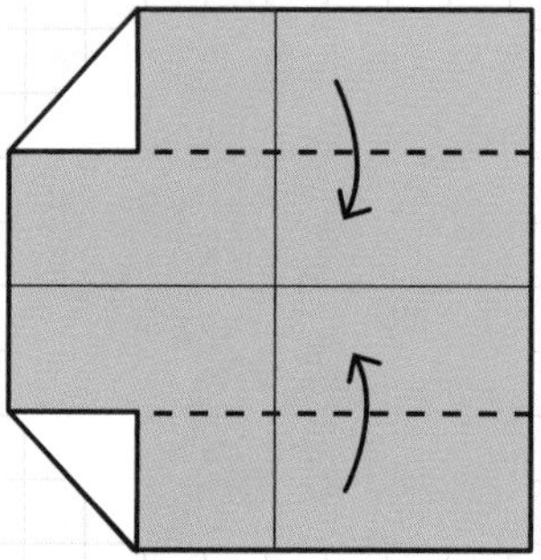

4 Fold the top edge down and the bottom edge up.

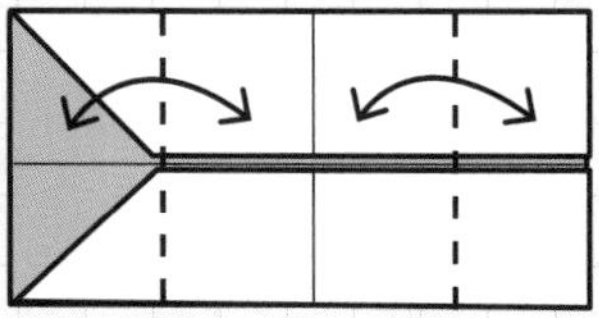

5 Fold and unfold.

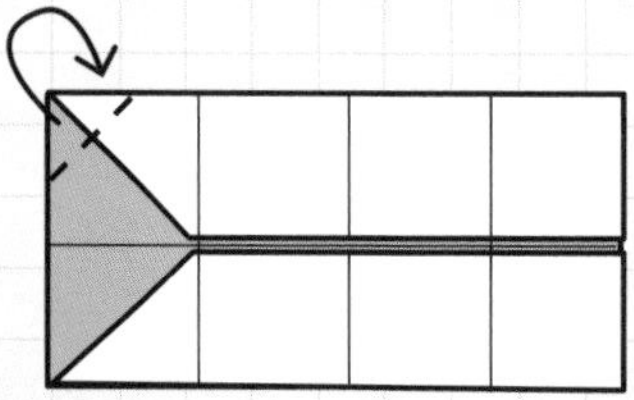

6 Fold the corner behind.

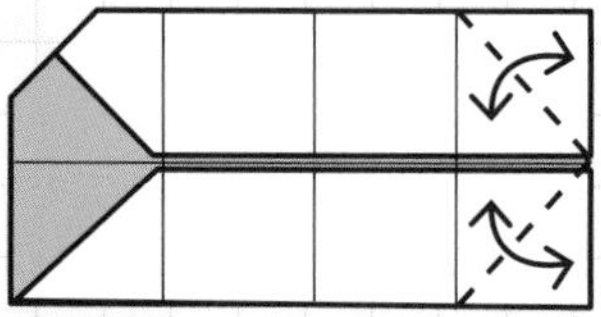

7 Fold and unfold the corners.

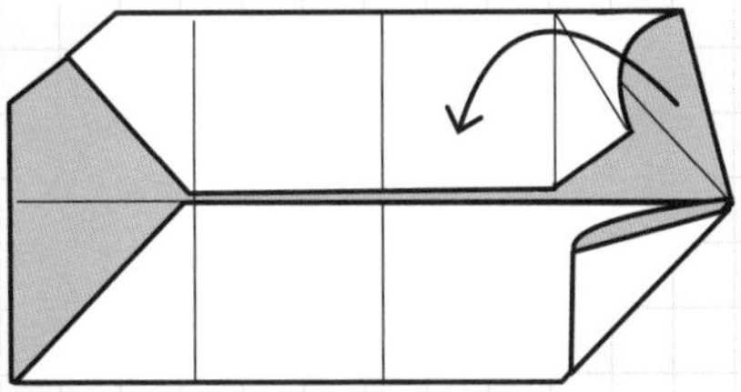

8 Lift the flap to open, put your finger in the pocket, and press down to make a triangle. Repeat on the bottom flap.

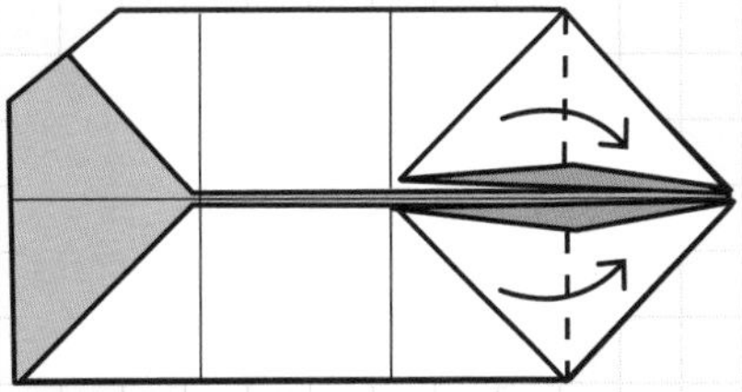

9 Fold to the right.

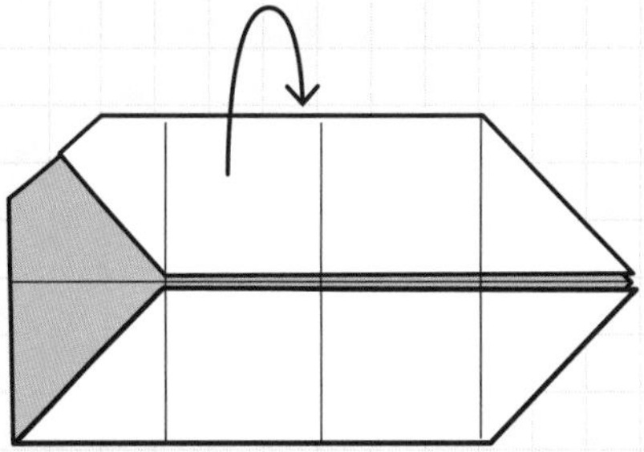

10 Fold the top edge to the back.

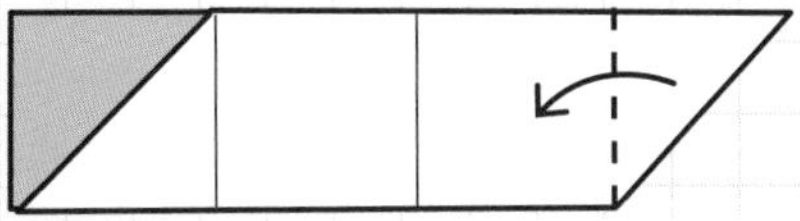

11 Fold the top flap to the left.

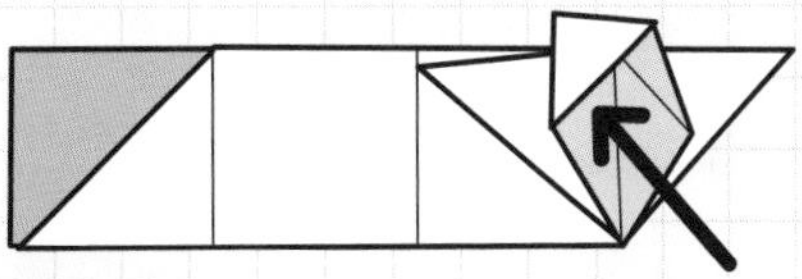

12 Open the middle pocket, put your finger in the pocket, and press to fold down.

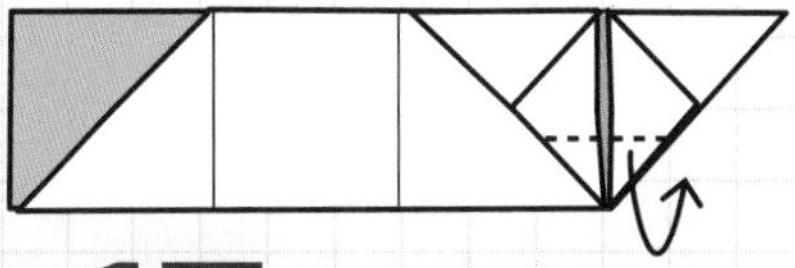

13 Fold the top point behind.

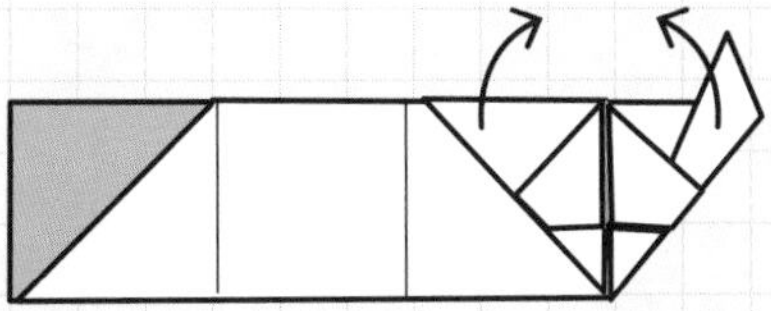

14 Fold the points in half up and behind the front flap.

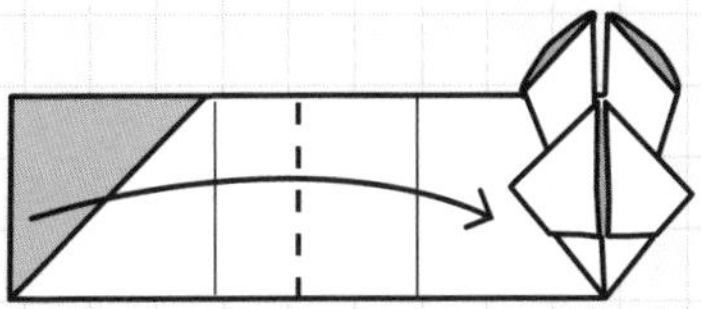

15 Fold the left edge in half.

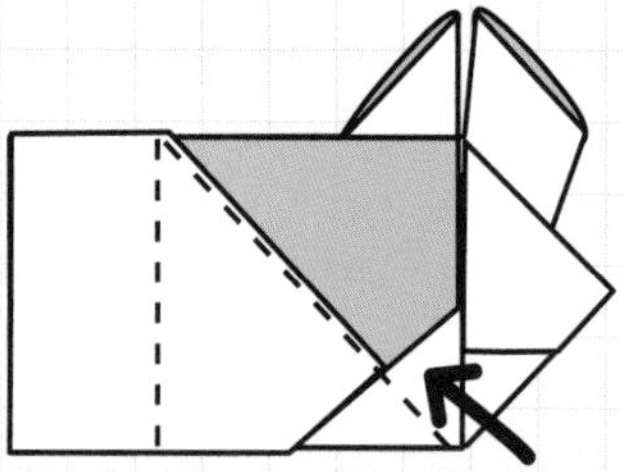

16 Lift and fold the outside flap so it turns inside out.

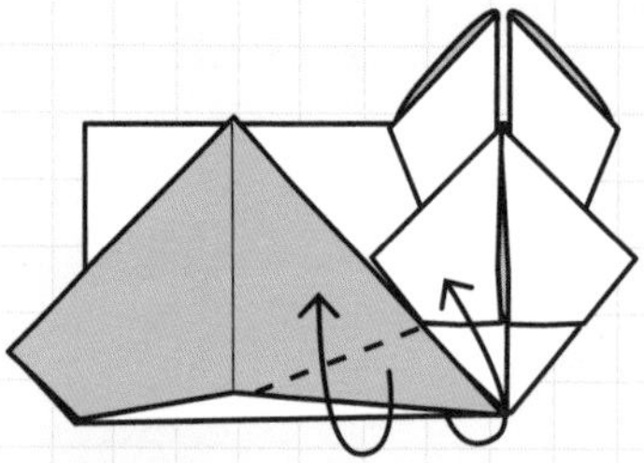

17 Make a crease, then fold to turn inside out.

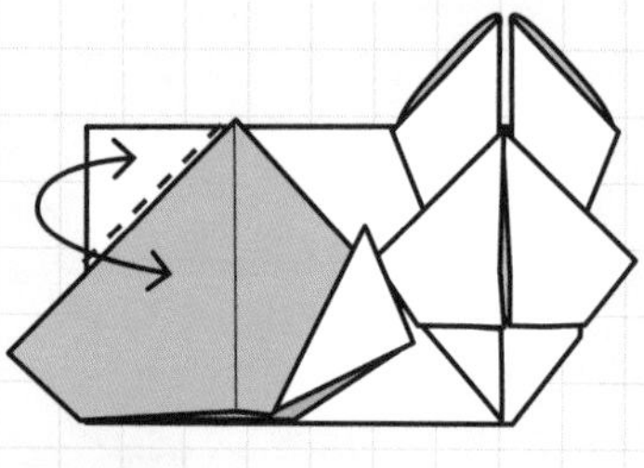

18 Fold and unfold.

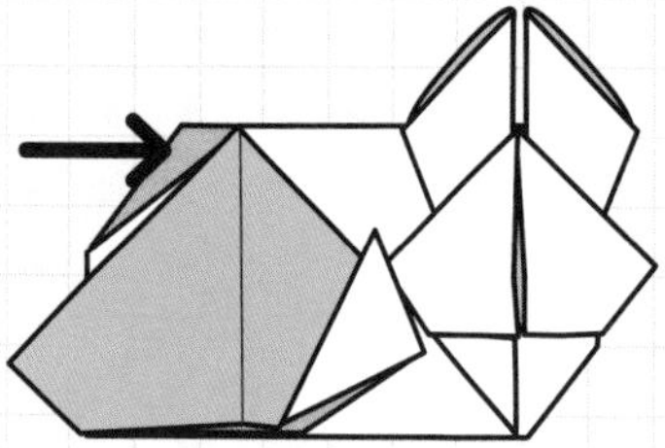

19 Tuck the corner inside.

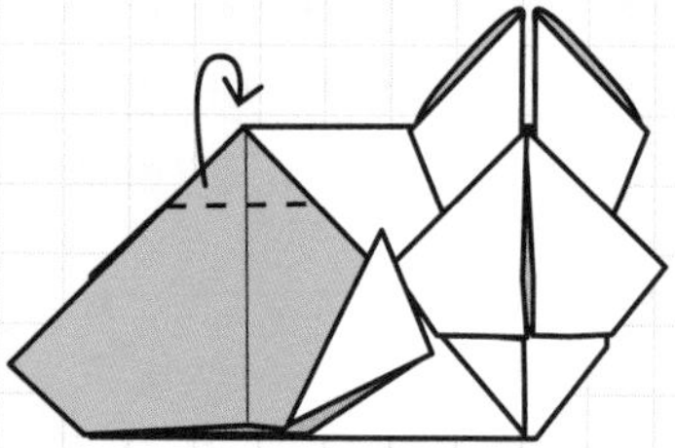

20 Fold the top point down. Add eyes and a nose to the hare, and an eye to the turtle. Now these 2 are the best of buds!

Find the Math!

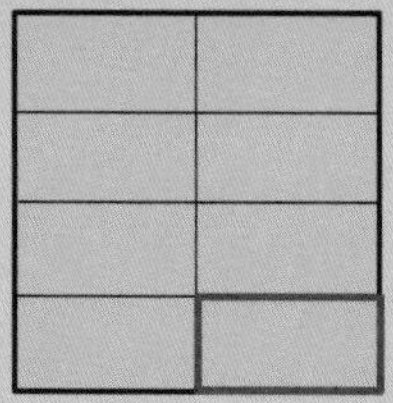

This picture shows step 3 of making a Tortoise and Hare. What fraction of the whole sheet of origami paper is the rectangle outlined in red?

ANSWER ON P. 105

Cat and Dog ★★★★★

There's one last kind of angle we haven't talked about: a **straight angle.** Straight angles measure 180°, even wider than obtuse angles—so wide that they're really just straight lines! To understand this better, look at step 11. The line at the very bottom of the paper is a straight angle made out of 2 90° angles on the black and orange triangles. 90 + 90 = 180, so they add together to make a flat line.

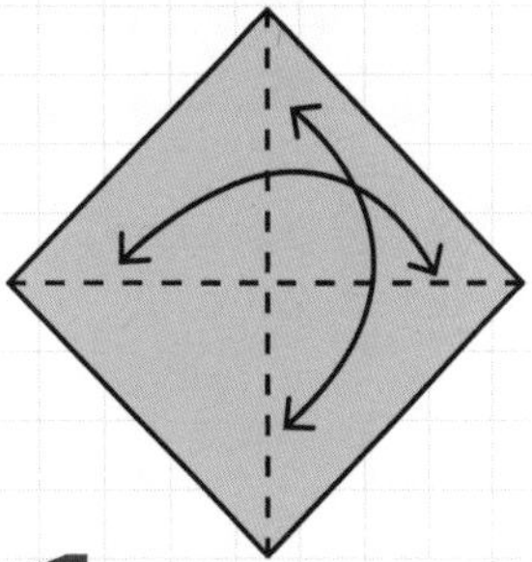

1 Fold and unfold.

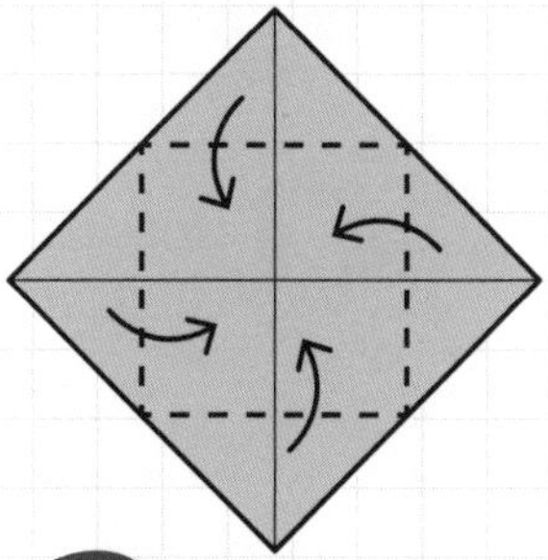

2 Fold the corners to the center.

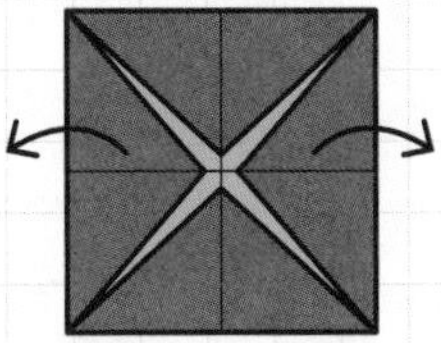

3 Open the left and right flaps.

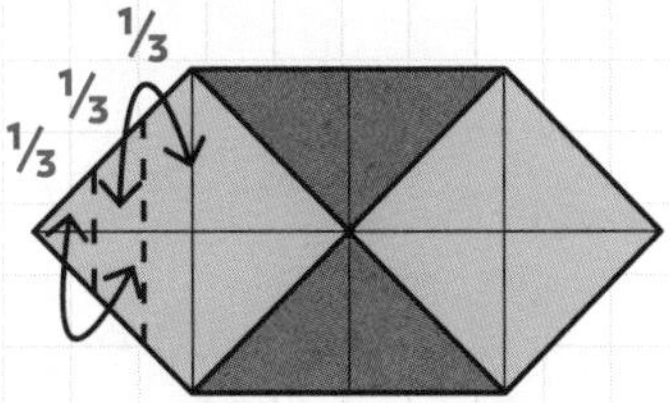

4 Fold the left triangle into thirds and unfold.

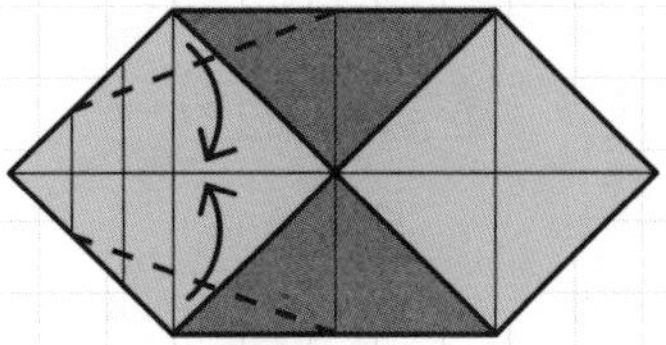

5 Fold.

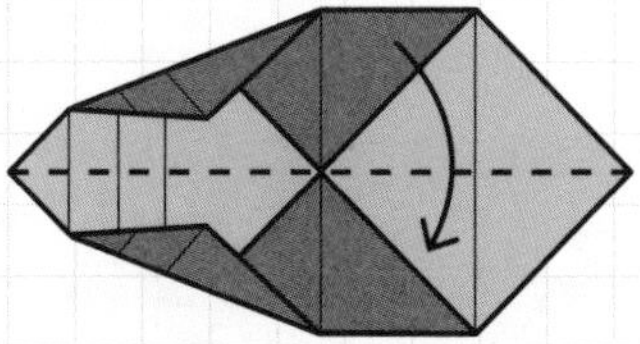

6 Fold in half down.

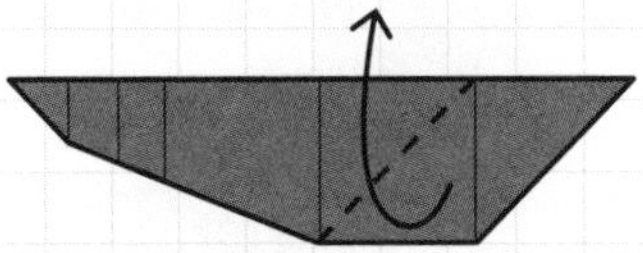

7 Fold up and unfold.

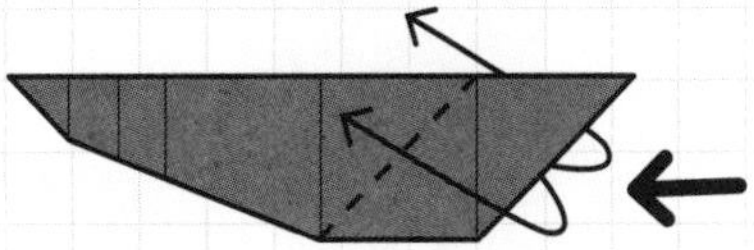

8 Fold back while turning the point inside out.

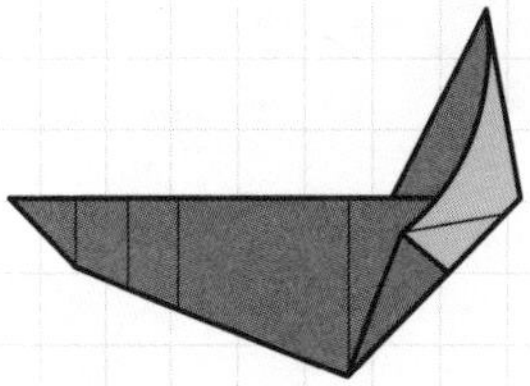

9 Fold flat along the crease.

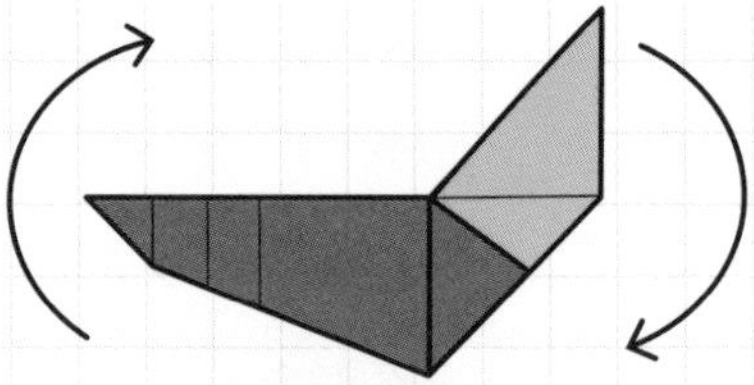

10 Rotate clockwise.

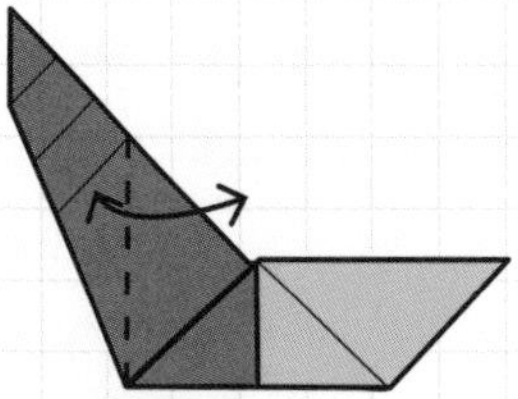

11 Fold and unfold.

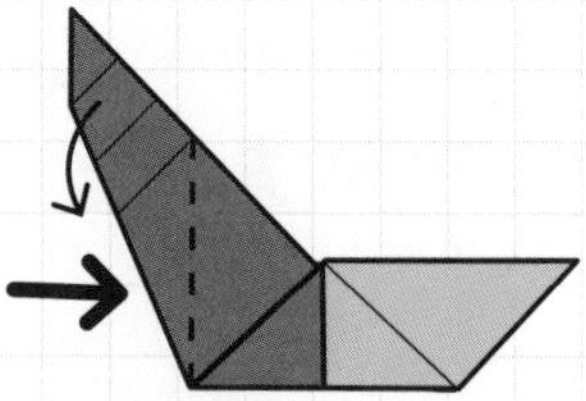

12 Open and press down to make the dog's head.

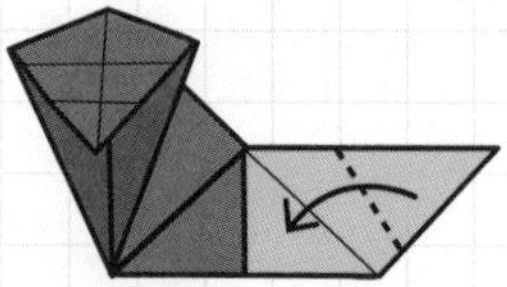

13 Fold the right point toward the center.

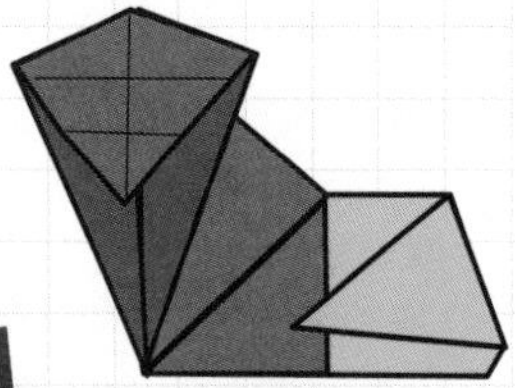

14

Flip over

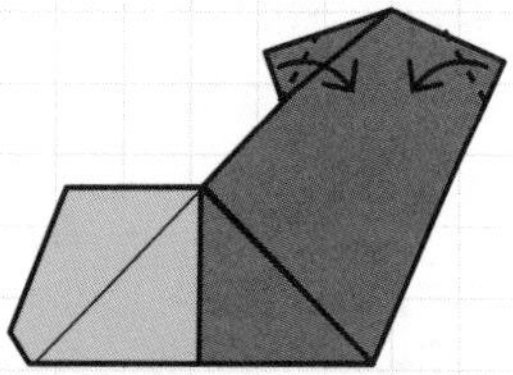

15 Fold the ears in.

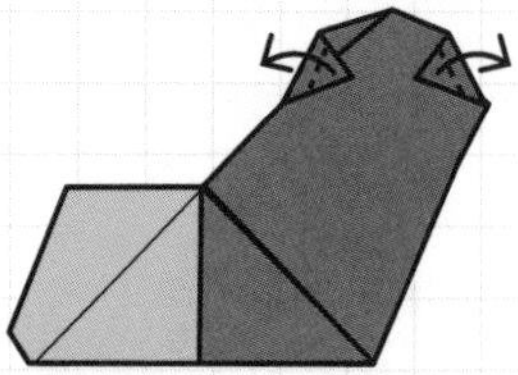

16 Fold the tips of the ears out.

Find the Math!

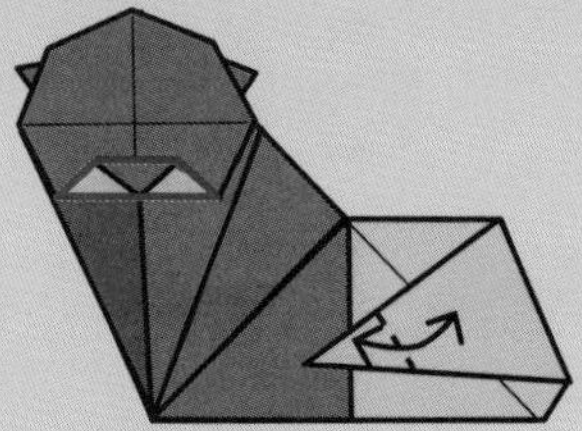

This picture shows step 20 of making a Cat and Dog. The shape outlined in red makes the dog's nose, but it also has a special name. What's this shape called?

ANSWER ON P. 105

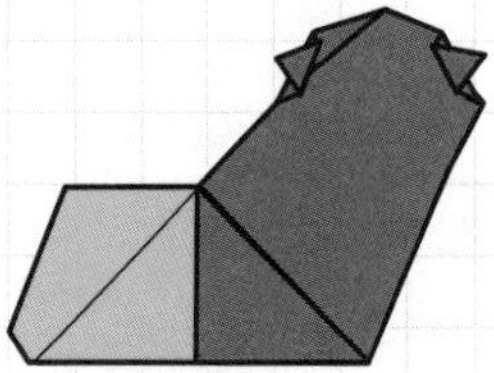

17

Flip over

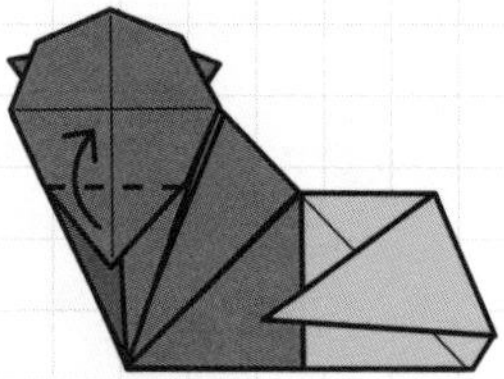

18 Fold the bottom of the dog's head up.

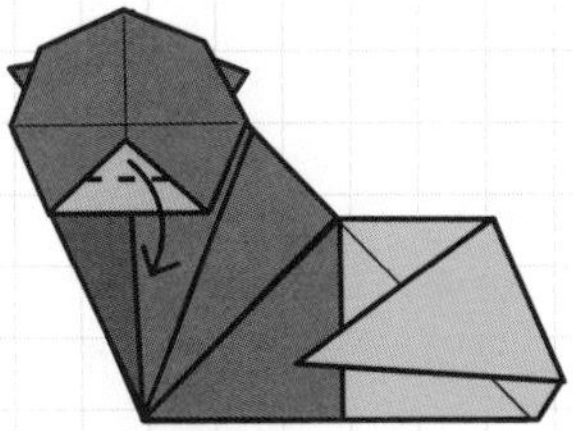

19 Fold the top point down.

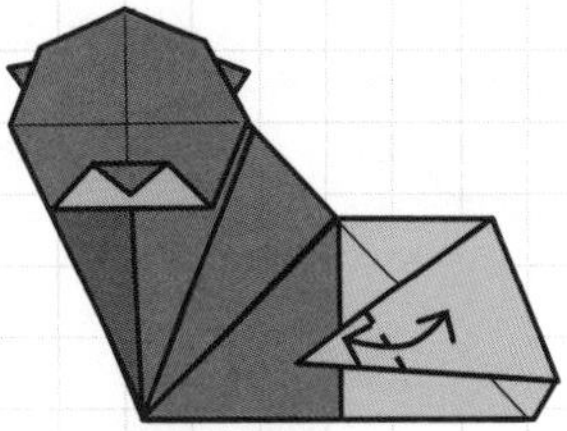

20 Fold and unfold.

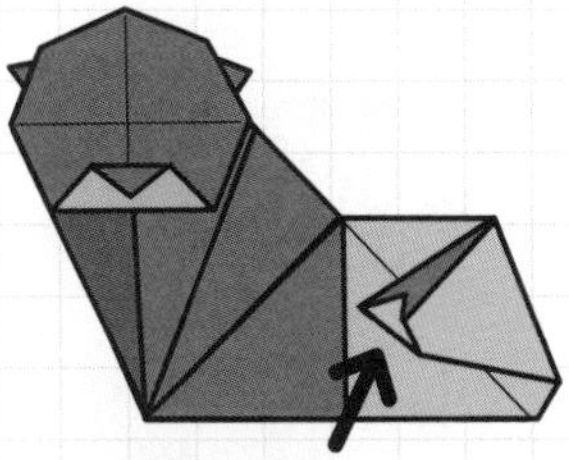

21 Lift and fold inside.

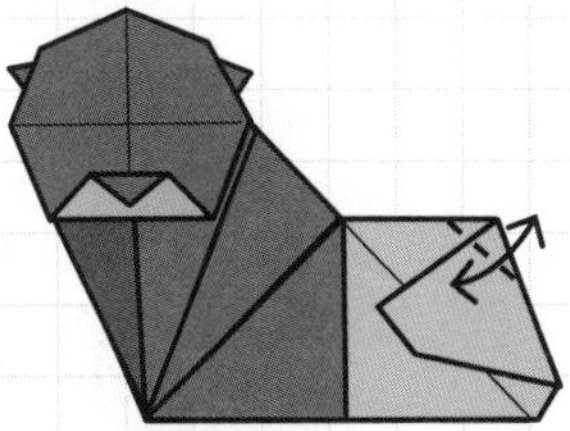

22 Fold and unfold.

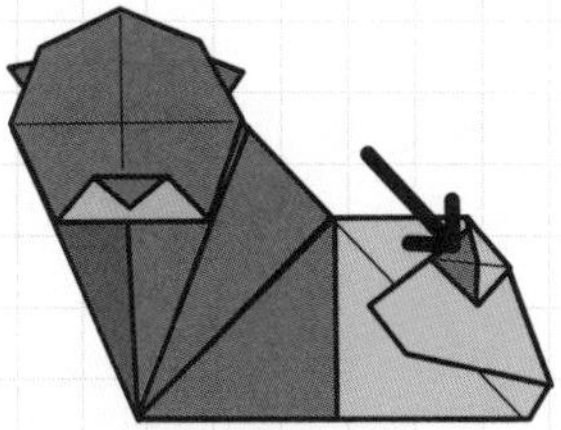

23 Lift to open, put your finger in the pocket, and press down.

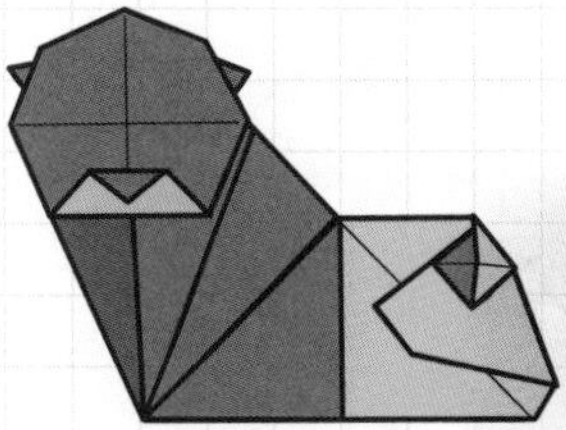

24 Add the sticker eyes. Now you have 2 new paper pets!

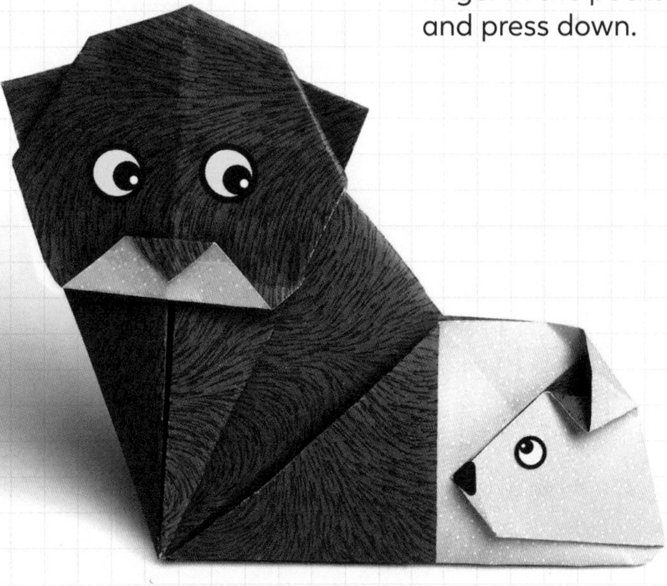

Four Frogs ★★★★★

To make these Four Frogs, you're going to have to repeat the same step a few times. Repeating is important in math, too. When you multiply one number by another (let's say 2 x 3), you're adding that first number to itself as many times as the second number says (2 + 2 + 2 = 6). Try counting how many times you repeat each step as you multiply 1 sheet of paper into 4 friendly amphibians.

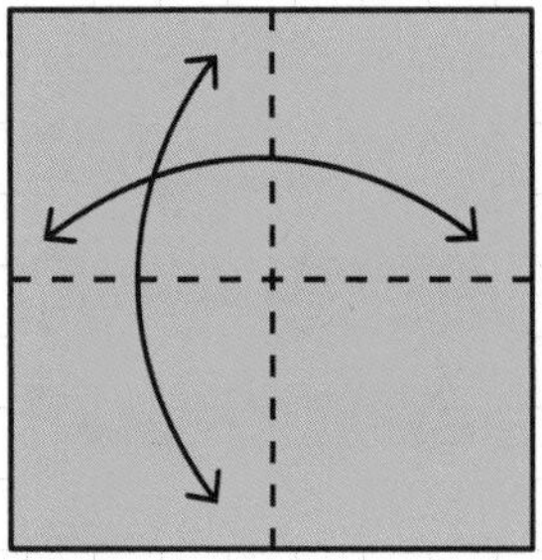

1 Fold and unfold.

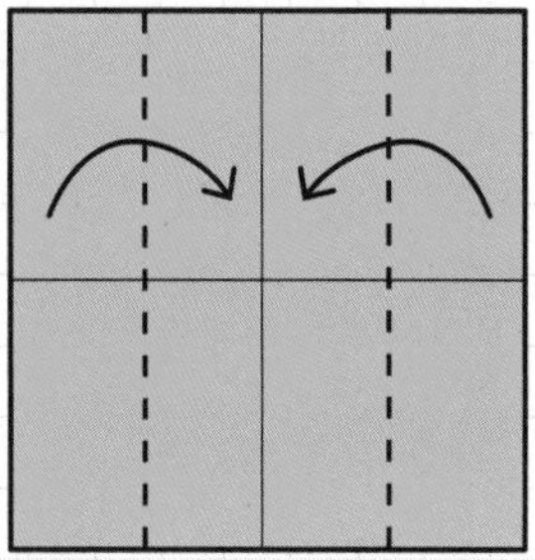

2 Fold the left and right edges to the center.

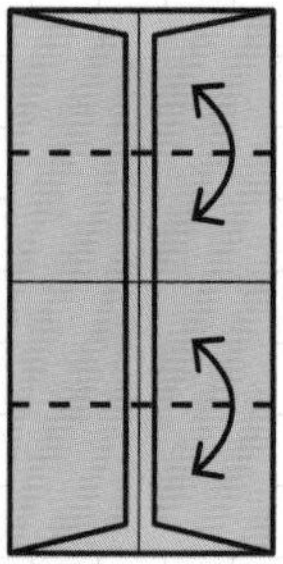

3 Fold and unfold.

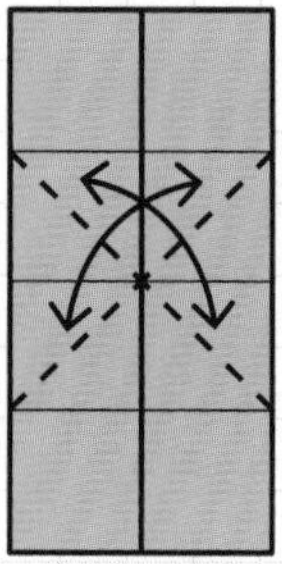

4 Make diagonal folds, then unfold.

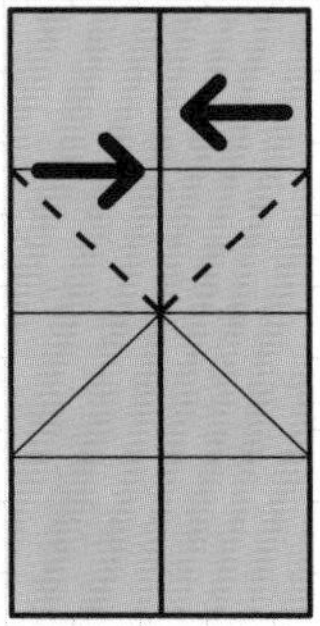

5 Lift to open the pockets.

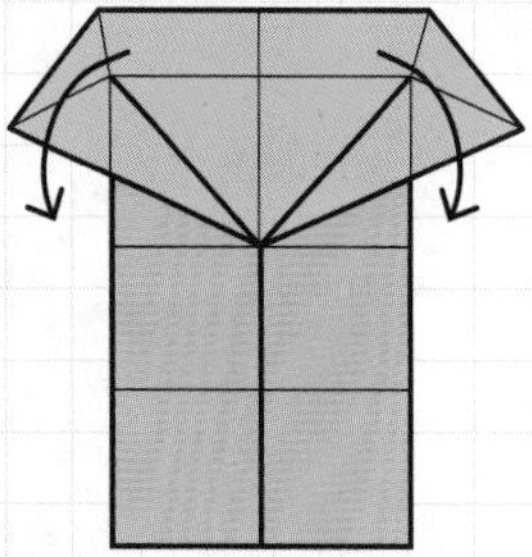

6 Press down to flatten.

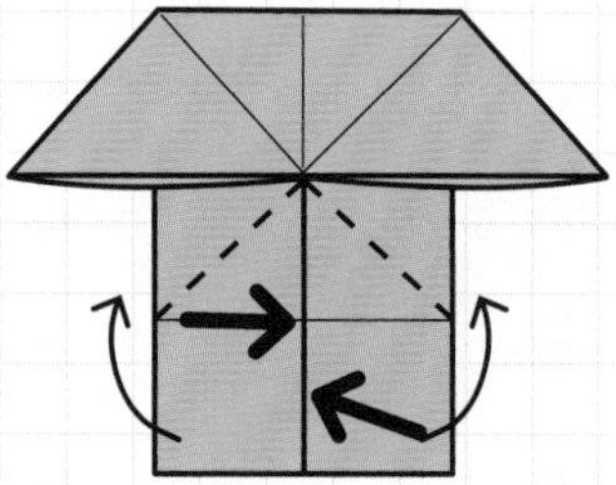

7 Repeat steps 5 and 6 on the bottom.

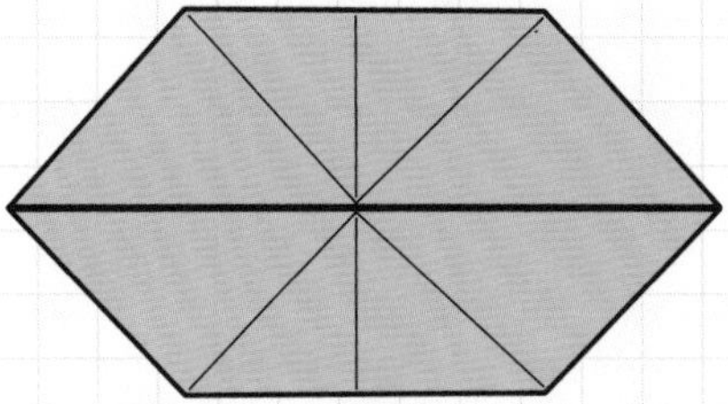

8

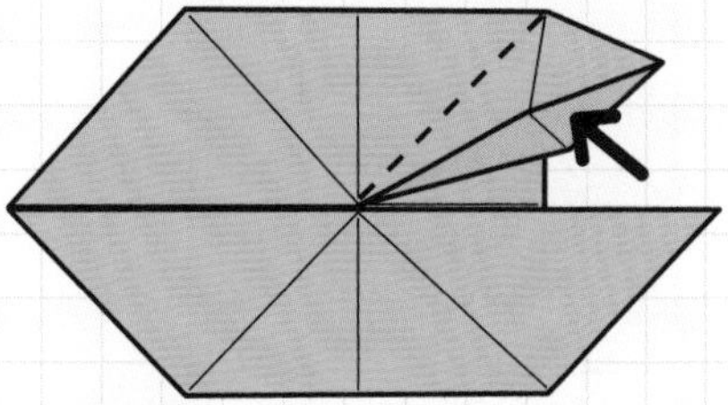

9 Lift up the top right flap and put your finger in the pocket.

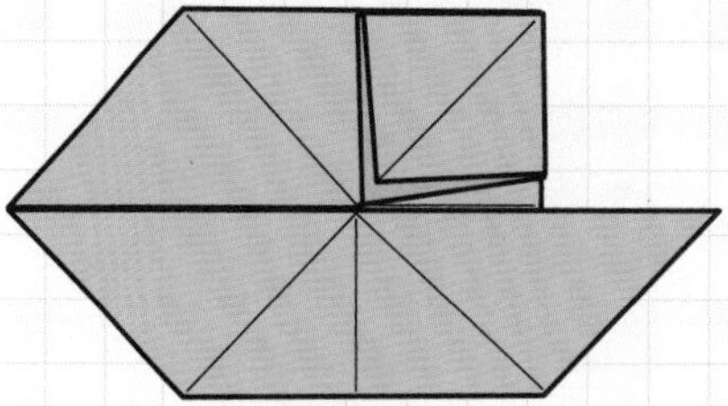

10 Squash down to make a square.

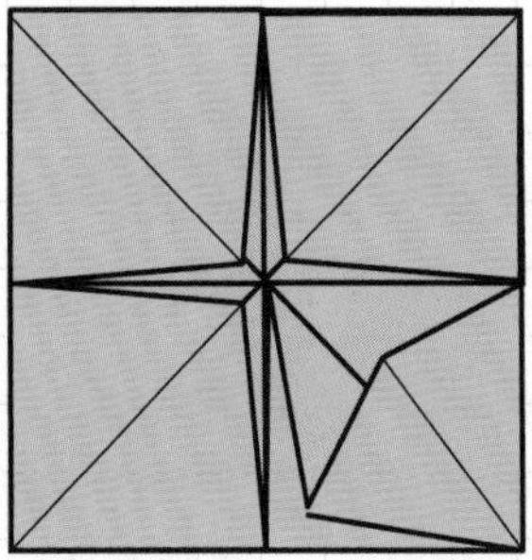

11 Repeat steps 9 and 10 on the other 3 corners.

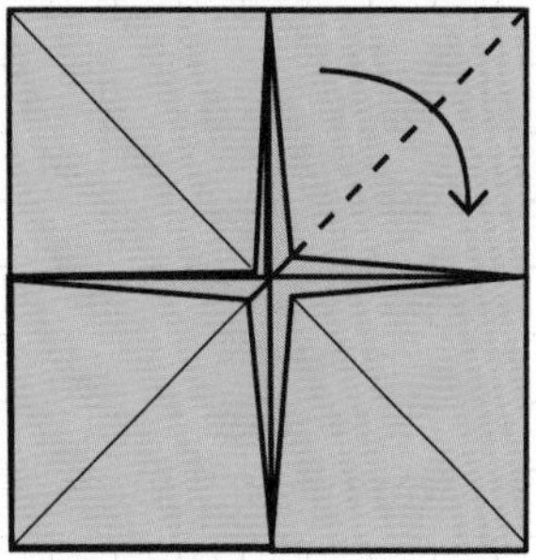

12 Lift the top corner and fold down.

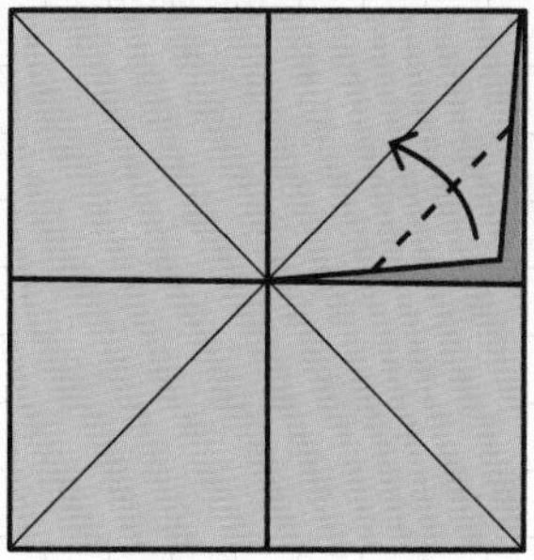

13 Fold the corner up.

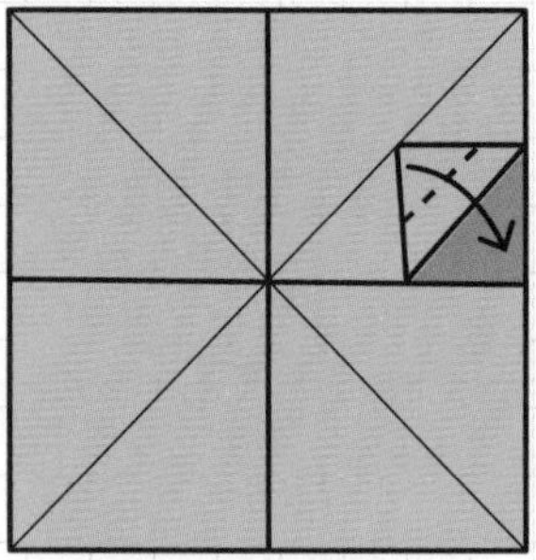

14 Fold the tip down.

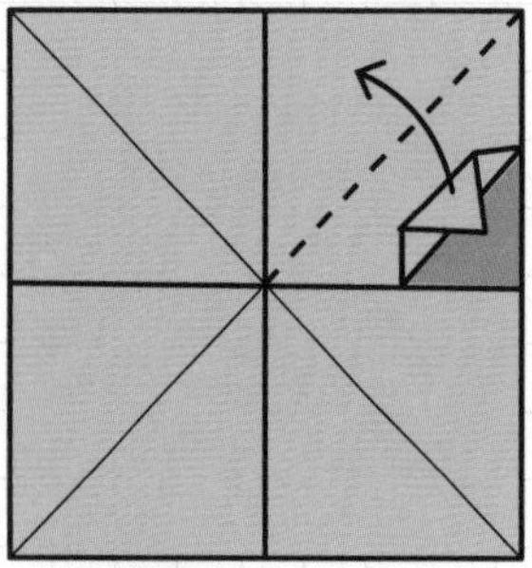

15 Swing the flap up.

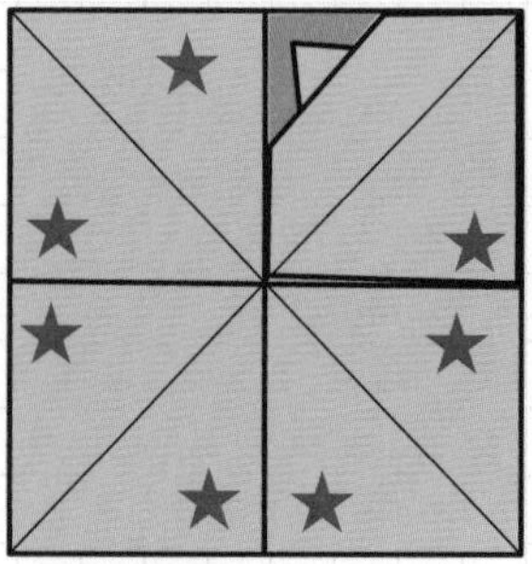

16 Repeat steps 12 through 15 in the places marked with a ★.

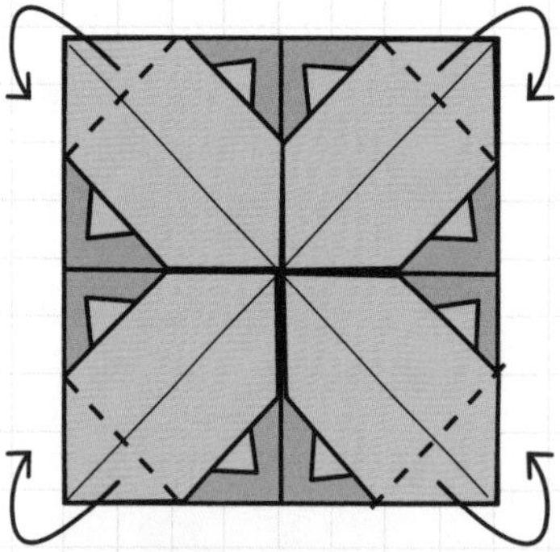

17 Fold the corners back. Add eyes and admire your lily pad full of frogs!

Find the Math!

This picture shows the finished Four Frogs. If there are 4 frogs sitting on the lily pad, and each frog has 2 eyes, how many eyes are there total?

ANSWER ON P. 105

Six Turtles ★★★★★

The Four Frogs (p. 68) taught us to imagine multiplication as repeating, but we can also understand it as grouping things together. Look at step 2. The solid lines divide the paper into 4 groups of squares, which each contain 4 smaller squares if you cut along the dotted lines. How many total squares are in 4 groups of 4? Count and see that 4 x 4 = 16! See what other groups you can find as you fold this group of Six Turtles.

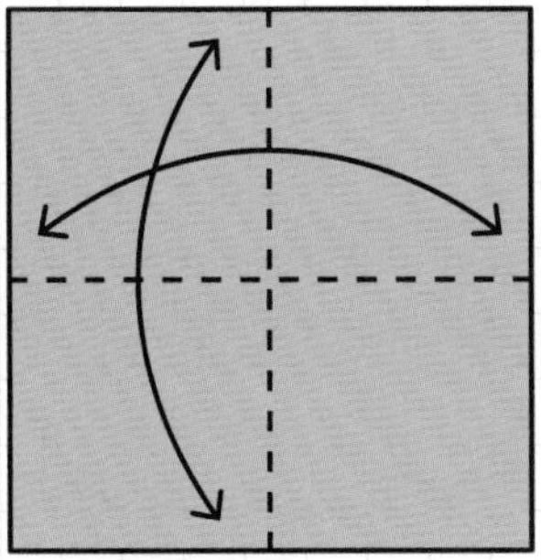

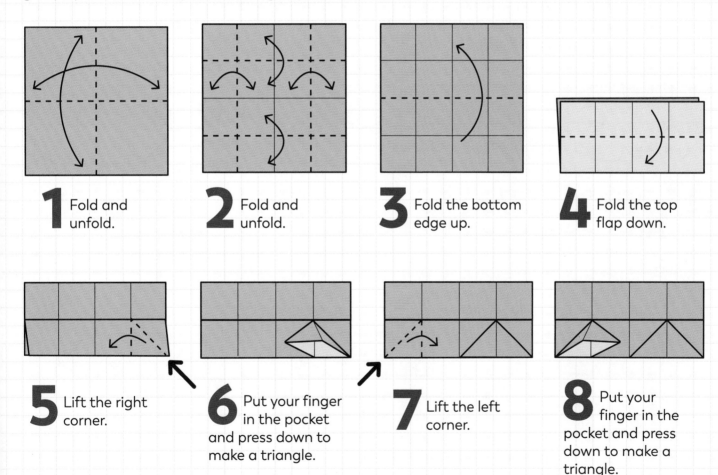

1 Fold and unfold.

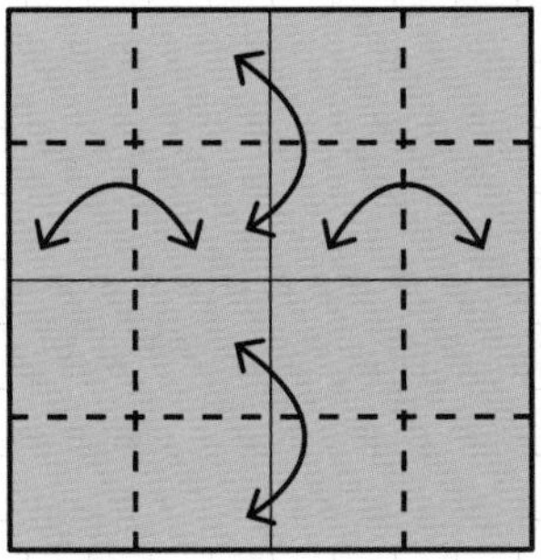

2 Fold and unfold.

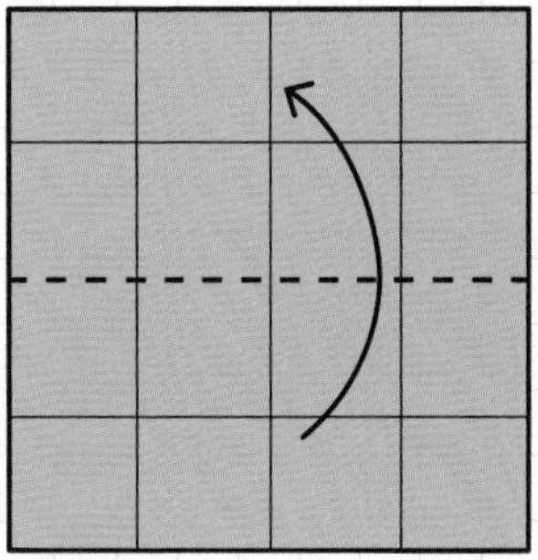

3 Fold the bottom edge up.

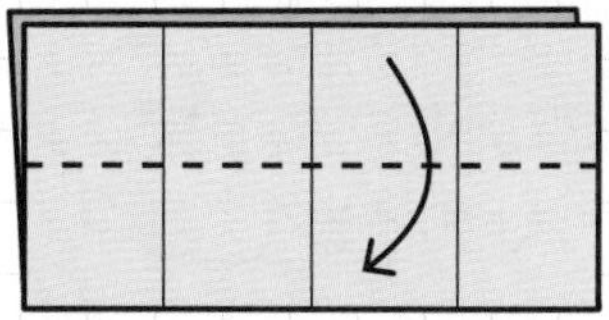

4 Fold the top flap down.

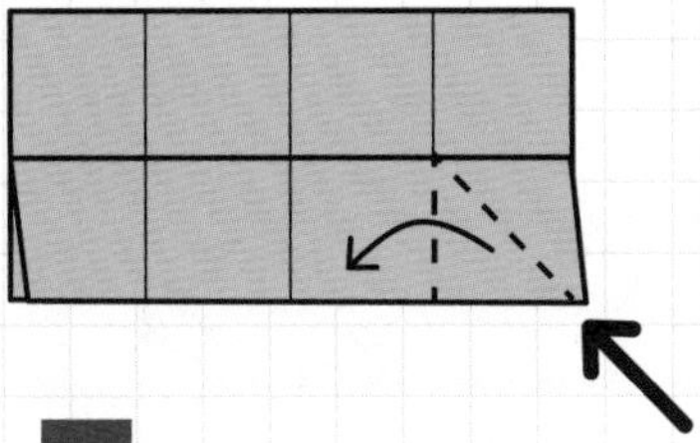

5 Lift the right corner.

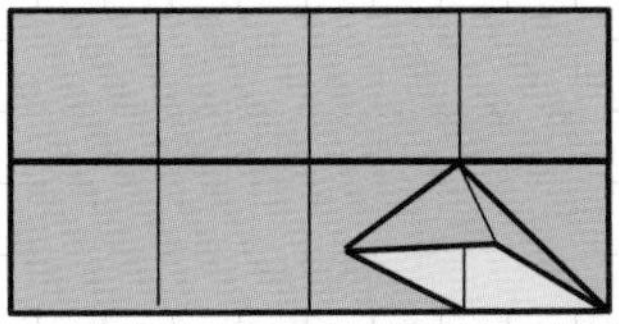

6 Put your finger in the pocket and press down to make a triangle.

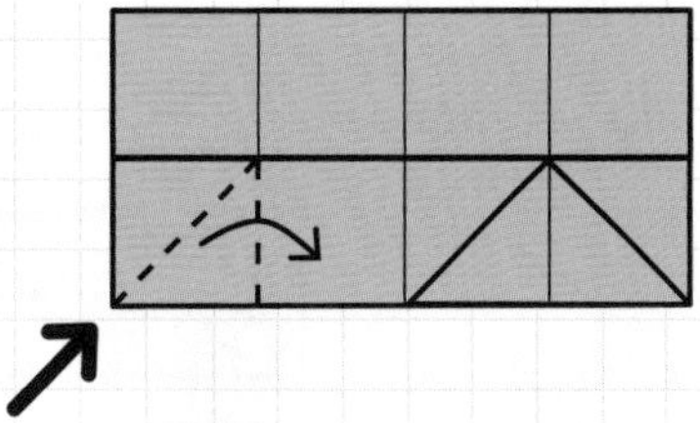

7 Lift the left corner.

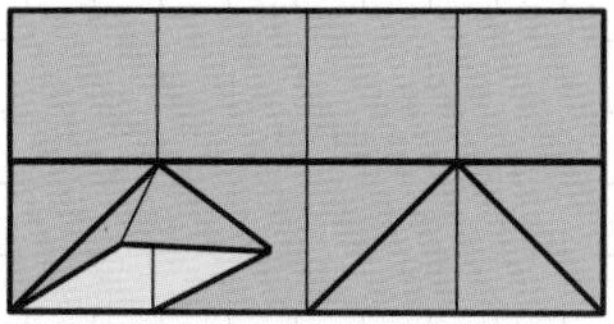

8 Put your finger in the pocket and press down to make a triangle.

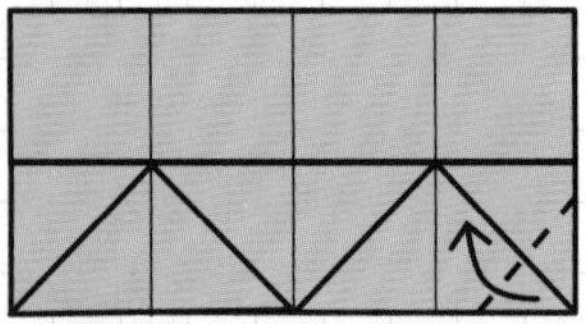

9 Fold the right corner up.

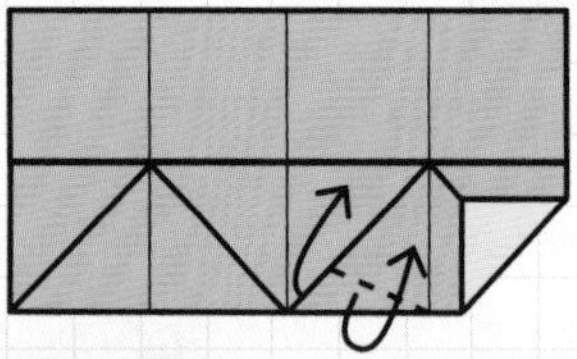

10 First, fold on the dotted line, then turn the flap inside out by spreading the pocket's edges out wide to make a big fold.

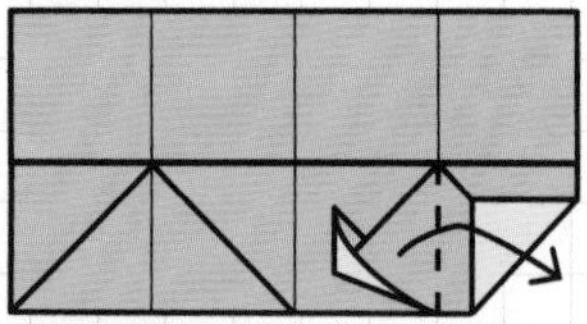

11 Fold to the right.

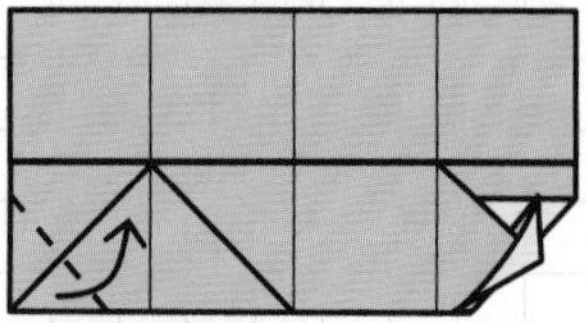

12 Fold the left corner up.

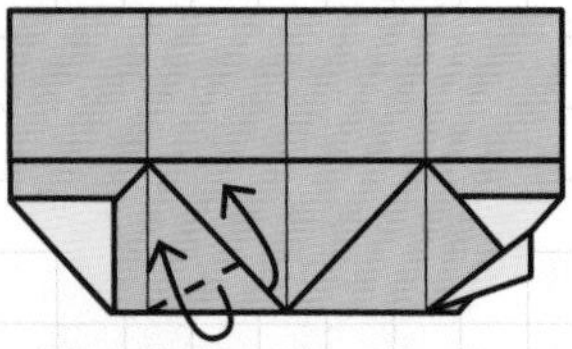

13 First, fold on the dotted line, then turn the flap inside out by spreading the pocket's edges out wide to make a big fold.

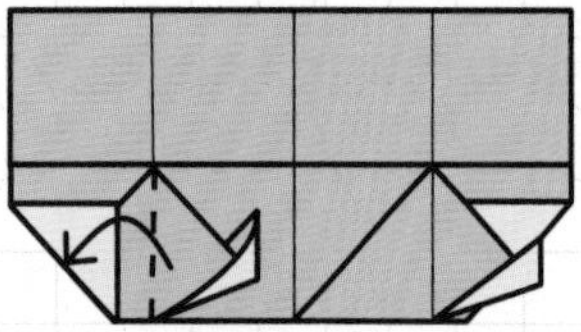

14 Fold to the left.

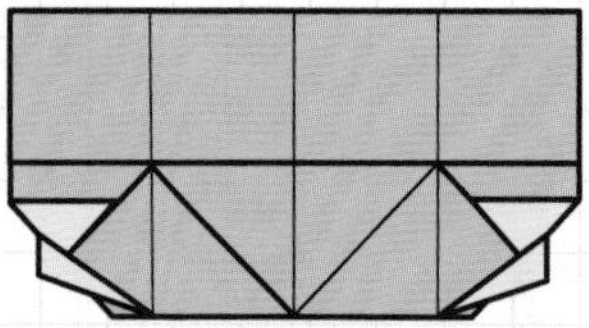

15

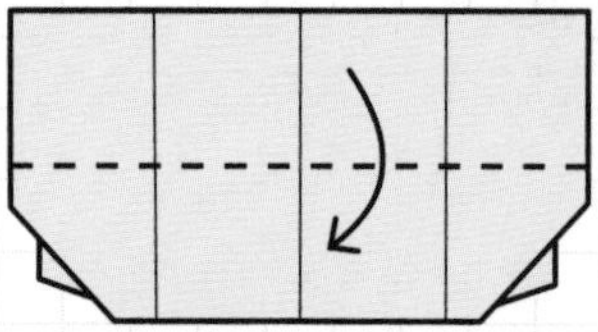

16 Fold the top edge down.

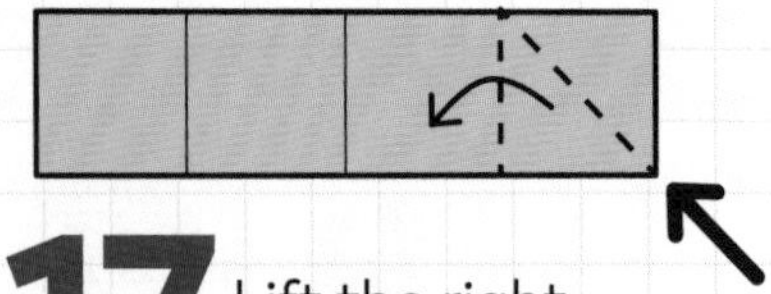

17 Lift the right corner.

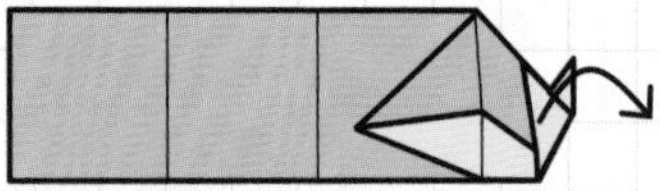

18 Put your finger in the pocket and press down. Pull the tip out a bit.

19 Repeat steps 17 and 18 on the left corner.

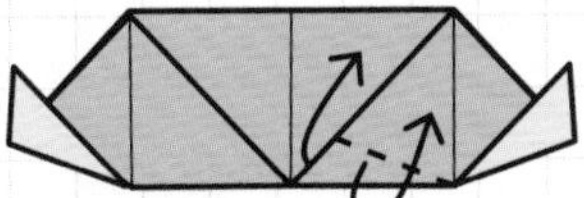

20 Fold to turn the flap inside out.

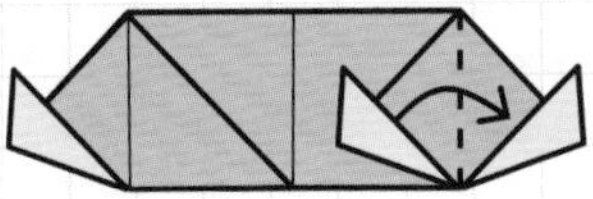

21 Fold to the right.

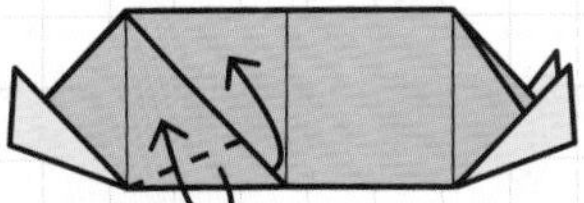

22 Fold to turn the flap inside out.

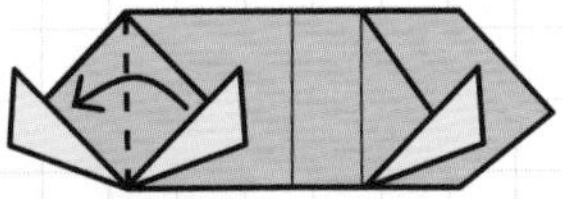

23 Fold to the left.

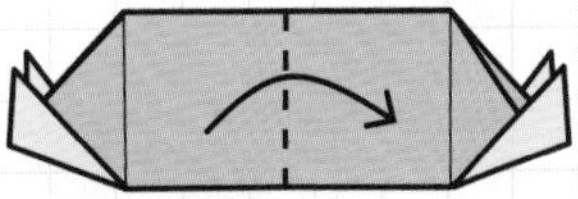

24 Fold in half to the right.

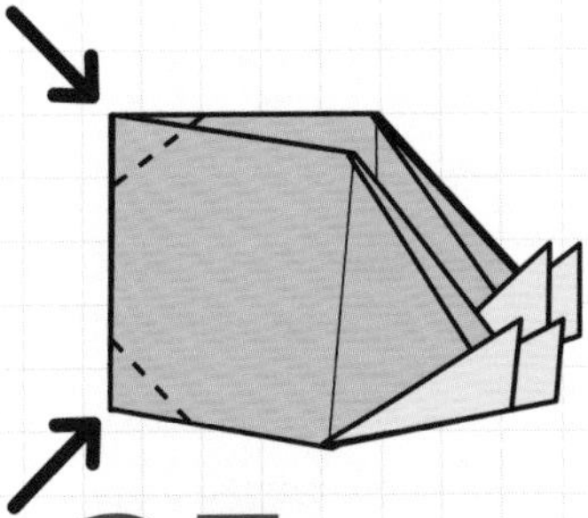

25 Tuck in the corners. Add the eyes and let the turtle party begin!

Find the Math!

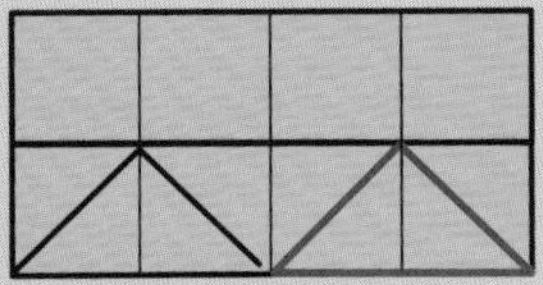

This picture shows step 7 of making Six Turtles. How many other triangles can you find that are the same shape as the one outlined in red?

ANSWER ON P. 106

Dogs on Boats

Remember how shapes with symmetry are the same on both sides? Sometimes, shapes can stay symmetrical even when we make changes to them. If you can't believe it, look at steps 5 and 6 of making the dog on the red boat. The dog's head is symmetrical before its ears are folded down—and after! As long as you make the exact same changes on both sides of a shape, it'll stay symmetrical the whole time.

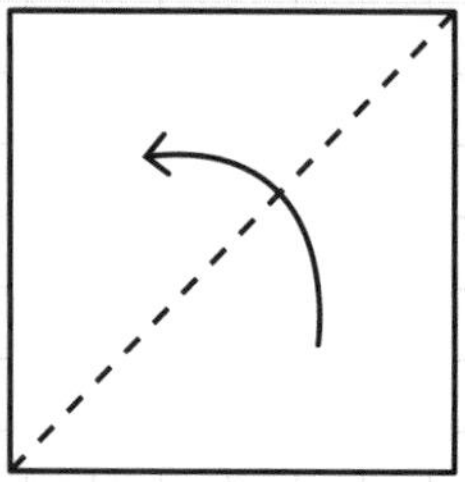

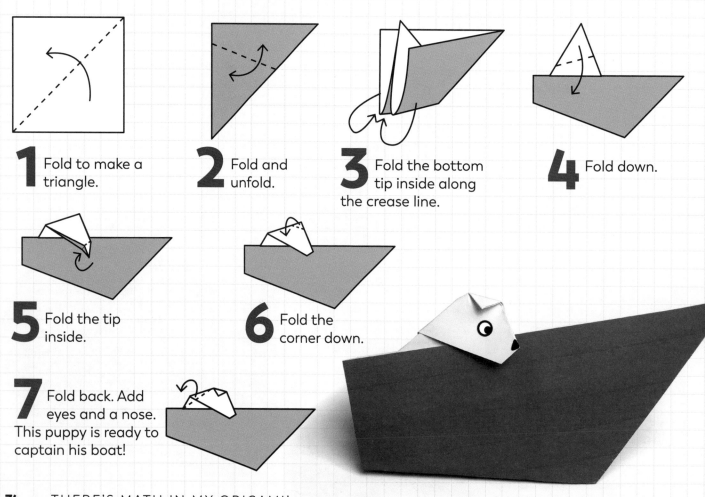

1 Fold to make a triangle.

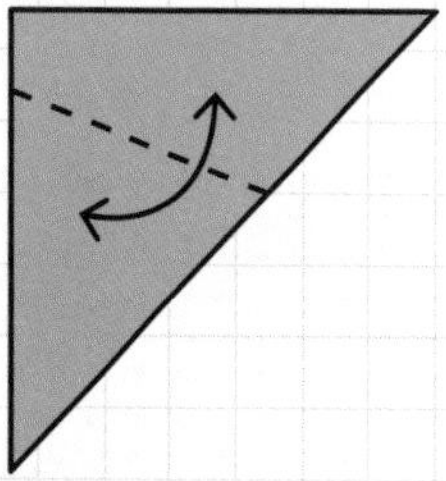

2 Fold and unfold.

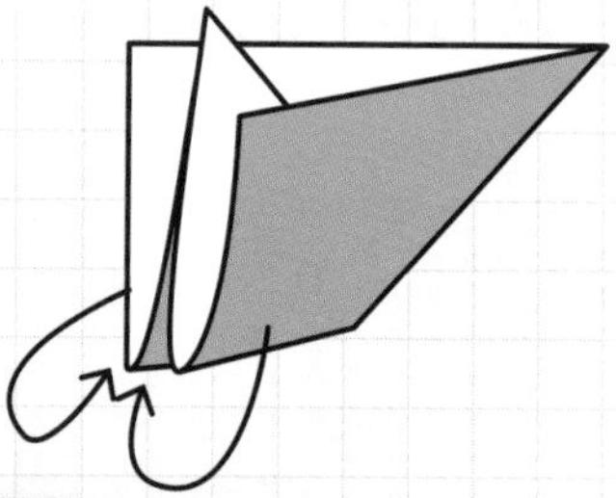

3 Fold the bottom tip inside along the crease line.

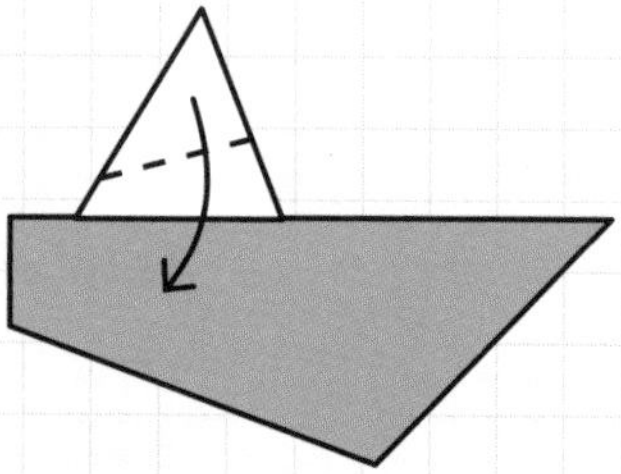

4 Fold down.

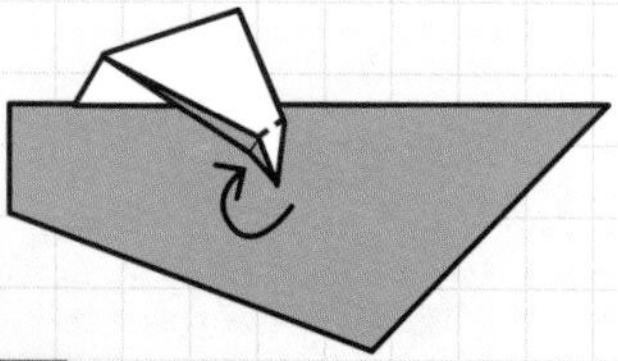

5 Fold the tip inside.

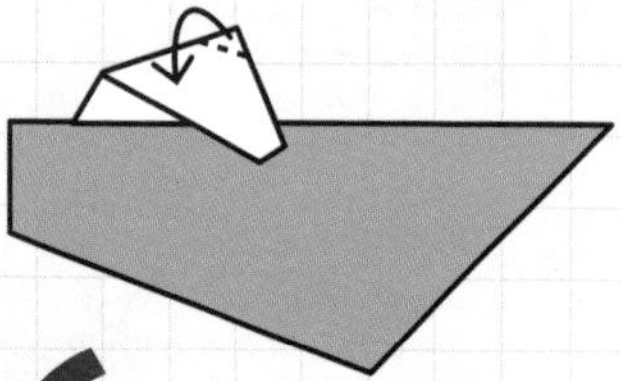

6 Fold the corner down.

7 Fold back. Add eyes and a nose. This puppy is ready to captain his boat!

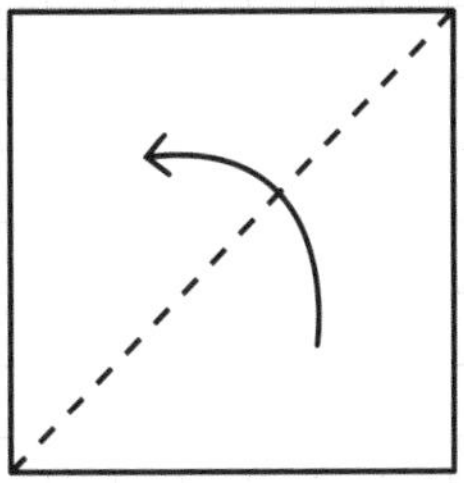

1 Fold to make a triangle.

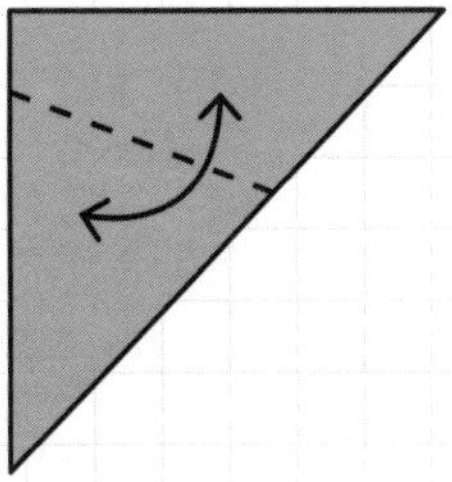

2 Fold and unfold.

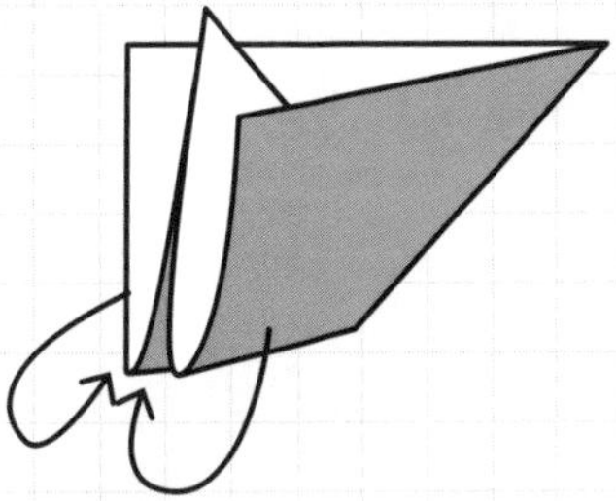

3 Fold the bottom tip inside along the crease line.

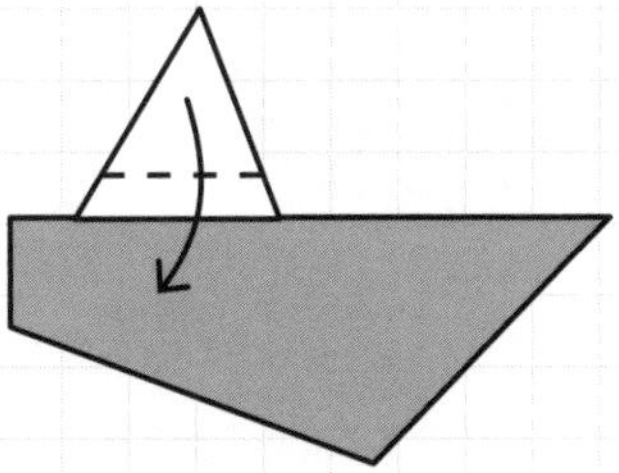

4 Fold straight down.

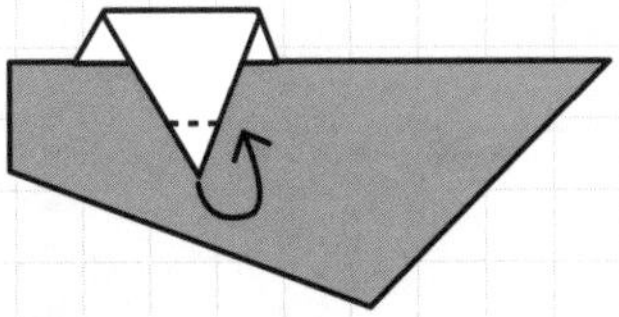

5 Fold the tip behind.

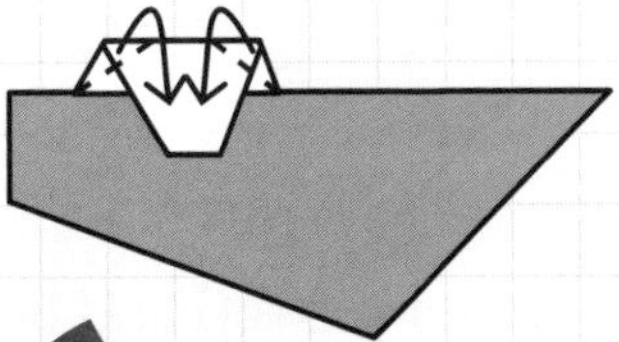

6 Fold the corners down.

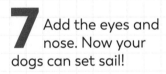

7 Add the eyes and nose. Now your dogs can set sail!

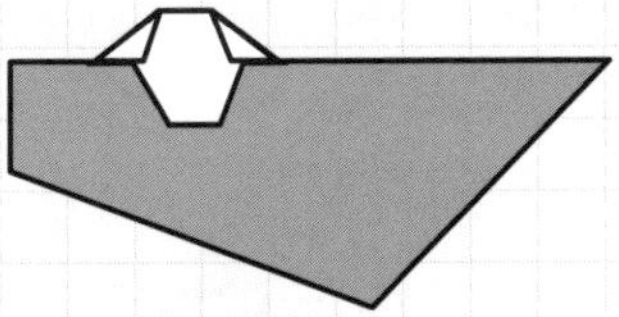

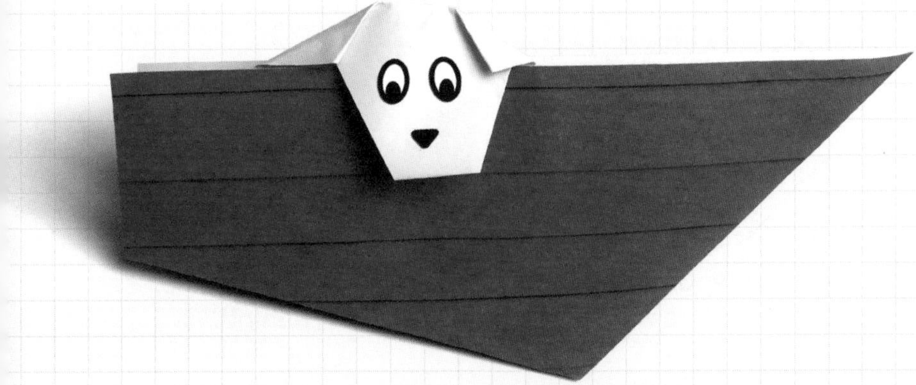

Find the Math!

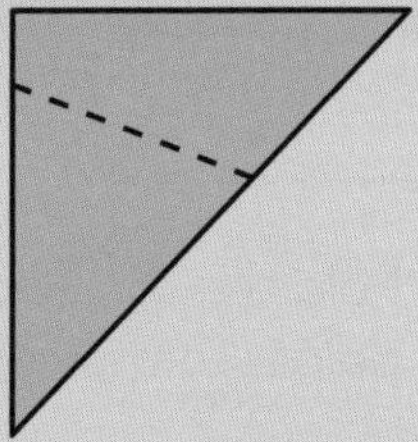

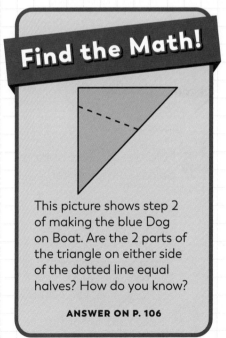

This picture shows step 2 of making the blue Dog on Boat. Are the 2 parts of the triangle on either side of the dotted line equal halves? How do you know?

ANSWER ON P. 106

Cat on a Mat ★★★★★

As we've seen with the different types of triangles, sometimes shapes' sides aren't all the same length. For example, look at the cat's pentagon-shaped head in step 11—the sides on the left and right are longer than the one on the bottom. Shapes like this are called **irregular** shapes (and shapes whose sides are all the same length are **regular**). This cat might be irregular, but it sure is cute!

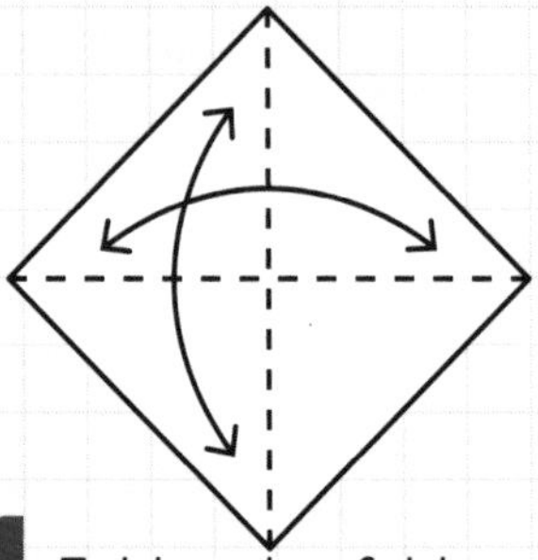

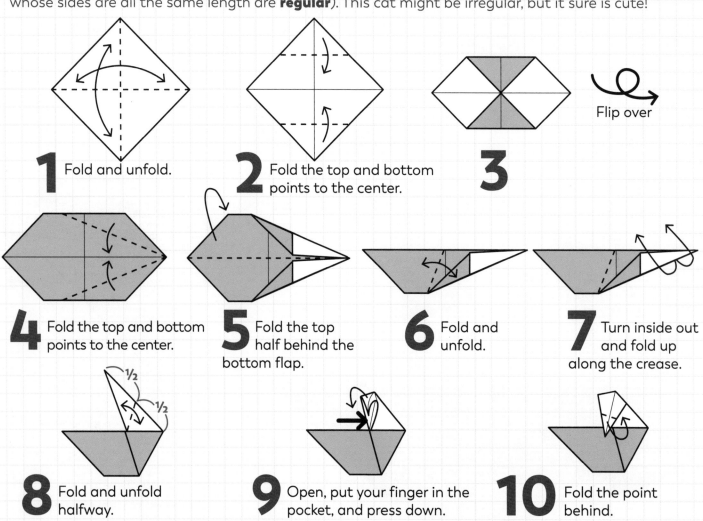

1 Fold and unfold.

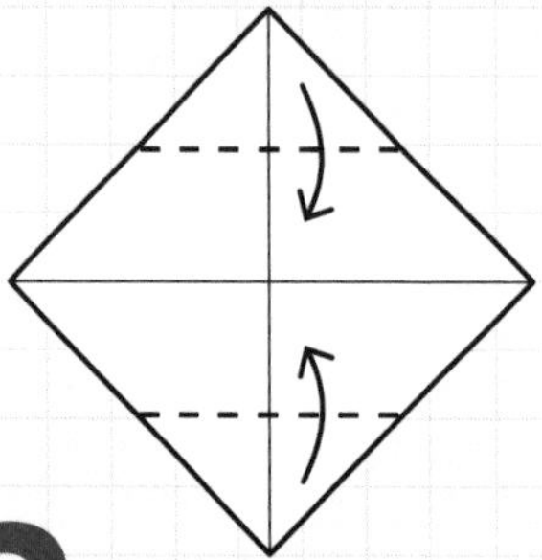

2 Fold the top and bottom points to the center.

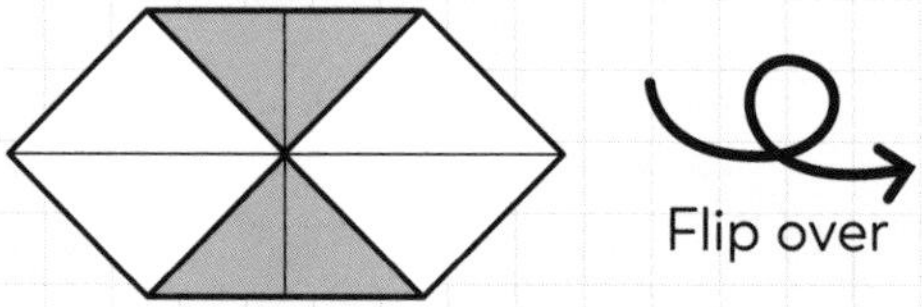

3 Flip over

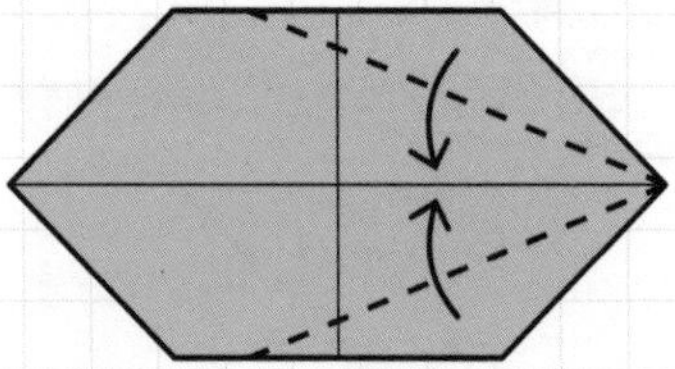

4 Fold the top and bottom points to the center.

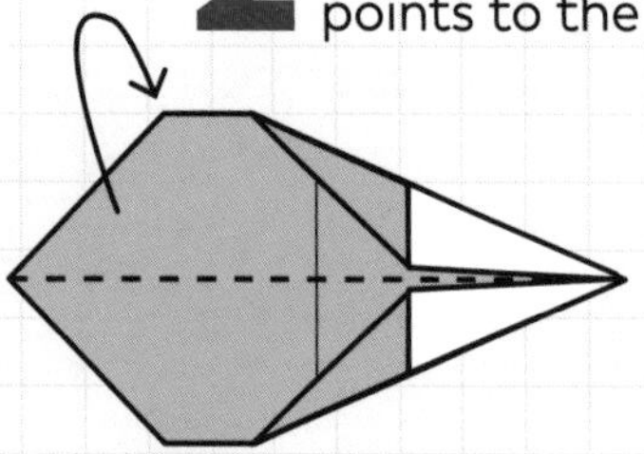

5 Fold the top half behind the bottom flap.

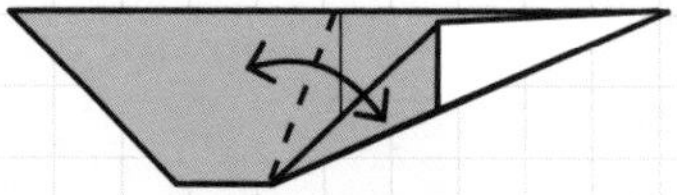

6 Fold and unfold.

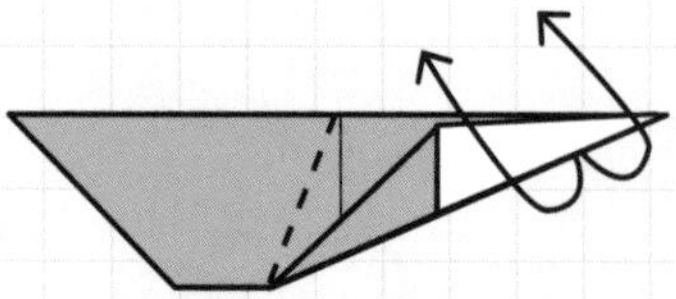

7 Turn inside out and fold up along the crease.

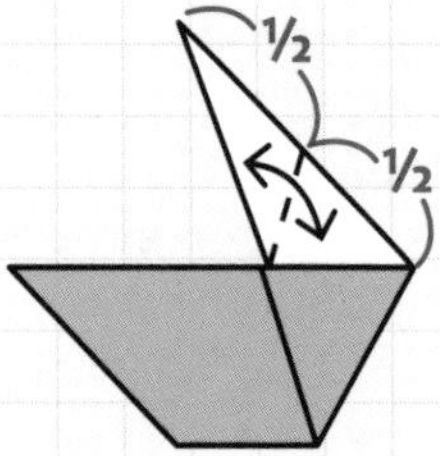

8 Fold and unfold halfway. ½ ½

9 Open, put your finger in the pocket, and press down.

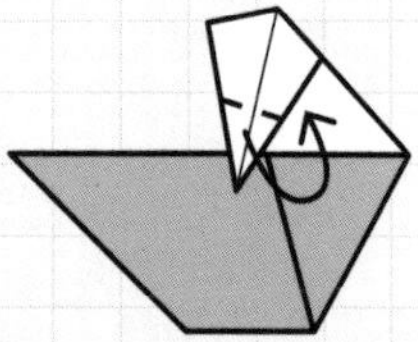

10 Fold the point behind.

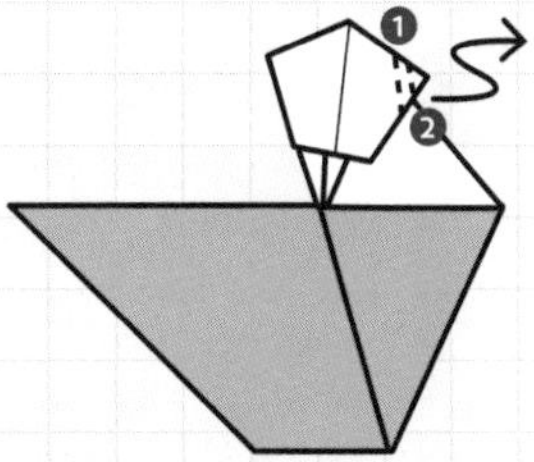

11 Fold the crease marked 1 to the back. Then, pull the part marked 2 to the front.

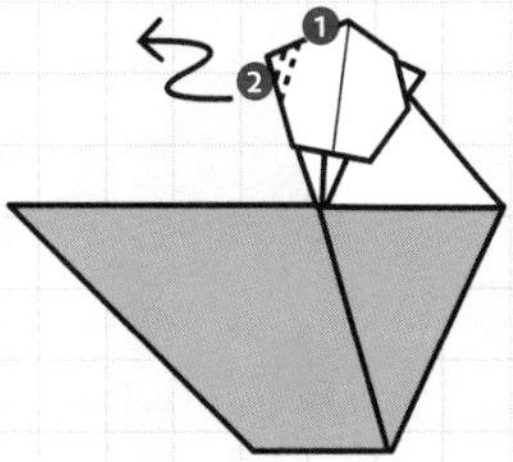

12 Repeat on the other side.

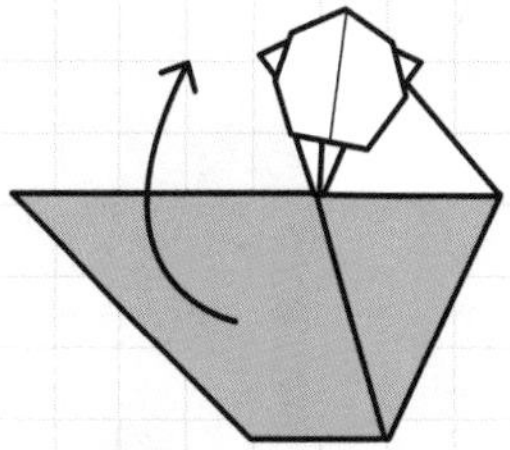

13 Fold up the bottom flap on top of the cat's head.

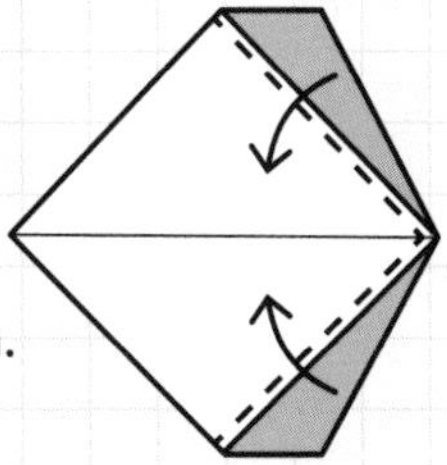

14 Fold in.

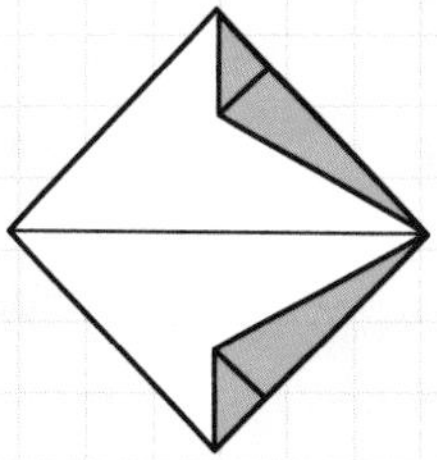

15

Flip over

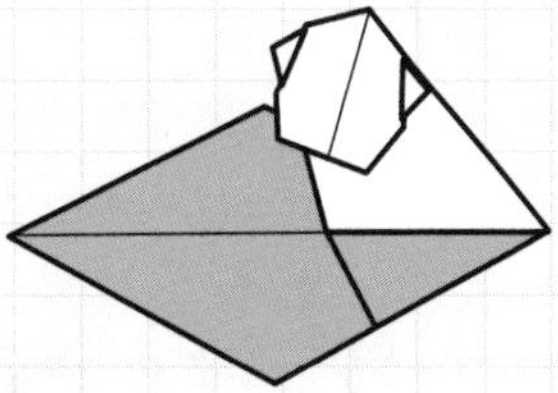

16 Stand the cat's head up and spread the cushion out underneath. Add eyes, a nose, and whiskers. Your cat is looking purrfect!

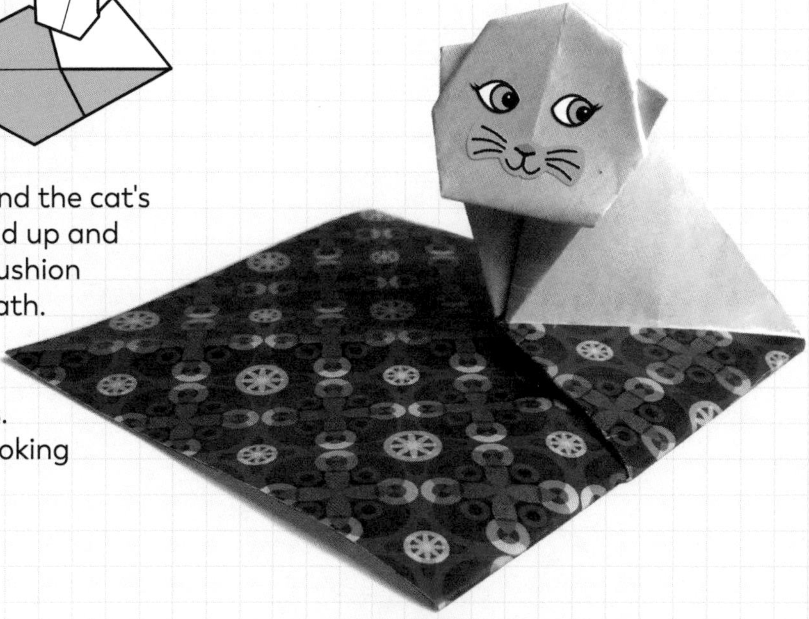

Find the Math!

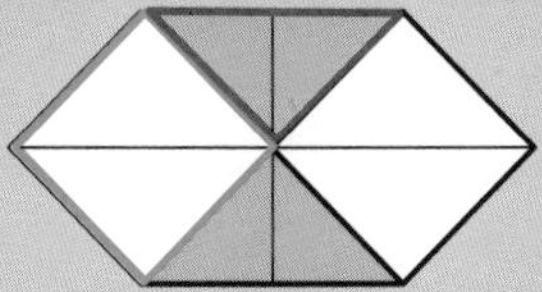

This picture shows step 3 of making a Cat on a Mat. How many of the triangles outlined in red will fit inside the square outlined in blue?

ANSWER ON P. 106

Play and Decorate

Who knew origami could be useful? Make toys and decorations using transformations and comparisons, then show off your art!

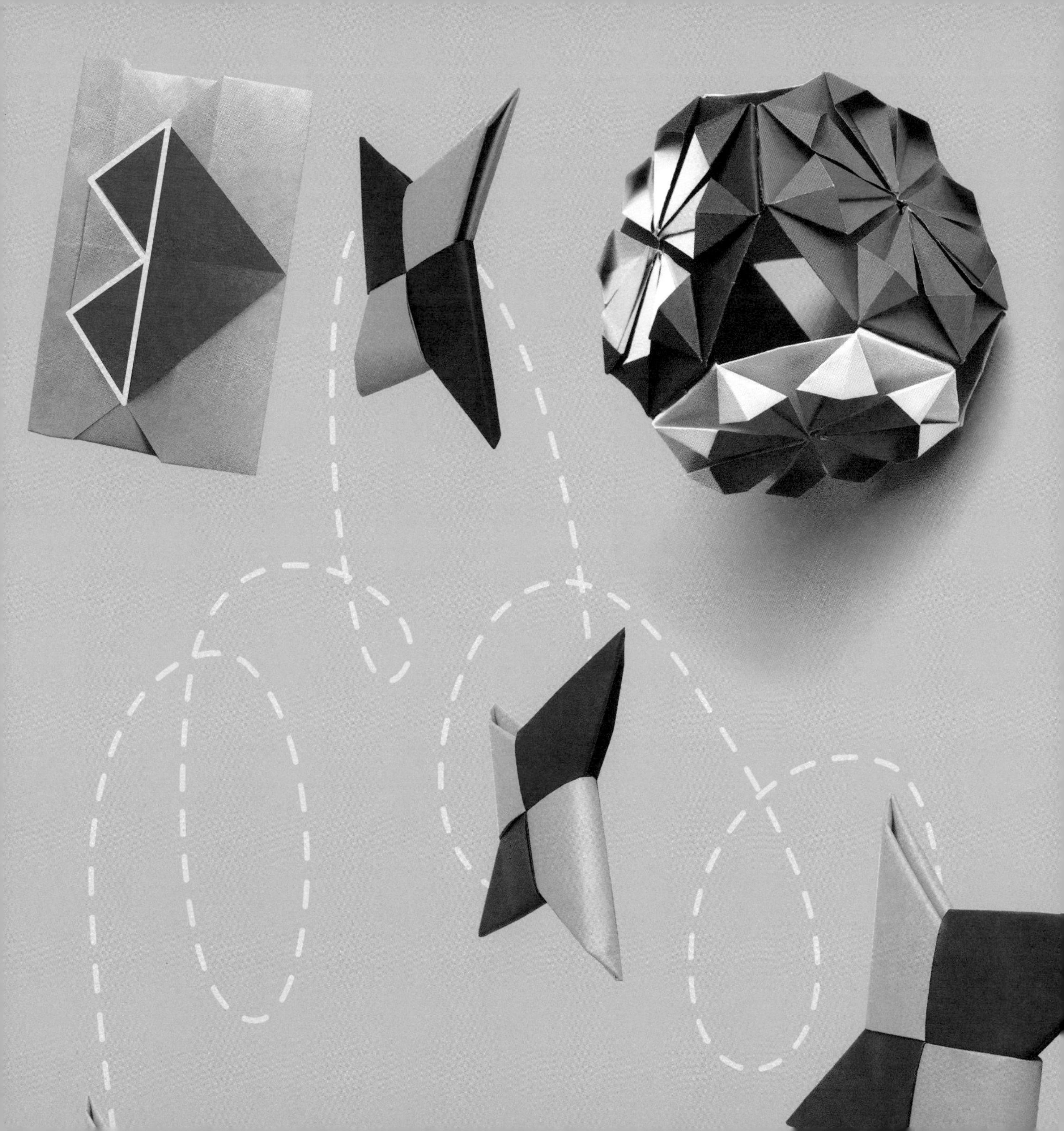

Spinning Top

While you watch the top spin, you can see that it has a type of symmetry called **rotational symmetry.** Shapes with rotational symmetry look the same after they're turned for less than a full rotation. To see what this means, hold the toothpick so the pink paper is on the top's sides. Turn it once, and the pink paper has moved to the top and bottom, but turn it again, and the sides are pink again—it's symmetrical!

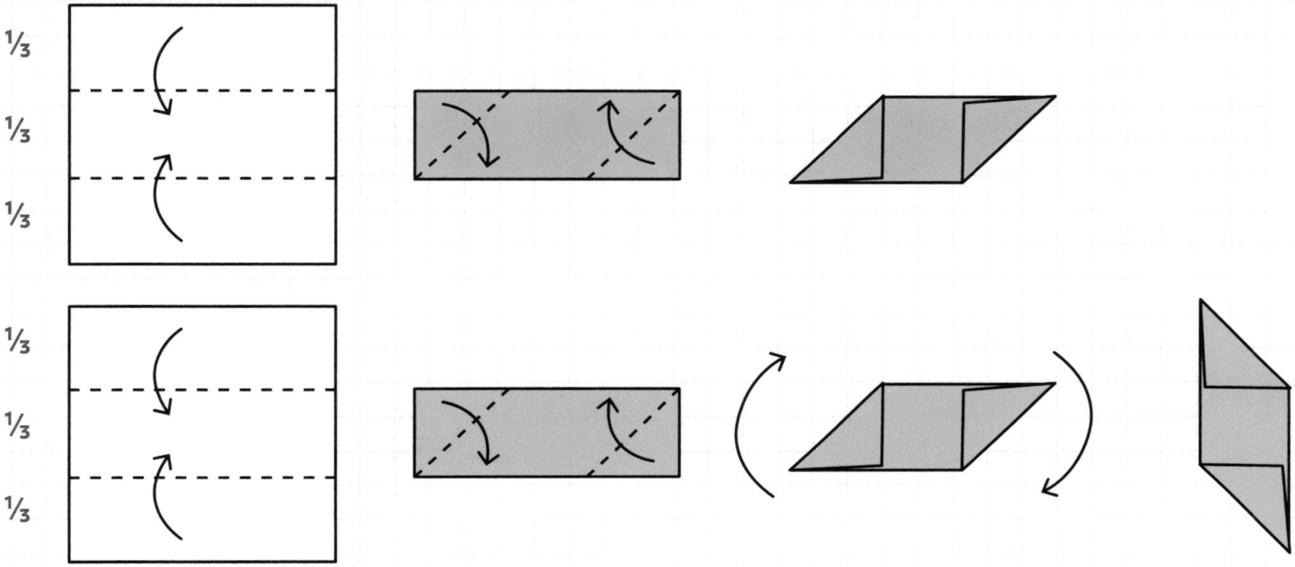

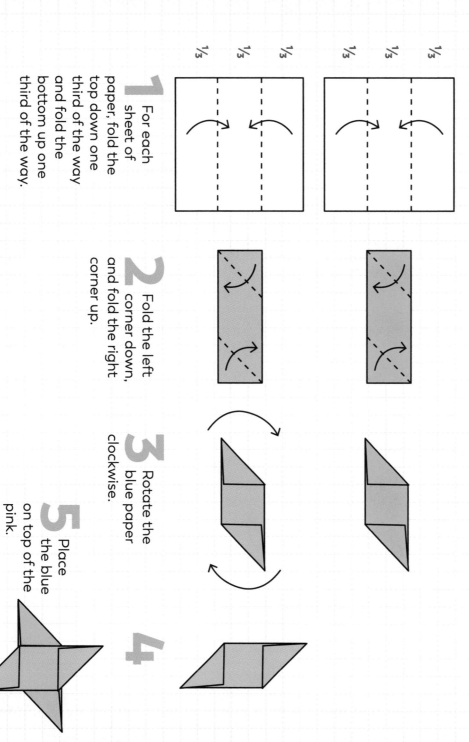

1 For each sheet of paper, fold the top down one third of the way and fold the bottom up one third of the way.

2 Fold the left corner down, and fold the right corner up.

3 Rotate the blue paper clockwise.

4

5 Place the blue on top of the pink.

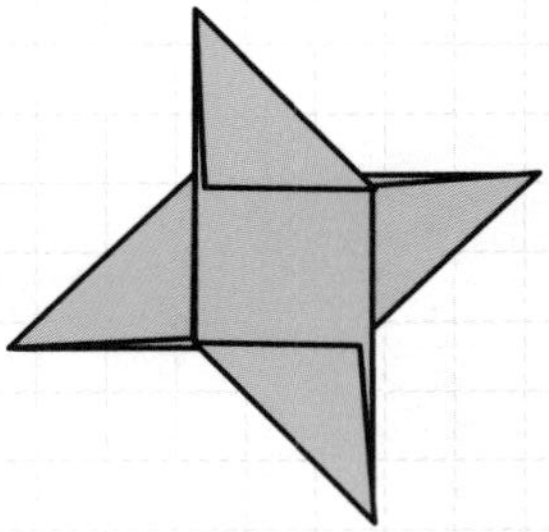

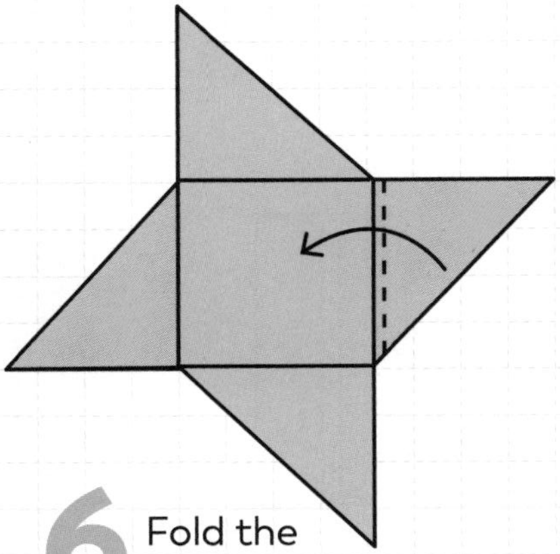

6 Fold the right pink point on top of the blue.

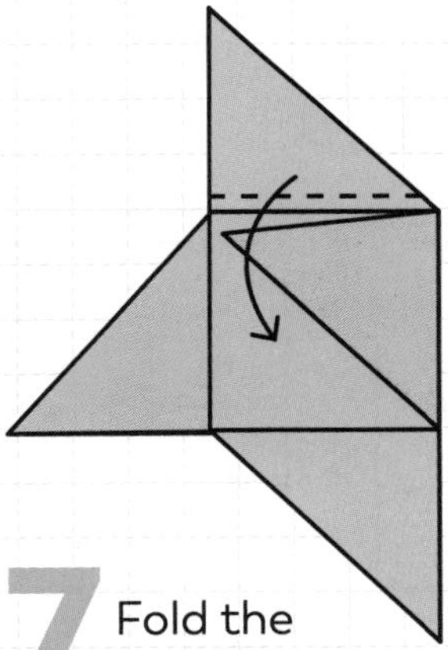

7 Fold the top blue point down.

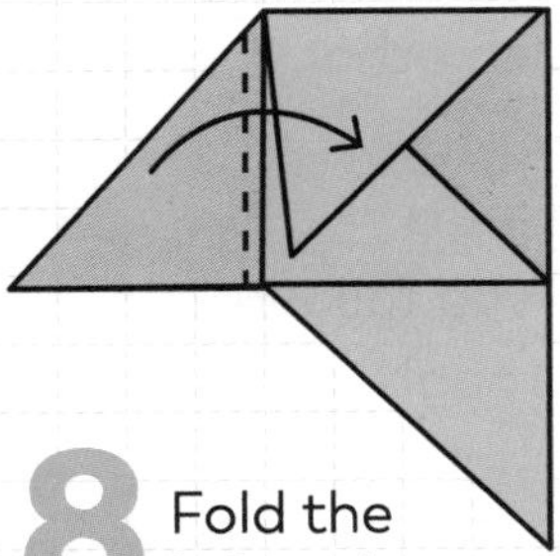

8 Fold the left pink tip on top.

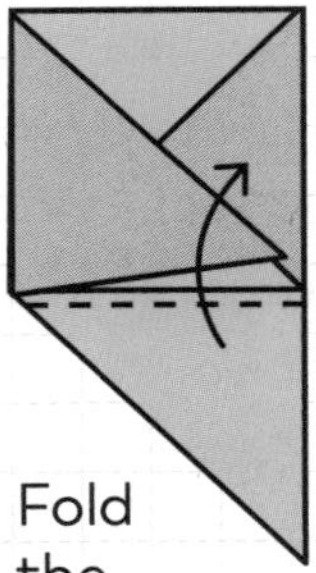

9 Fold the bottom blue point up. Tuck it into the pink pocket.

10 Stick a toothpick into the center. Push one third of the toothpick through the middle.

11 Hold the toothpick, then twist and release it at the same time. Watch it spin!

Find the Math!

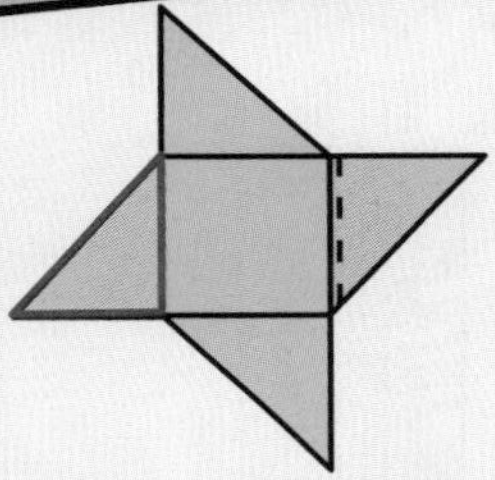

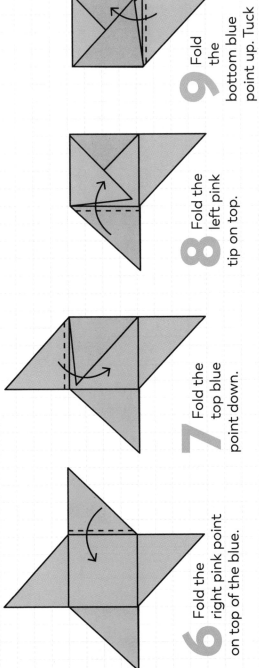

This picture shows step 6 of making a Spinning Top. How many other triangles that are the same as the one outlined in red can you find in the origami shape? (It's OK if the colors are different as long as the shapes are the same.)

ANSWER ON P. 106

Ninja Star

When lines cross over each other, we say they **intersect.** The finished Ninja Star gives us a great example of this. If you follow the two straight lines through the center, you can see that they intersect right in the middle, where all of the colors meet. Something to puzzle over: Can you imagine 2 straight lines that intersect in more than 1 place?

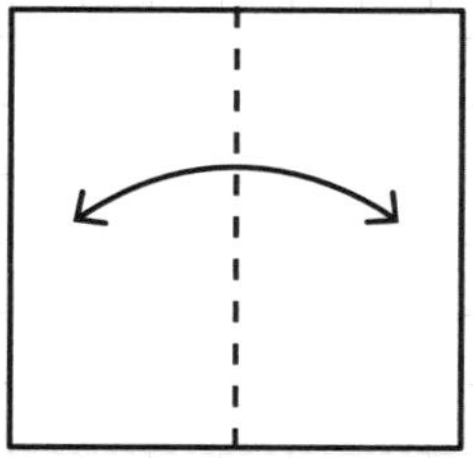

1 Fold and unfold.

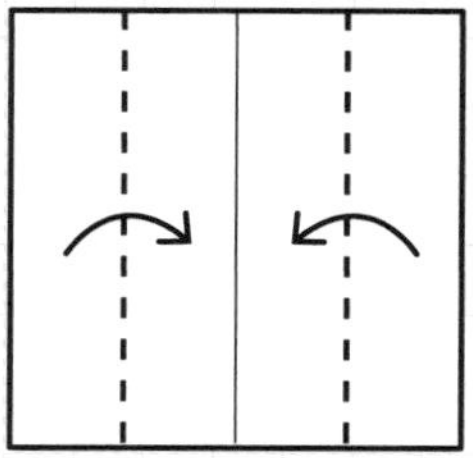

2 Fold the outer edges in to the center crease.

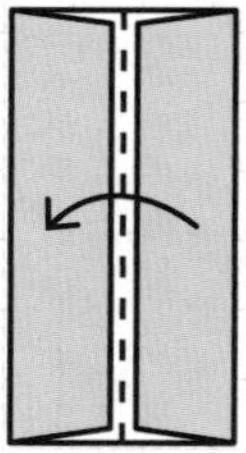

3 Fold to the left.

4 Fold the corners.

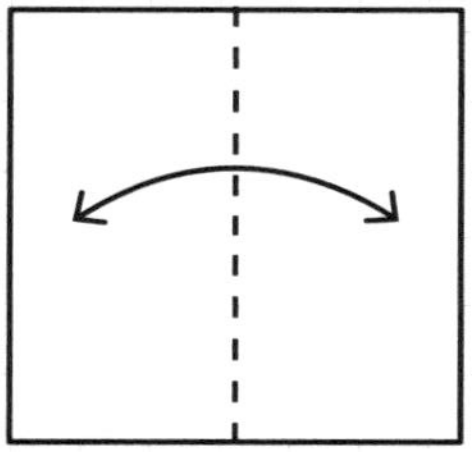

1 Fold and unfold.

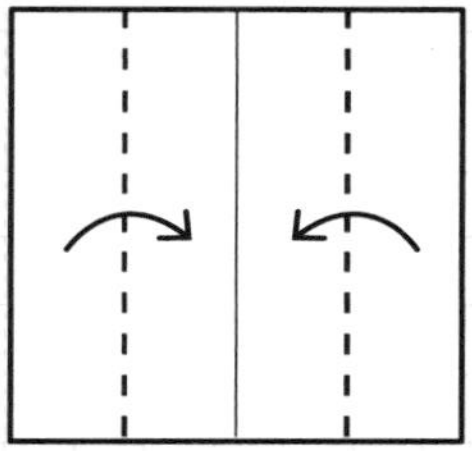

2 Fold the outer edges in to center crease.

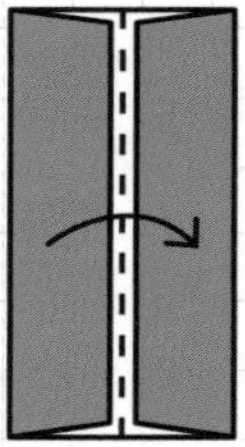

3 Fold to the right.

4 Fold the corners.

Find the Math!

This picture shows step 5 of making a Ninja Star. How many of the triangles outlined in red fit into the shape outlined in blue?

ANSWER ON P. 106

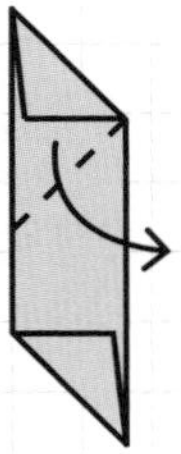

5 Fold the top point to the right.

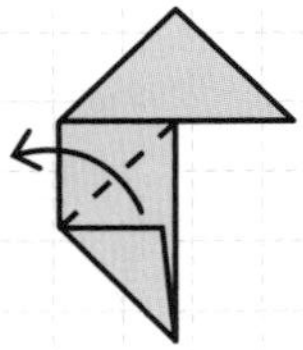

6 Fold the bottom point to the left.

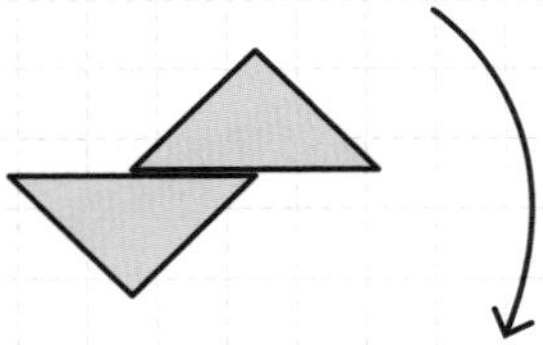

7 Rotate clockwise.

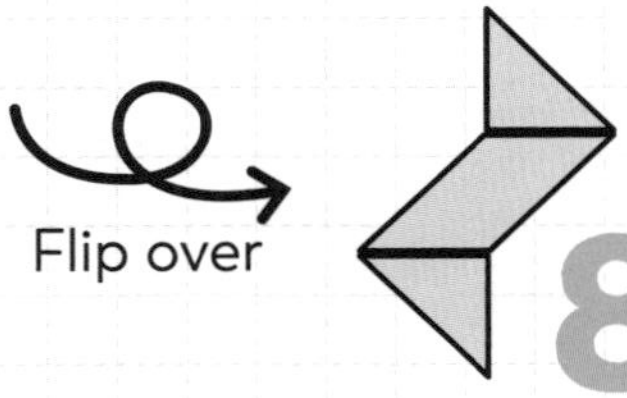

8

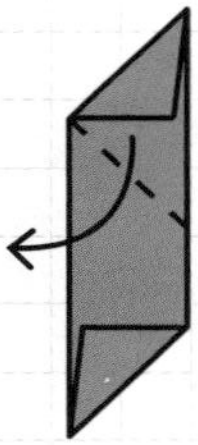

5 Fold the top point to the left.

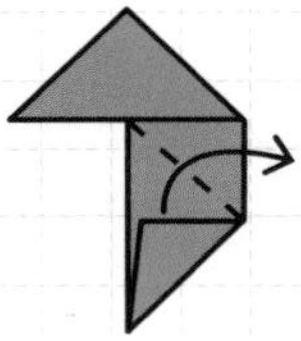

6 Fold the bottom point to the right.

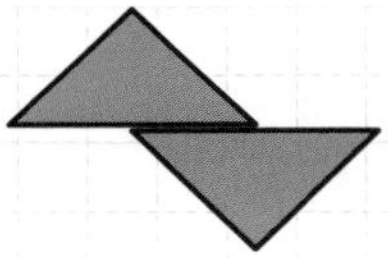

7 Place on top of 8.

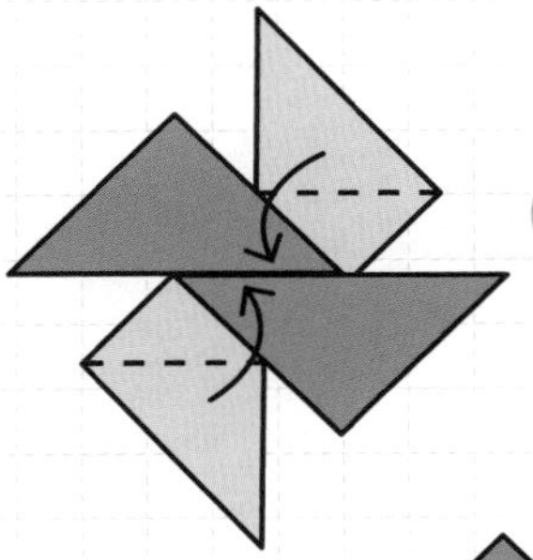

9 Fold and tuck in.

10

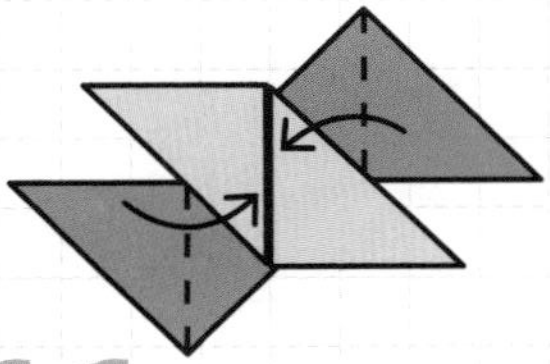

11 Fold and tuck in.

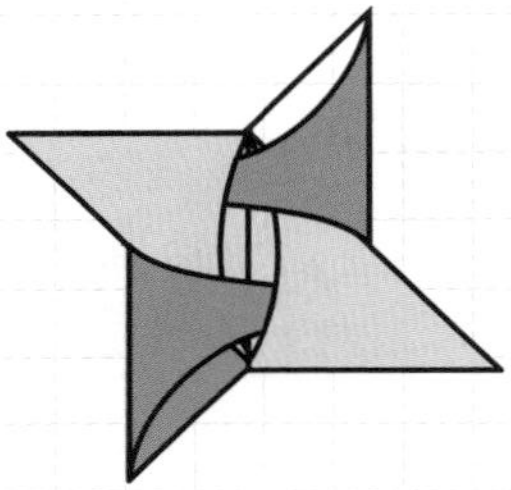

12 Flatten your star. To throw, grip one of the points and flick your wrist as you let go. Practice hitting a target to hone your ninja skills!

Star

When we turn a shape, besides needing to know if we should spin it clockwise or counterclockwise, we also want to know how far we should turn it. One way to talk about this is using **degrees,** just like we would for angles. Turning the shape upside down (like we do with one of the triangles in step 10) means turning it 180°. Turn it upside down twice, and it comes all the way back around to the beginning—that's 360°. Spin, spin, spin the triangles and see how the star changes!

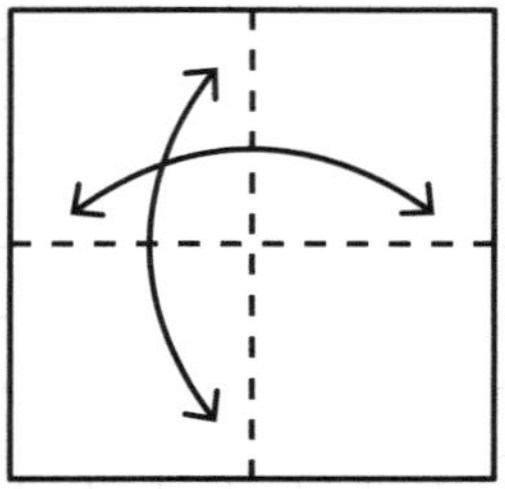

1 Fold and unfold.

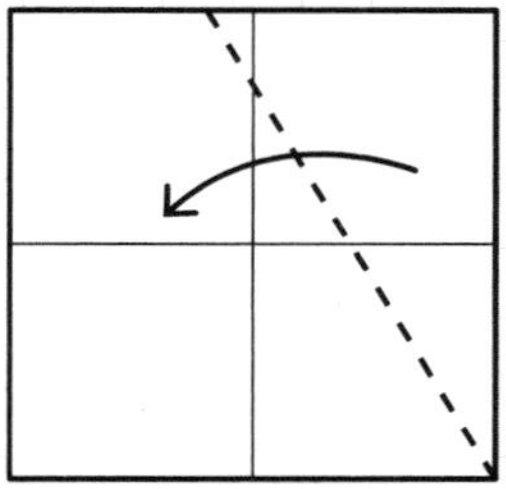

2 Fold to the left.

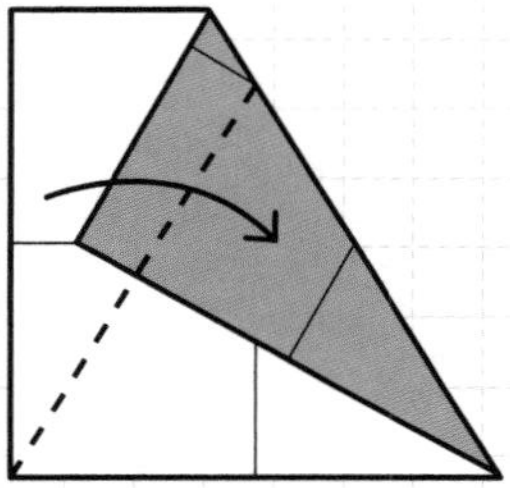

3 Fold to the right.

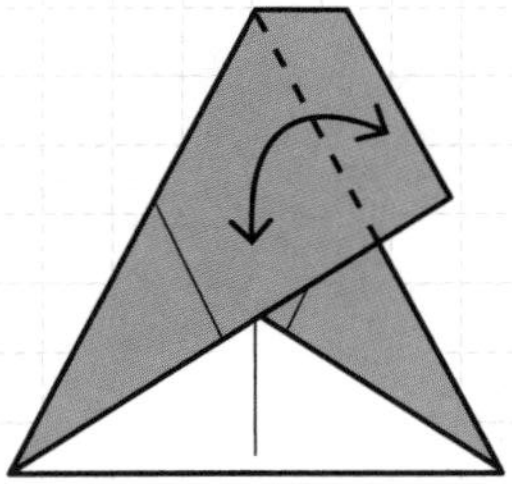

4 Fold and unfold.

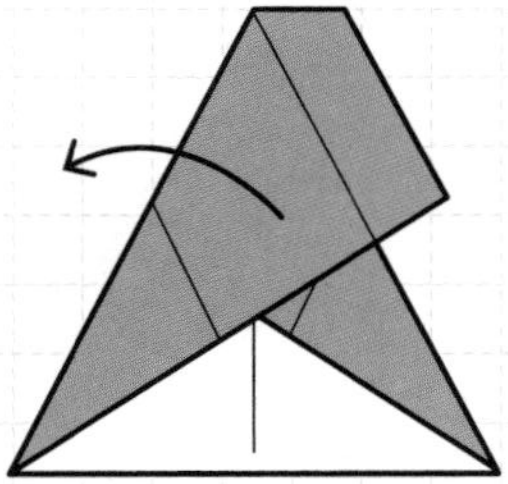

5 Swing the flap open.

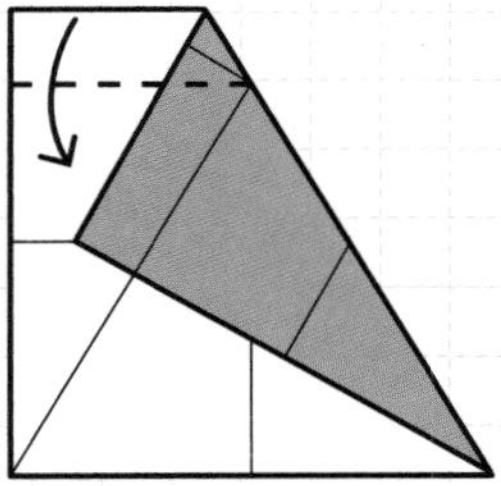

6 Fold the top edge down.

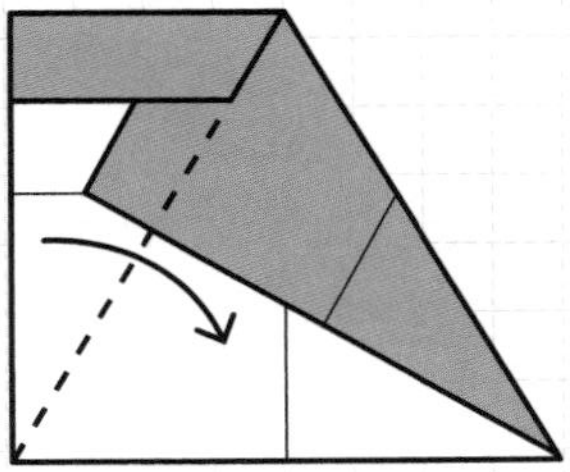

7 Fold to the right.

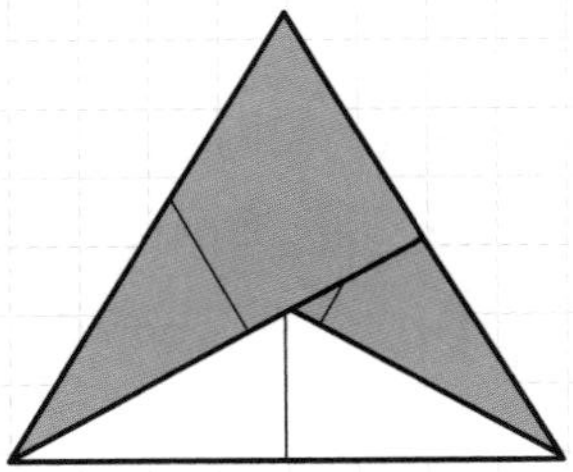

8

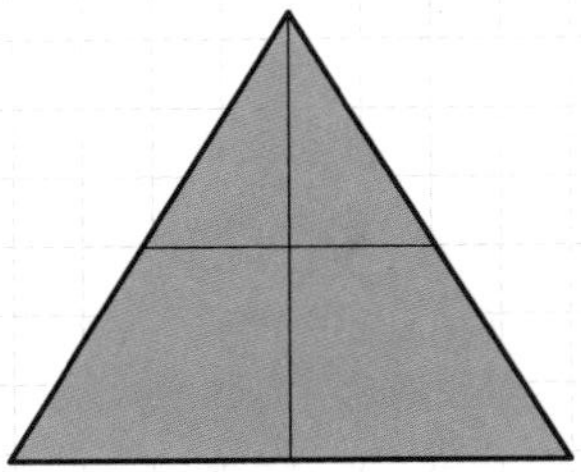

9 Repeat steps 1 through 8 to make 1 more triangle.

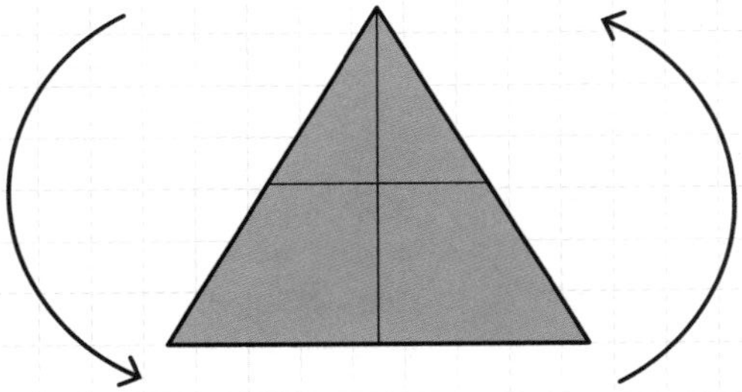

10 Turn 1 of the triangles upside down and combine to make the star.

Find the Math!

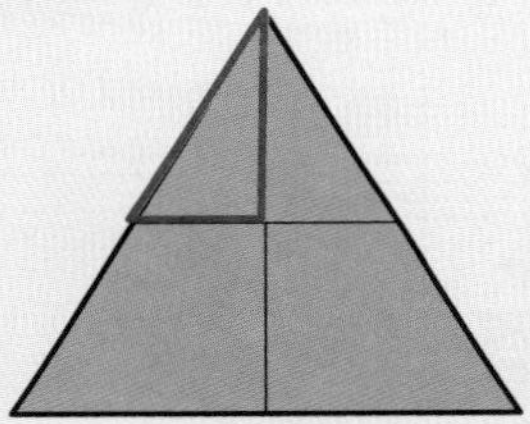

This picture shows step 10 of making a Star. Can you find any other triangles that are similar to the one outlined in red?

ANSWER ON P. 106

Kitty Candy Box

When you think of a **kite,** you probably imagine a toy you play with on a windy day, but there's also a special shape called a kite we can find in the Kitty Candy Box. Think you can tell what it is? If you guessed a shape like the ones in step 8 with dotted lines through the middle, you're right—a kite is a quadrilateral that has 2 pairs of sides that are the same length and have edges touching each other.

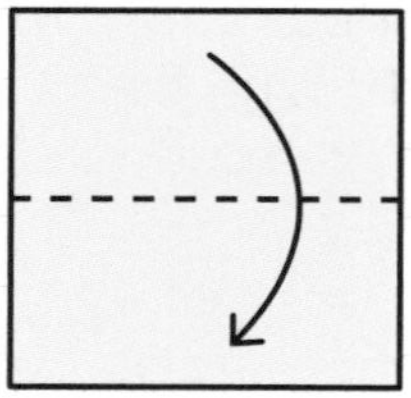

1 Fold down.

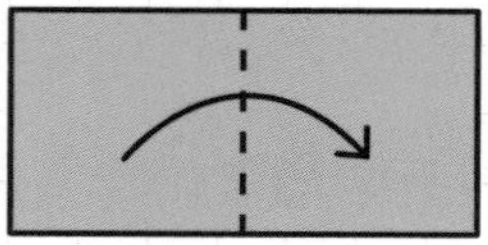

2 Fold to the right.

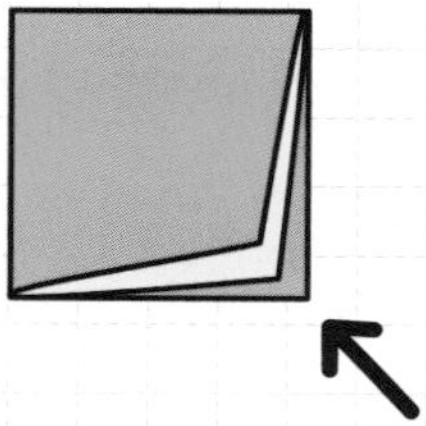

3 Put your finger in the pocket and press down, following the crease line as you fold into a triangle.

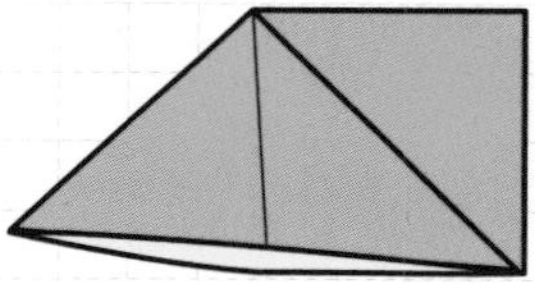

4 Flip over and repeat on the other side.

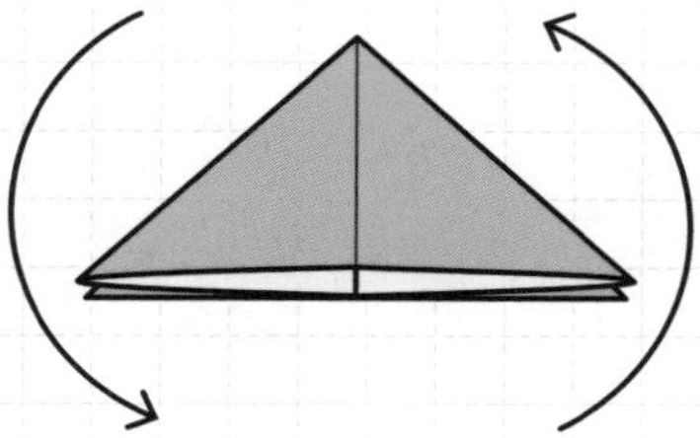

5 Rotate 180° clockwise.

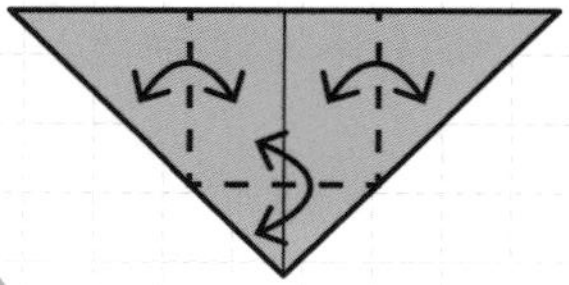

6 Fold the bottom point up, then unfold. Fold and unfold the left and right sides.

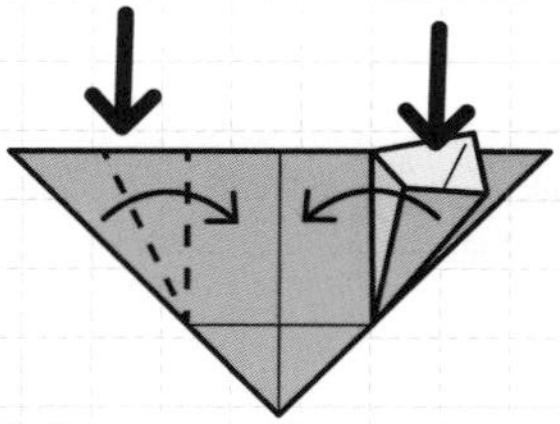

7 Put your finger in the pocket and squash down along the crease lines.

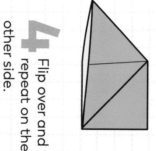

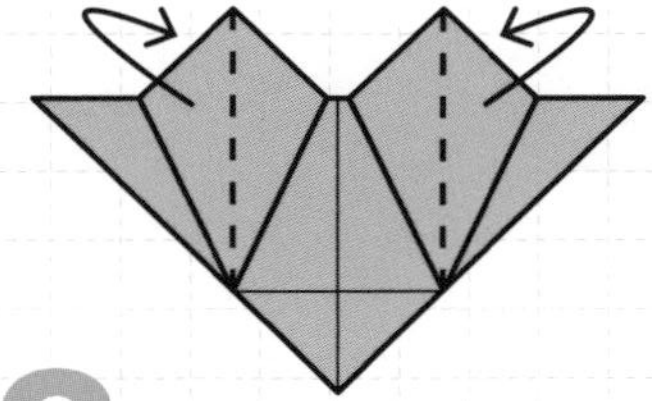

8 Fold the outer half of each side behind the flap.

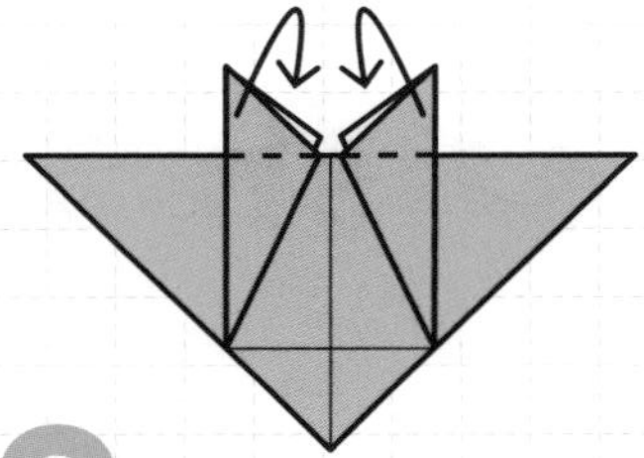

9 Fold the top points back.

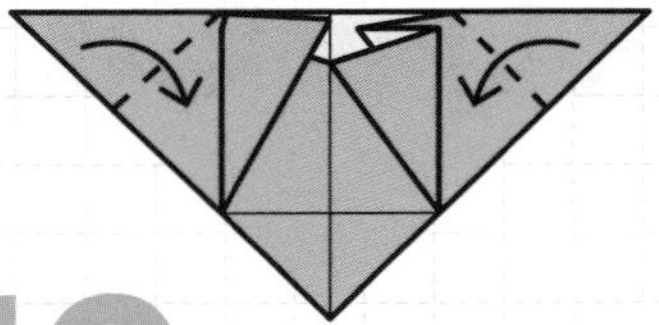

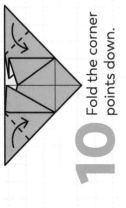

10 Fold the corner points down.

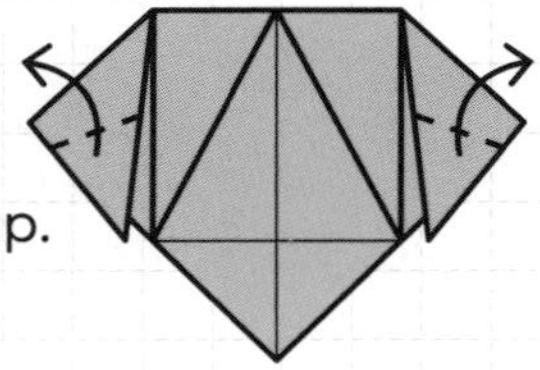

11 Fold up.

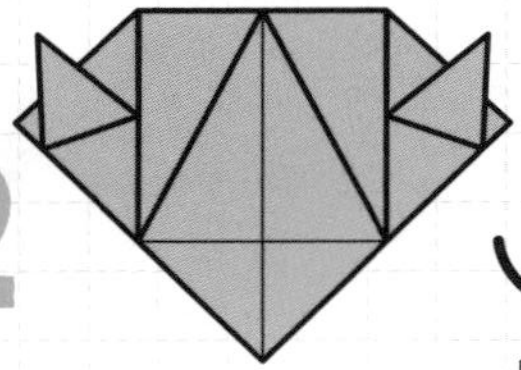

12

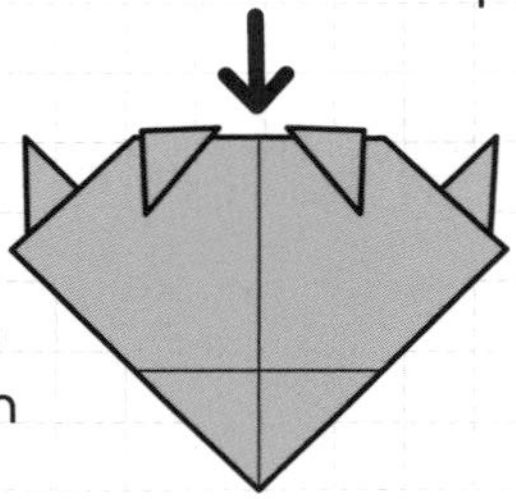

13 Pull open from the top first, then from the sides. Flatten the creases in the bottom and sides of the box.

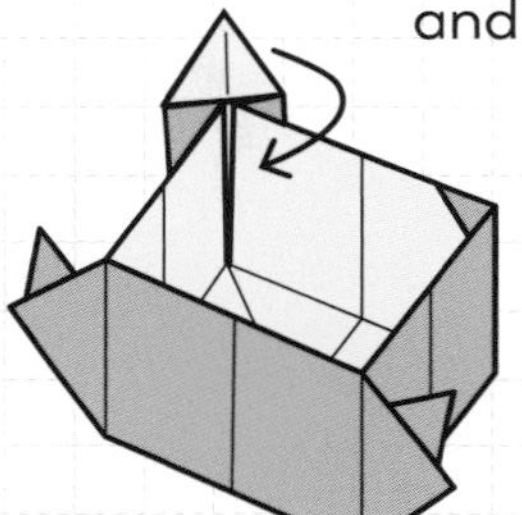

14 Fold the corner flaps up and over the back corners. Tape them down if you want. Add eyes, a nose, and whiskers, and this kitty is ready to eat some candy!

Find the Math!

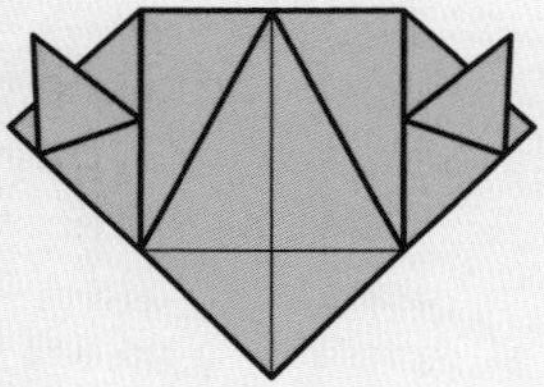

This picture shows step 12 of making a Kitty Candy Box. Are all of the triangles in the picture right triangles? And if not, what kind of triangles are the others?

ANSWER ON P. 107

Little Candy Dish

Just like ordinary 2D shapes, 3D shapes have versions that are regular and irregular. Remember the Boxy Balloon (p. 18)? The balloon had 6 sides, and we called it a cube because each of those sides was a square. But all 3D shapes with 6 sides are also called **hexahedrons,** whether they're regular like the Boxy Balloon or irregular like the Little Candy Dish.

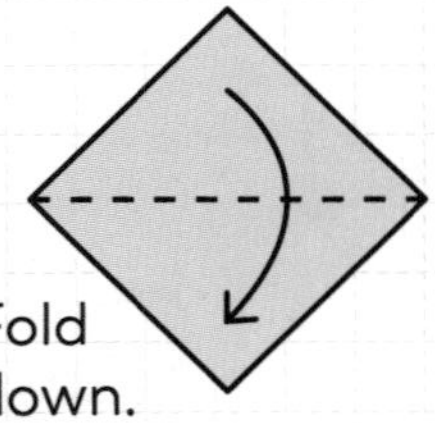

1 Fold down.

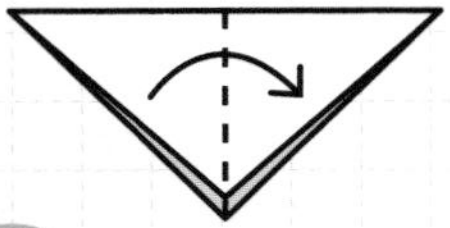

2 Fold in half to the right.

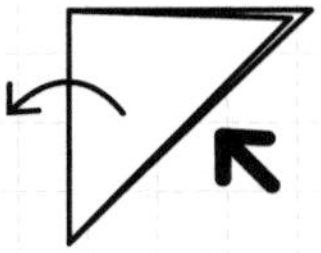

3 Put your finger in the pocket and press down, following the crease line to fold.

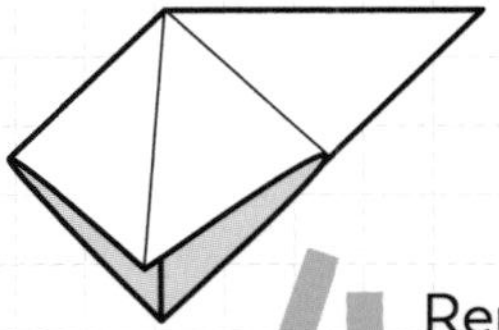

4 Repeat on the other side.

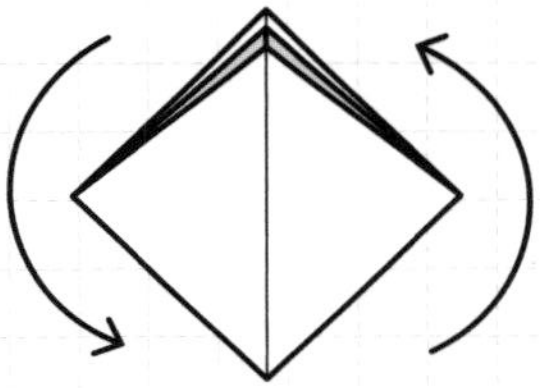

5 Rotate so the open end is on top.

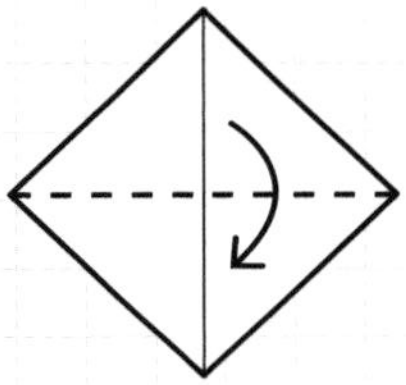

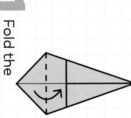

6 Fold the top flap down and repeat on the other side.

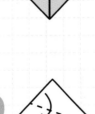

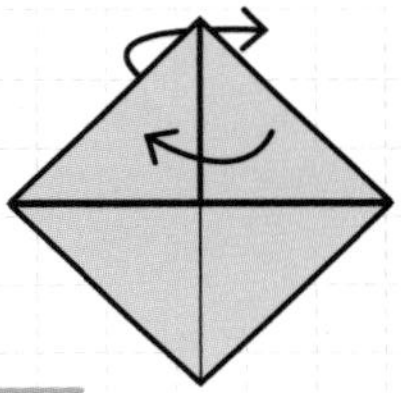

7 Fold the top right flap to the left and the back flap to the right.

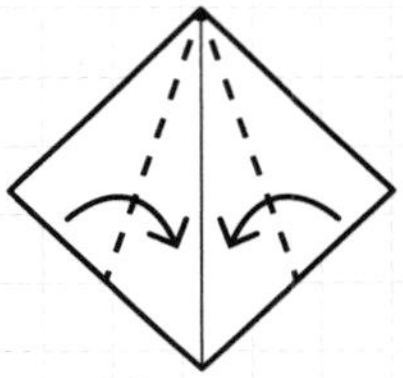

8 Fold the top flap's points to the center crease.

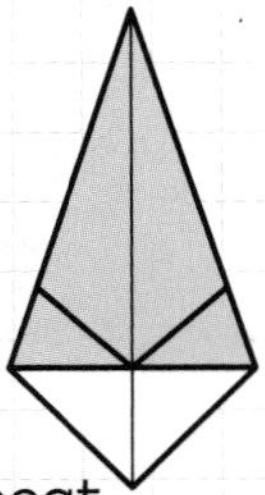

9 Repeat on the other side.

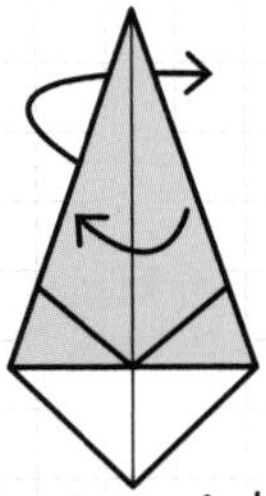

10 Fold the top right flap to the left and the back flap to the right.

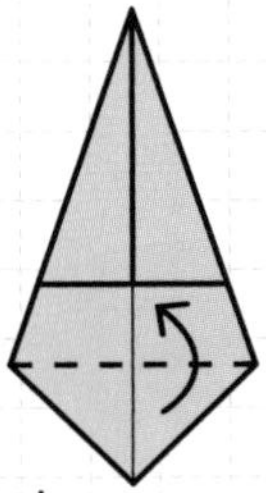

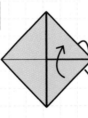

11 Fold the bottom tip of the top flap up.

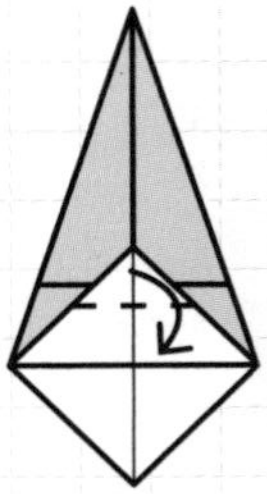

12 Fold down.

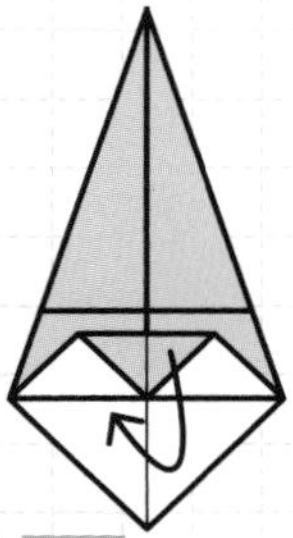

13 Tuck the flap under and inside the pocket. Repeat steps 11 and 12 on the other side.

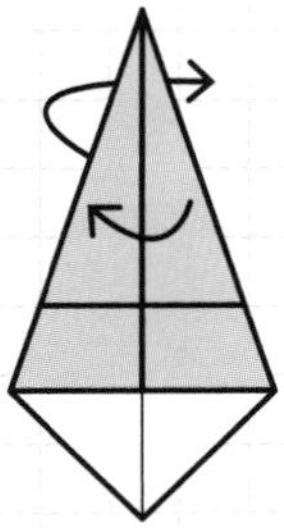

14 Fold the top right flap to the left and the back flap to the right.

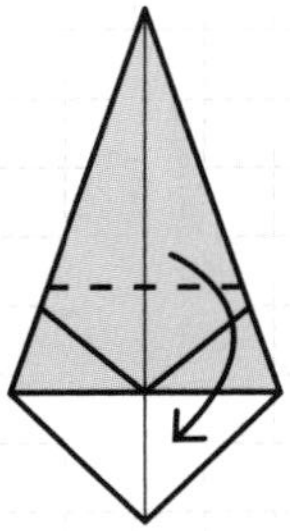

15 Fold the top point down. Repeat on the other side.

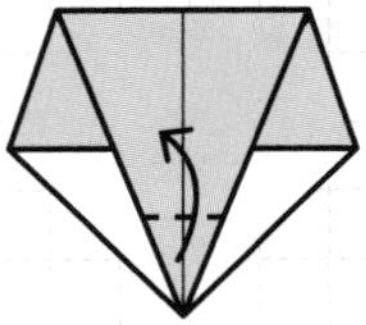

16 Fold up. Repeat on the other side.

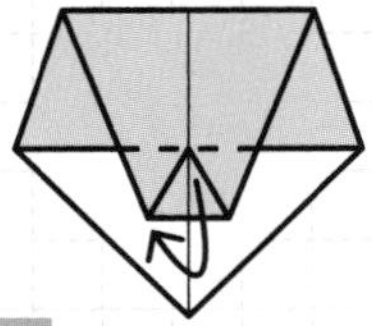

17 Fold and tuck the folded flap inside the pocket. Repeat on the other side.

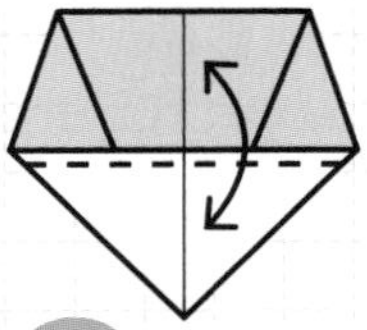

18 Fold and unfold.

Find the Math!

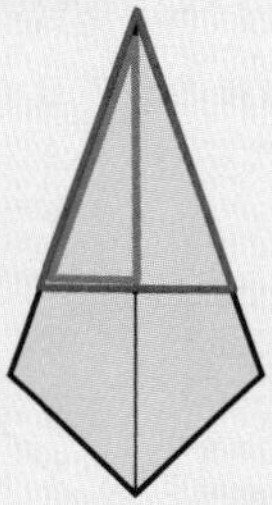

This picture shows step 11 of making a Little Candy Dish. How many times larger is the red triangle than the blue triangle?

ANSWER ON P. 107

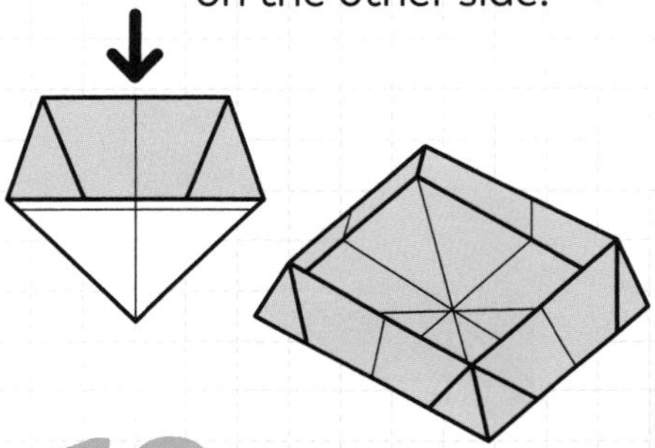

19 Spread the box opening apart and flatten the bottom so the box stands up. Fill it with your favorite treats for a fancy snack!

Spiral Envelope

The Spiral Envelope is the perfect project to teach us about **rotation.** In this type of transformation, a shape is turned around an imaginary center point so that it faces a different way. Looking at the final picture, start at the top triangle. If you rotated it 90° to the right, you'd get the triangle on the right of the envelope, and rotating it the same amount twice more will give you the bottom and left triangles. Around and around it goes. . . .

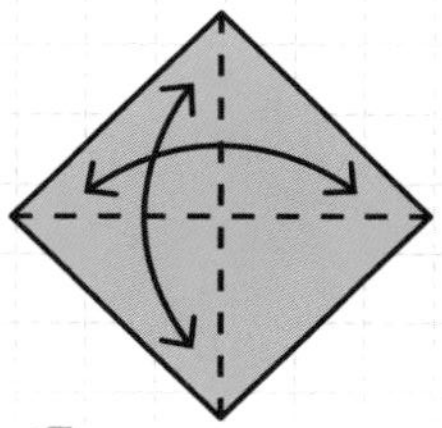

1 Fold and unfold.

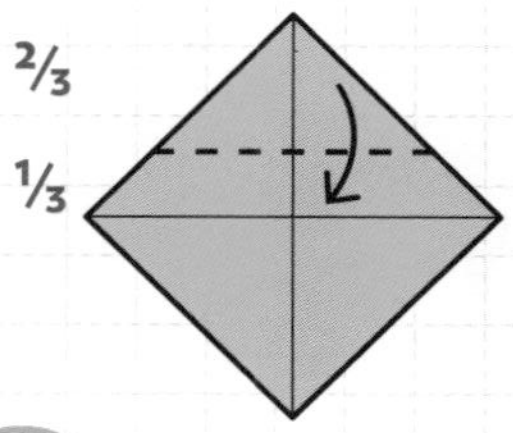

2 Fold the top point two thirds of the way down.

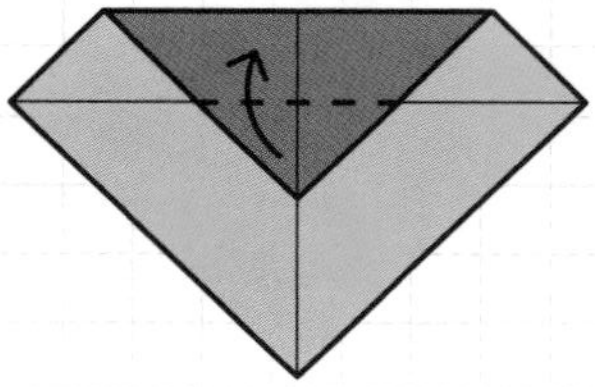

3 Fold the point up to meet the top edge.

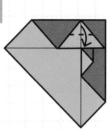

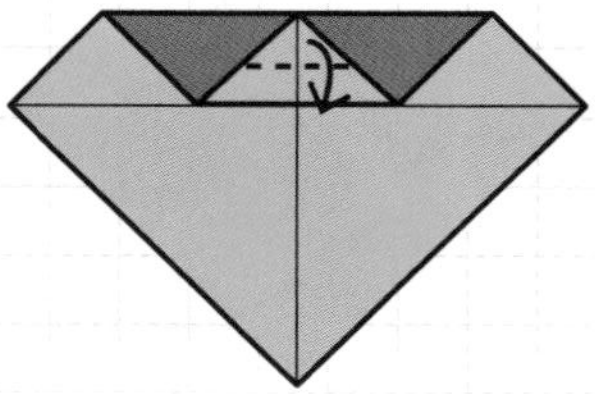

4 Fold down.

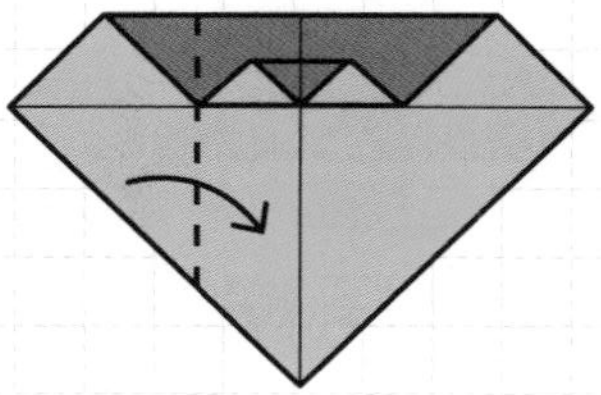

5 Fold the left point to the right.

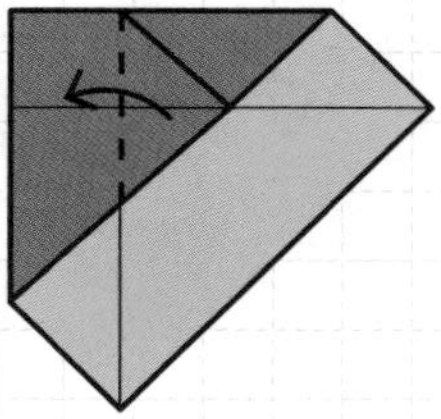

6 Fold to the left edge.

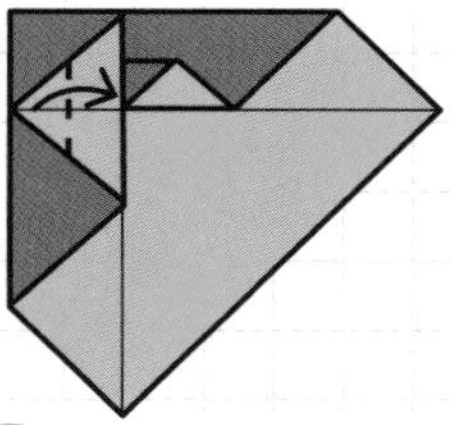

7 Fold the point to the right.

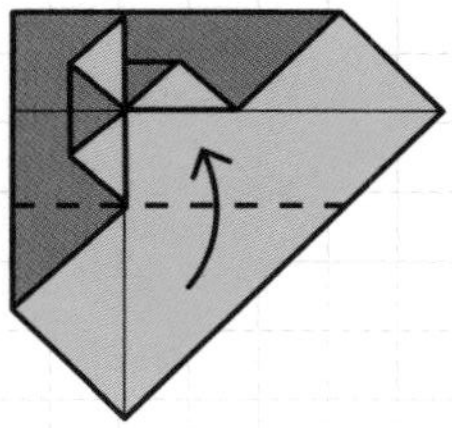

8 Fold in half up.

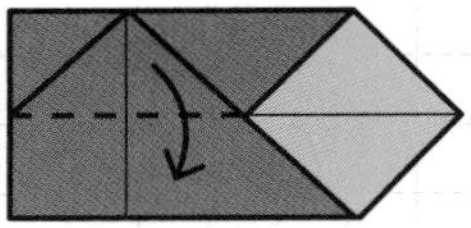

9 Fold the top point down.

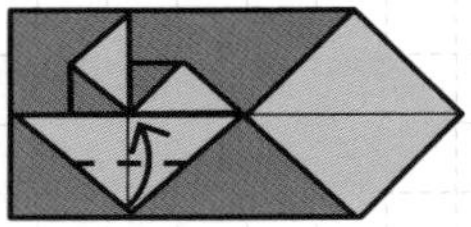

10 Fold the point up.

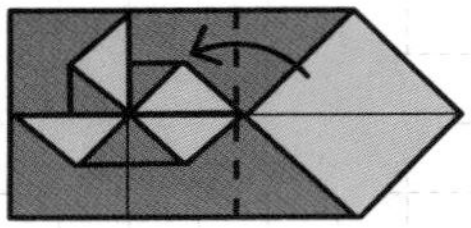

11 Fold in half to the right.

12 Fold the top point to the right.

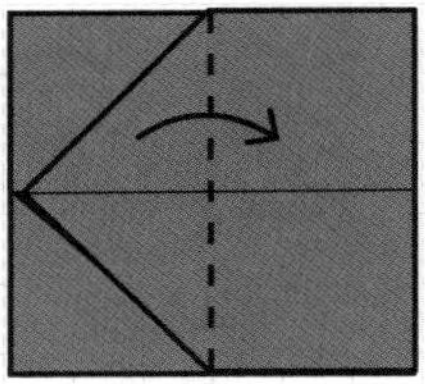

13 Fold the right point in to the center.

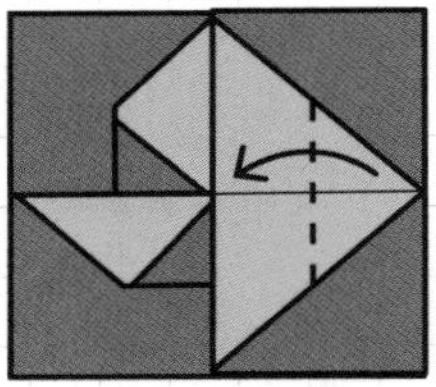

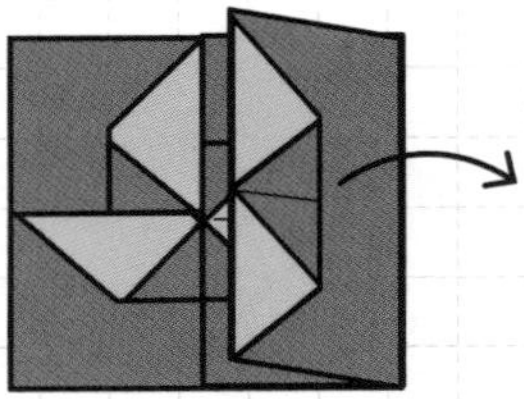

14 Open the right flap.

Find the Math!

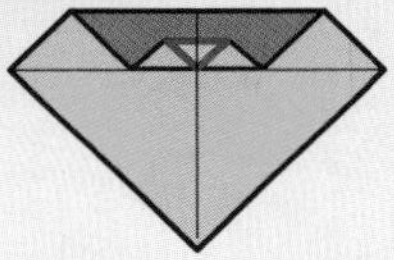

This picture shows step 5 of making a Spiral Envelope. How many other triangles that are the same as the one outlined in red can you find in the origami shape? (It's OK if the triangles are different sizes, different colors, or rotated in different directions as long as the shapes are the same.)

ANSWER ON P. 107

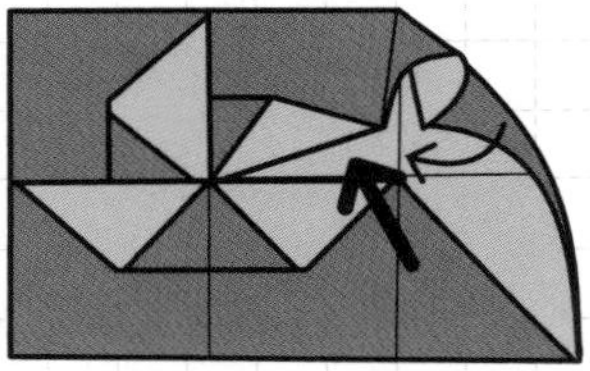

15 Lift the flap and fold the right edge into the pocket on the top right side, tucking it inside. Now your envelope is finished and ready to send to a friend!

Fancy Letters

Inside these letters, we can find a new type of transformation called **translation.** Translating a shape means moving it up and down or side to side (or both) without changing anything else about its shape or size. Look at step 9 of the first letter and focus on the 2 triangles that make the top points of the heart. If you moved the left triangle over to the right, it would match exactly—that's translation! See if you can find other examples hiding in the rest of the steps.

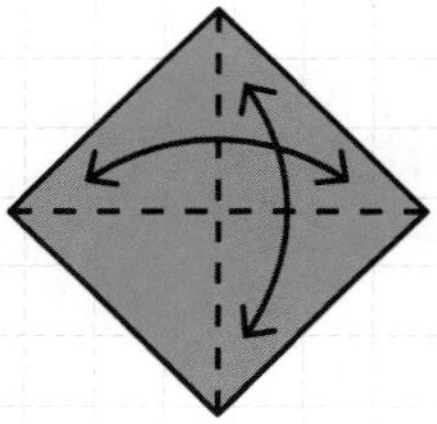

1 Fold and unfold.

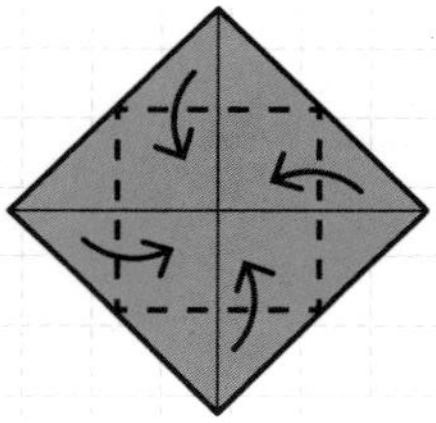

2 Fold all 4 corners to the center.

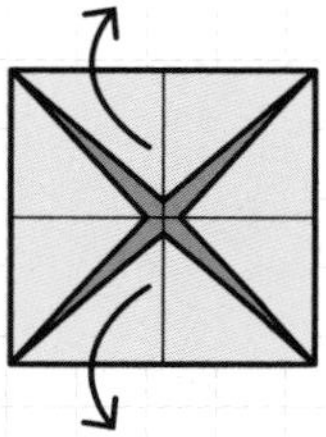

3 Open the top and bottom flaps.

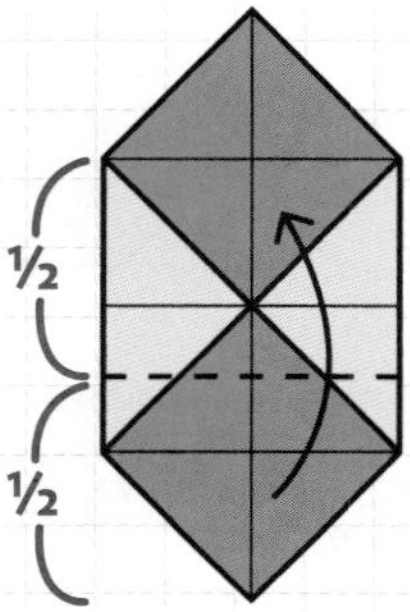

4 Fold the bottom point up.

5 Fold the point down to the bottom edge.

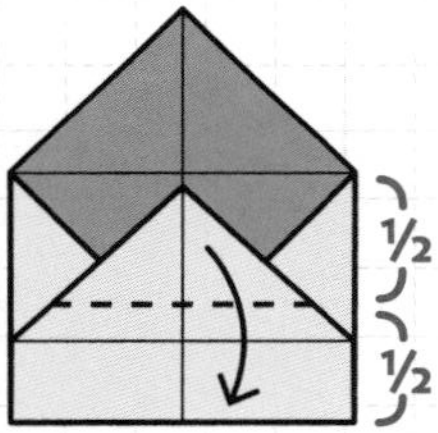

6 Fold the top point down to the bottom edge.

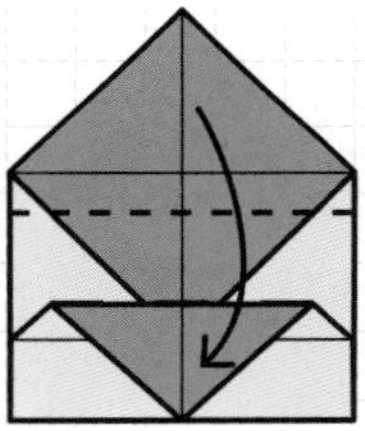

7 Fold the point up.

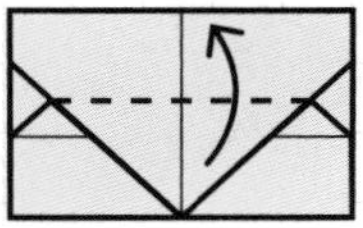

8 Fold the point down.

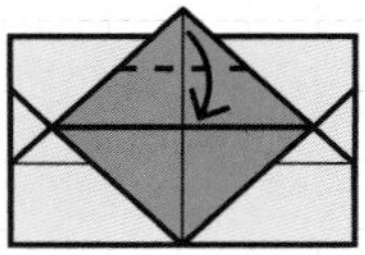

9 Use tape or glue to finish the letter if you want. Send this heart to someone you love!

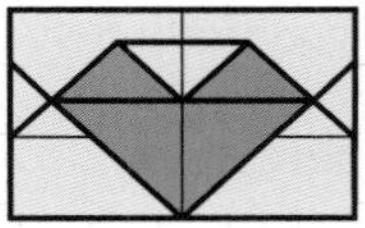

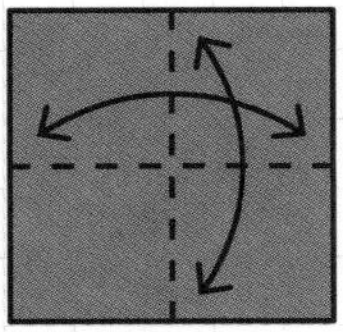

1 Fold and unfold.

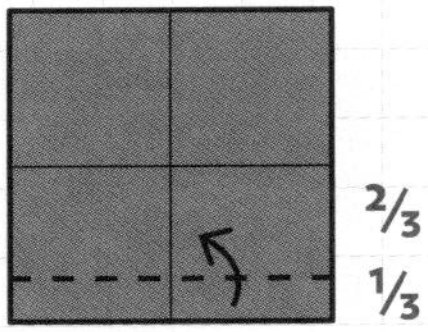

2 Fold the bottom one third of the way up.

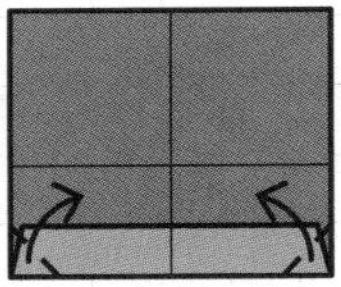

3 Fold the corners in.

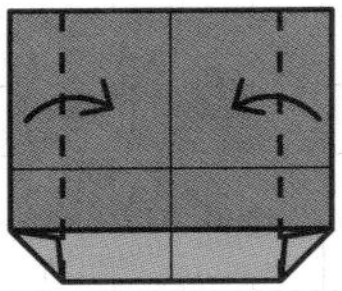

4 Fold the left and right edges in.

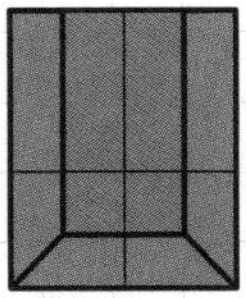

5

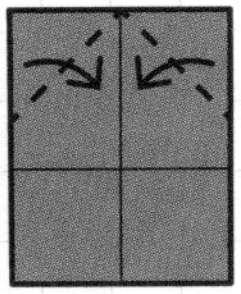

6 Fold the top corners to the center crease.

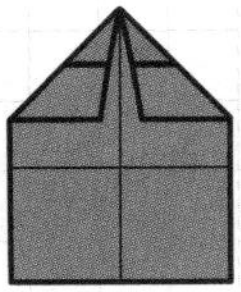

7

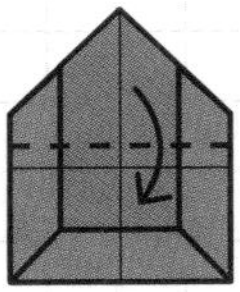

8 Fold the top point down to meet the bottom edge.

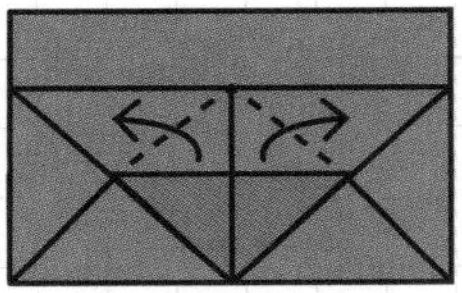

9 Fold the flaps over.

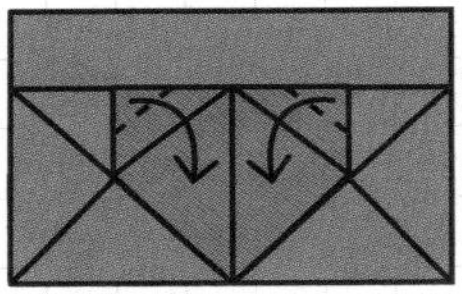

10 Fold the corners down.

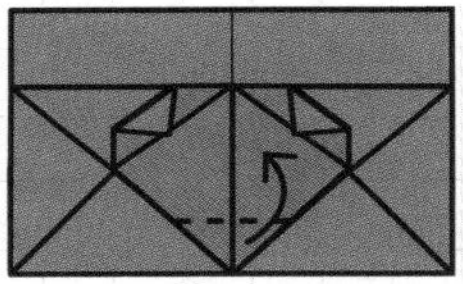

11 Fold the bottom point up. Add eyes and a nose to make a super cute puppy!

Find the Math!

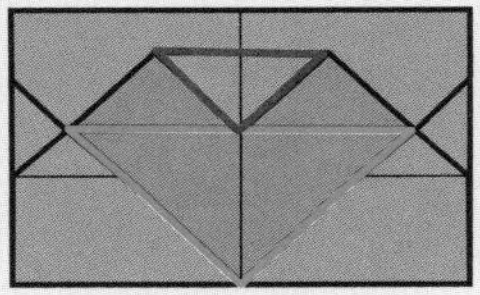

This picture shows the finished heart-shaped Fancy Letter. The triangle outlined in red is just like the triangle outlined in blue. What are shapes that are the same shape but different sizes called?

ANSWER ON P. 107

Flower Ornament

We're going to meet another 3D shape while working on step 9 of the Flower Ornament. When you lift the flap and expand the pocket, it makes a **square pyramid,** which has 4 triangle sides sitting on top of a square base (here, this is the empty space your finger goes through). Flattening the pyramid in the next step shows how 3D shapes are built by combining 2D shapes—just like this ornament is built by combining 6 origami flowers!

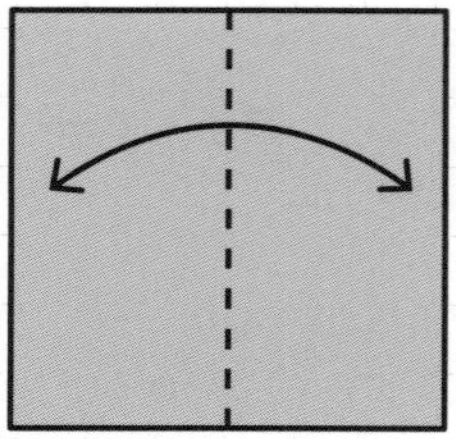

1 Fold and unfold.

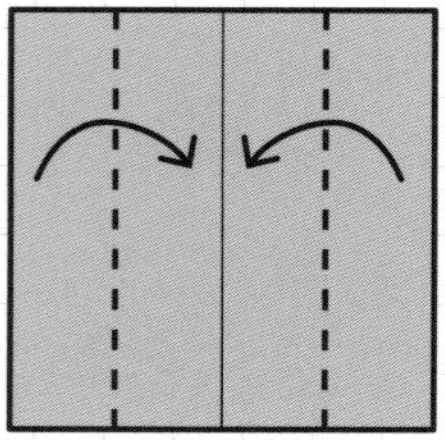

2 Fold the left and right sides to the center crease.

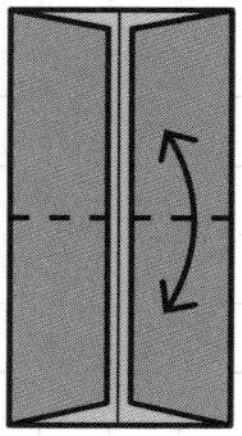

3 Fold down.

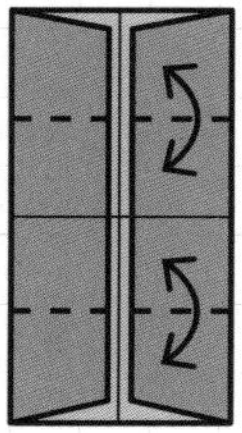

4 Fold and unfold.

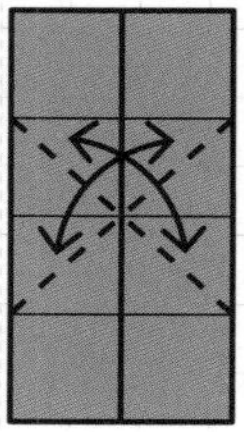

5 Fold and unfold.

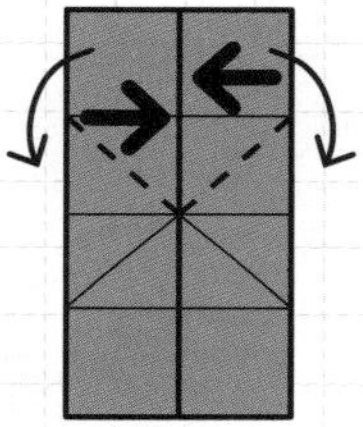

6 Lift the flaps open.

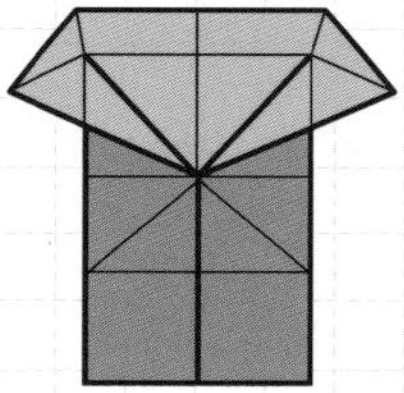

7 Press down along the creases.

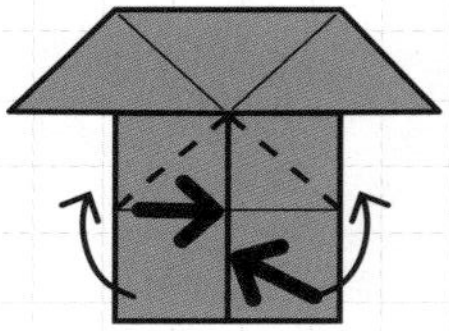

8 Repeat on the bottom.

9 Lift the flap, put your finger in the pocket, and press down along the crease. Repeat 3 times with the other sections.

10 Fold in.

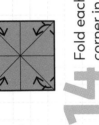

11 Lift the flap and press down.

12 Repeat steps 9 and 10 on the places marked with ★.

13

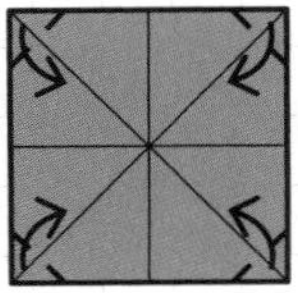

14 Fold each corner in.

15

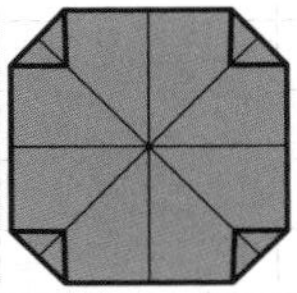

16 Make 6 flowers. Try making each one a different color.

17 Turn each flower over and put a little glue on the folded tabs. Then, stick all of the parts together 1 by 1.

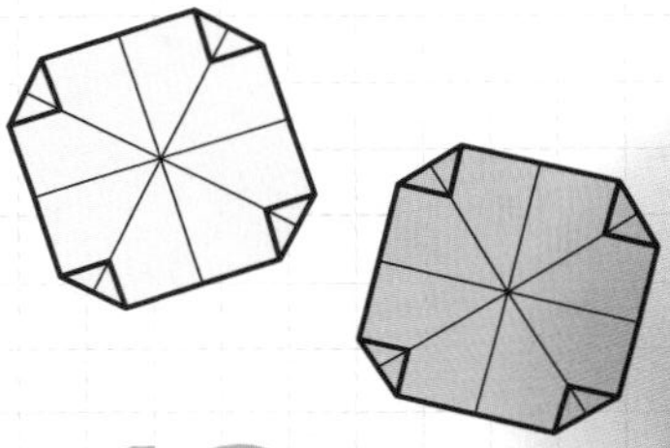

18 Tape 1 end of a piece of string to the top. You can display your ornament by taping the other end to the ceiling, or maybe looping it around a branch. Beautiful!

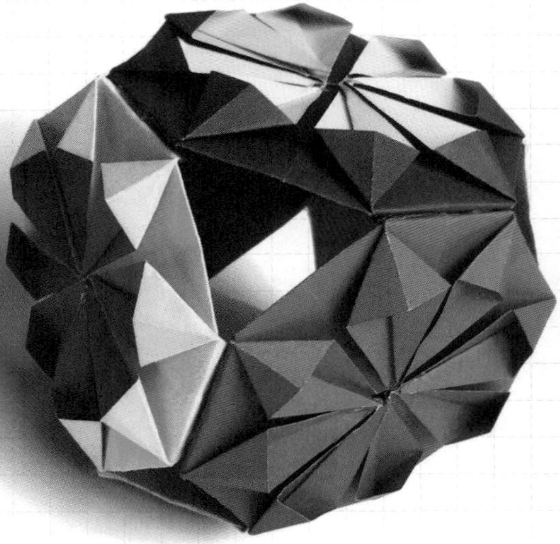

Find the Math!

This picture shows step 9 of making a Flower Ornament. The shape outlined in blue is the same as the one outlined in red. What is the name for shapes that are the same, like the red and blue ones are?

1. **Twin shapes**
2. **Congruent shapes**

ANSWER ON P. 107

Math Magic Tricks

Do some magic with just a piece of paper! These tricks are helpful if you want to come up with some origami art of your very own.

Trick 1: Create 2 Identical Shapes

You can make 2 of the exact same shape by matching up the origami papers' corners neatly and cutting along the fold.

Make 2 identical triangles

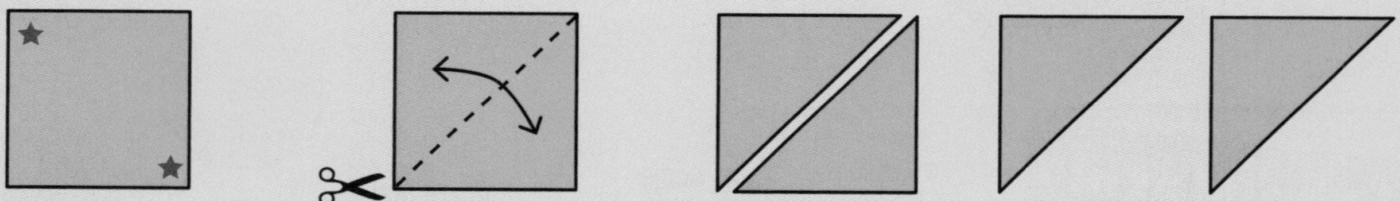

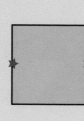

1 Match up the corners marked with ★, then fold and unfold the paper.

2 Cut along the crease.

3 Try rotating the marked triangle. See? The two triangles are exactly the same.

Make 2 identical rectangles

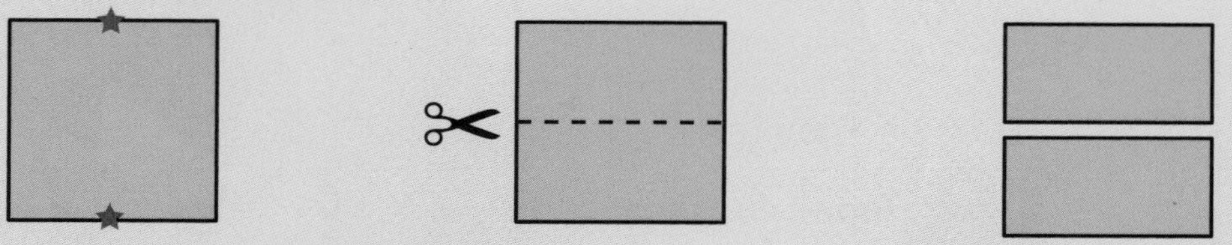

1 Match up the sides marked with ★, then fold and unfold the paper.

2 Cut along the crease.

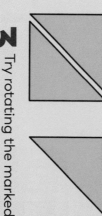

Look! The rectangles are identical.

Trick 2: Turn a Rectangle into a Square

Is your origami paper a rectangle instead of a square? No problem!

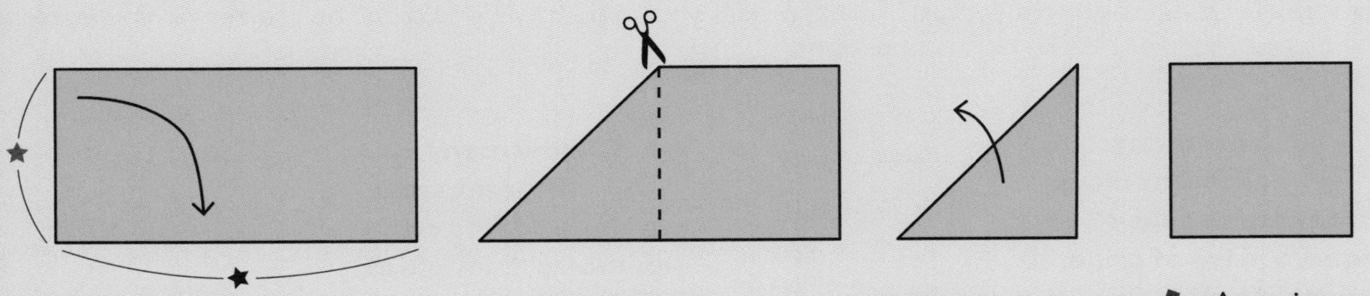

1 Fold the side marked ★ over to match up with the side marked ★.

2 Cut along the dotted line.

3 Unfold.

4 Amazing—it's now a square!

Trick 3: Make Right Angles

You can make right angles with any shape of paper just by folding the paper 2 times.

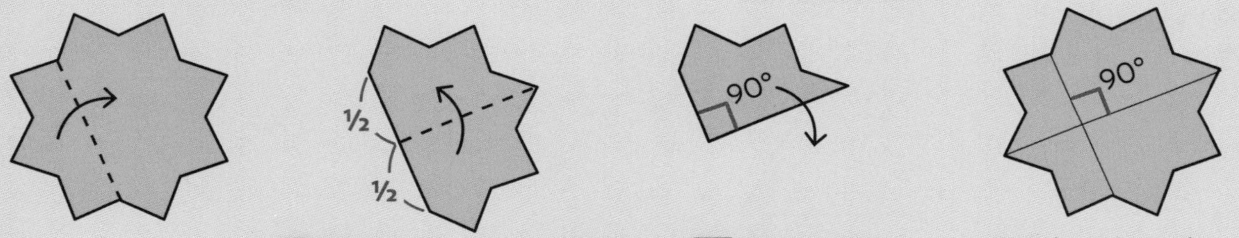

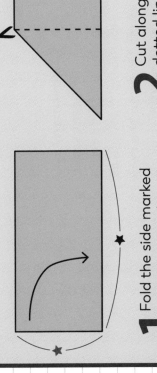

1 Fold the paper anywhere you like.

2 Find the spot in the middle of one of the sides. Fold it carefully so that the 2 edges on either side of the central fold match up exactly.

3 Open the folds you made in steps 1 and 2.

That's right—the corner where the two creases meet is a 90° angle!

Bonus Brain Teasers

Hungry for more math challenges? Test the skills you've built while folding the projects in this book by answering these tricky bonus questions.

1 **How many different ways are there to fold a square piece of origami paper in half 1 time so the edges line up neatly?**

2 **How many different ways are there to fold an equilateral triangle in half 1 time so the edges line up neatly?**

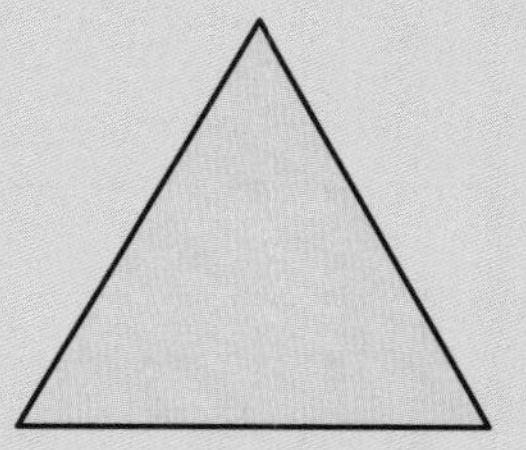

3 **Which of these triangles cannot be made by folding a piece of origami paper (a square) 1 time? Choose 3.**

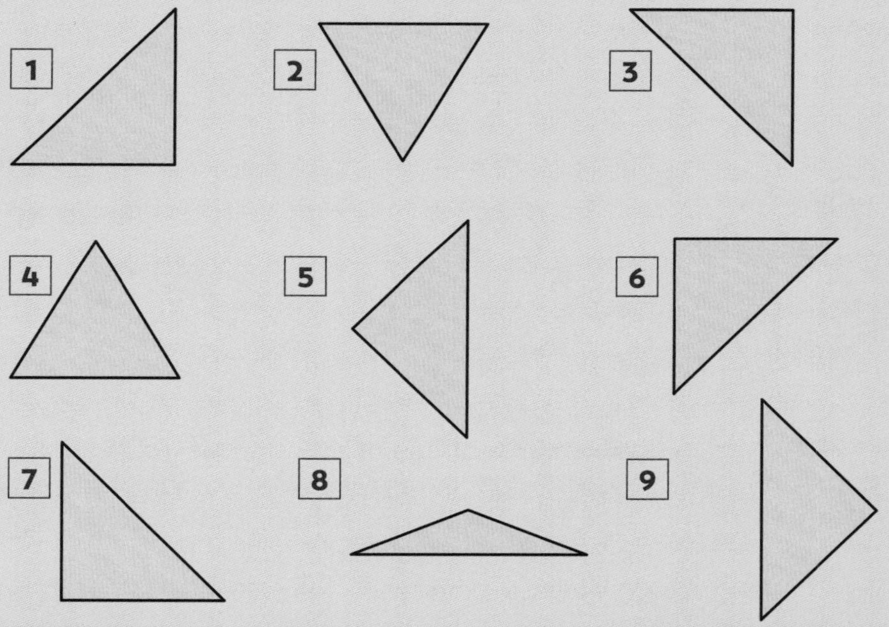

ANSWERS ON P. 101

4 **Which of the following shapes can be made using just 1 piece of origami paper cut in half to make 2 right triangles? Choose 3.**

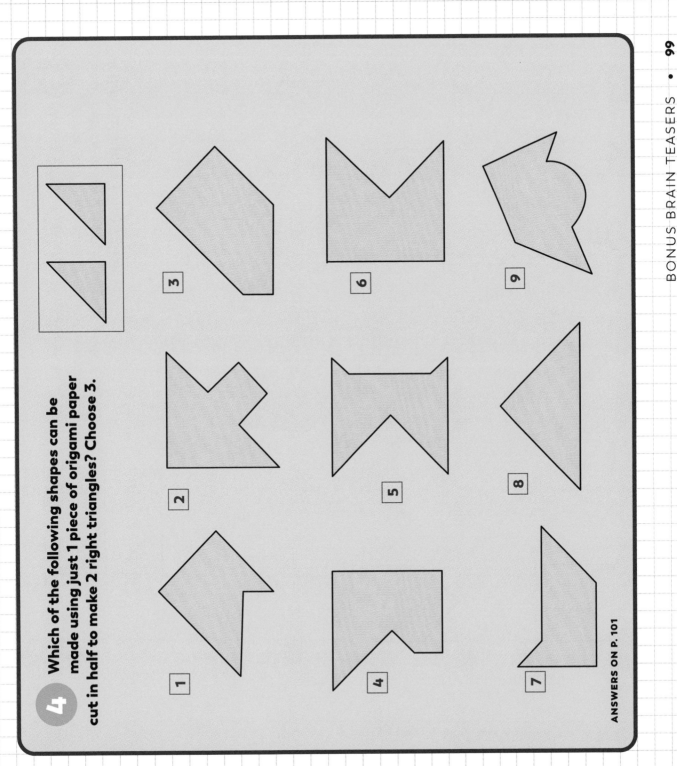

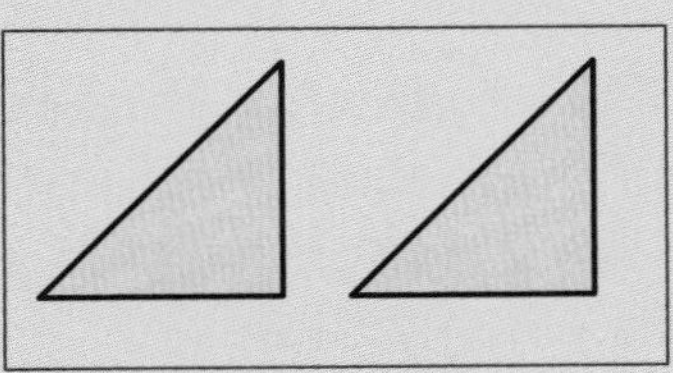

1

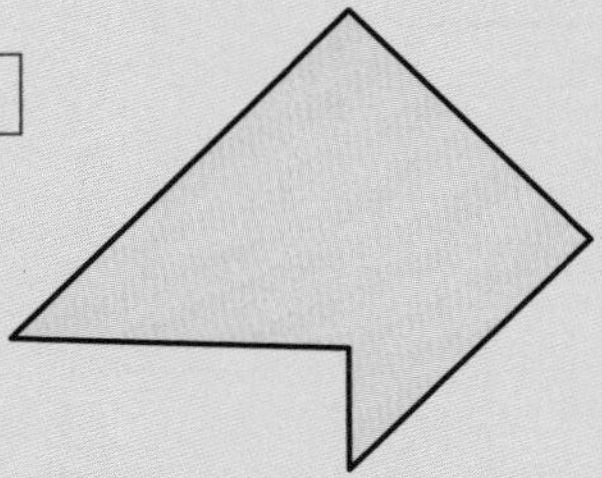

2

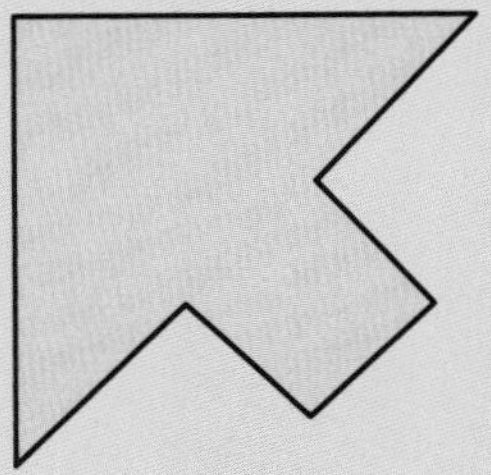

3

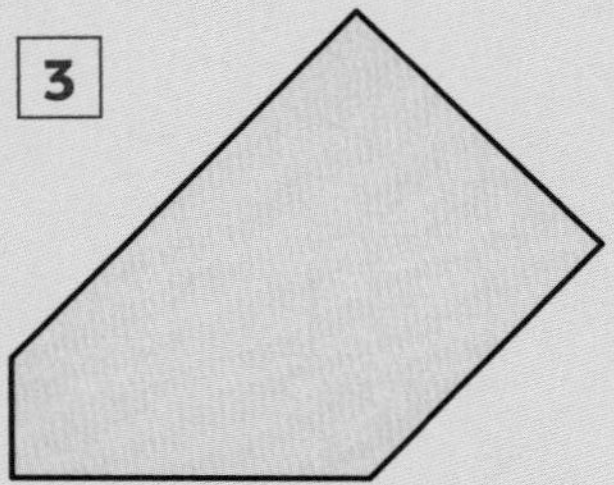

4

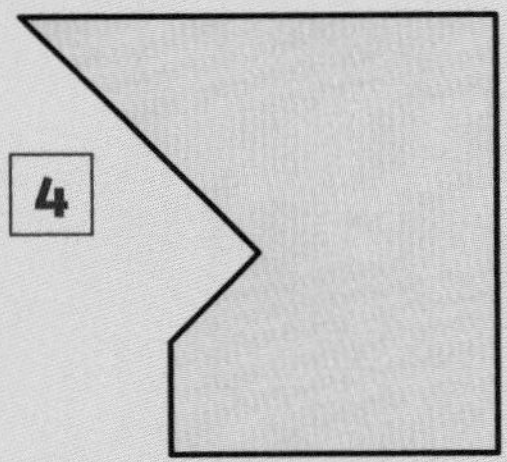

5

6

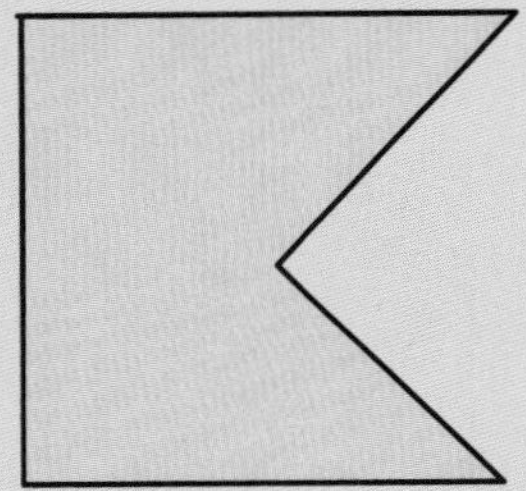

7

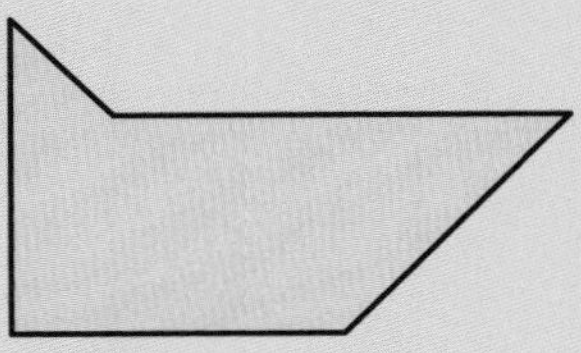

8

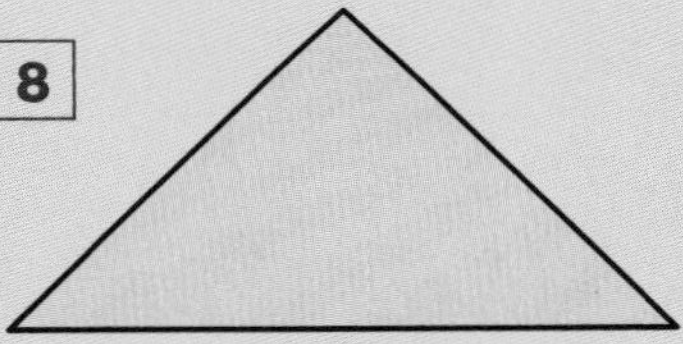

9

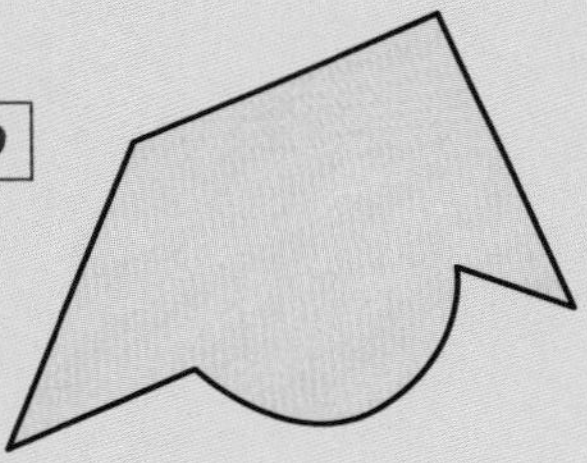

ANSWERS ON P. 101

5 **Which of the following shapes can be made using 2 pieces of origami paper cut in half to make 2 right triangles each (4 right triangles total)? Choose 3.**

1

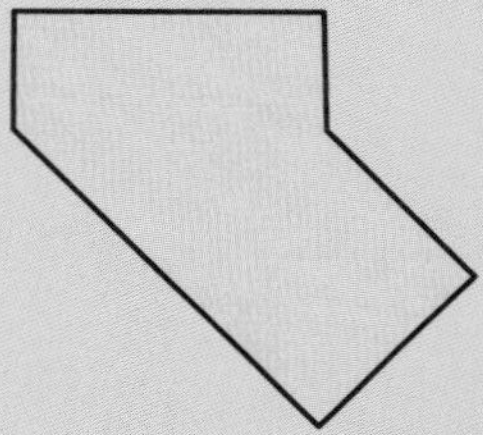

2

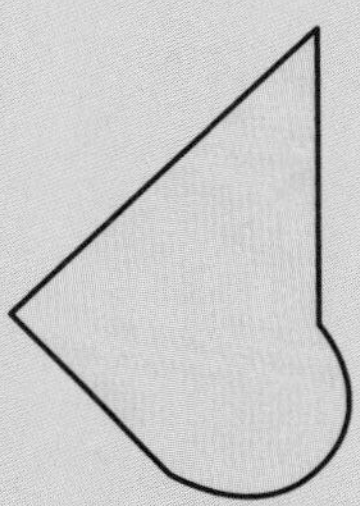

3

4

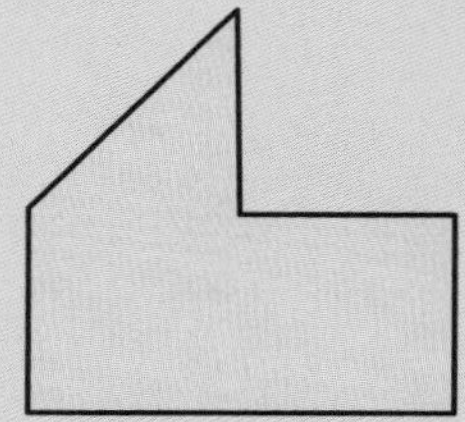

5

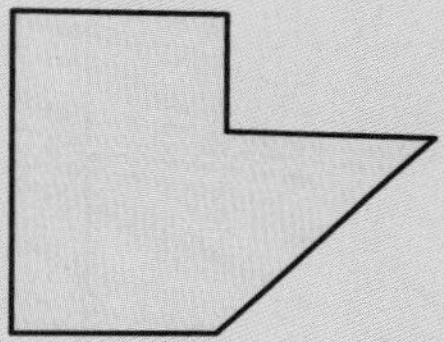

6

7

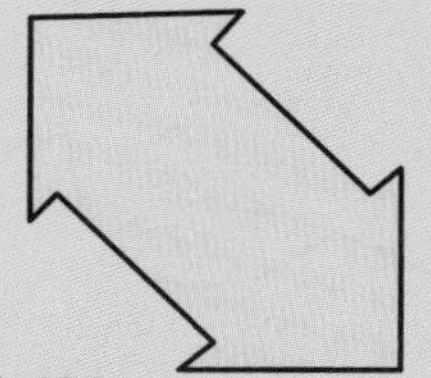

8

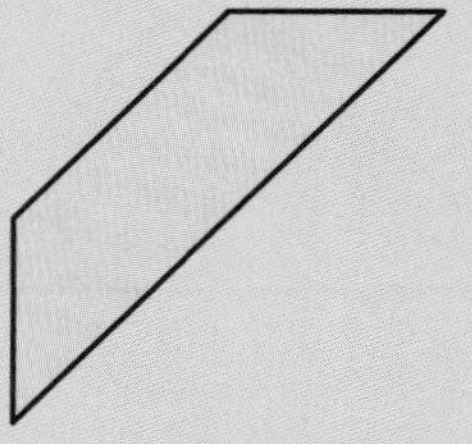

9

ANSWERS ON P. 101

Bonus Answers

1 **4 ways:** The edges and corners line up neatly when a square is folded along these dotted lines.

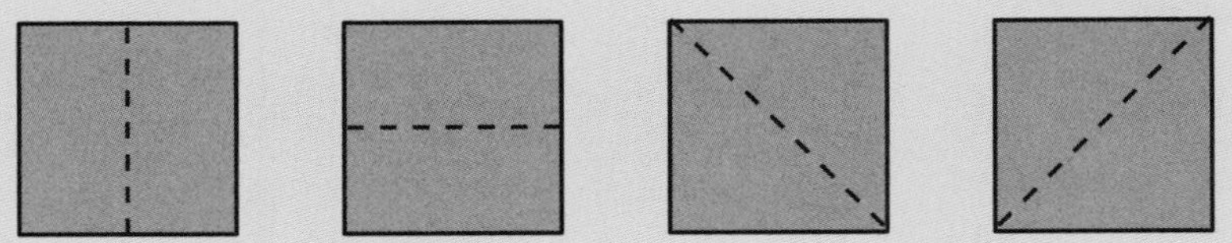

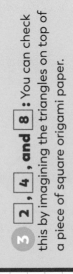

2 **3 ways:** The corners line up neatly when a triangle is folded along these dotted lines.

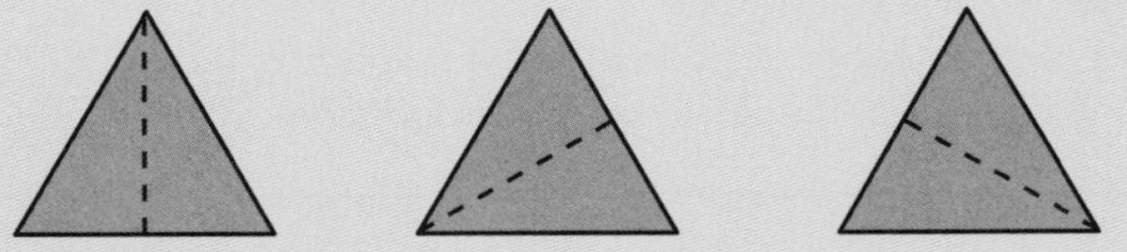

3 **2, 4, and 8:** You can check this by imagining the triangles on top of a piece of square origami paper.

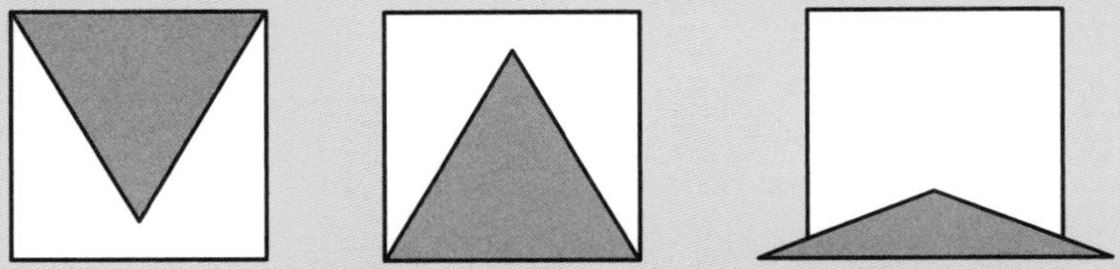

4 **1, 7, and 8:** The black lines show how triangles can be used to make these shapes.

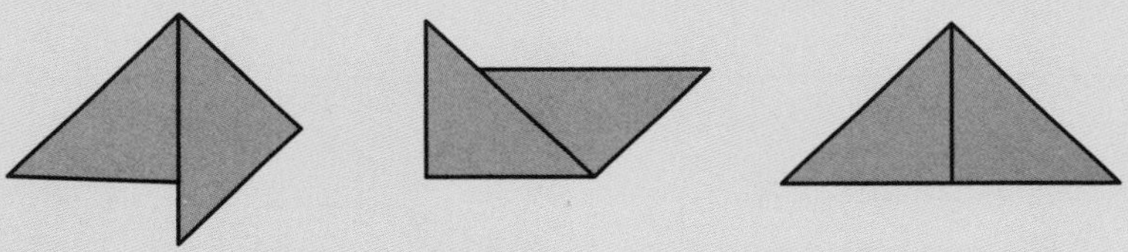

5 **3, 6, and 7:** The black lines show how triangles can be used to make these shapes.

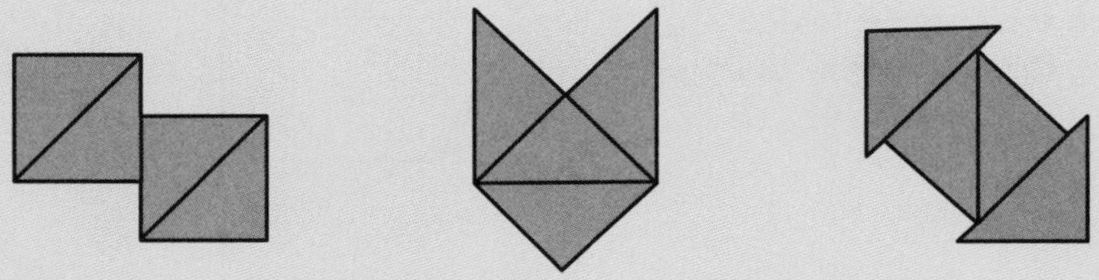

Find the Math! Answers

Airplane (p. 12)

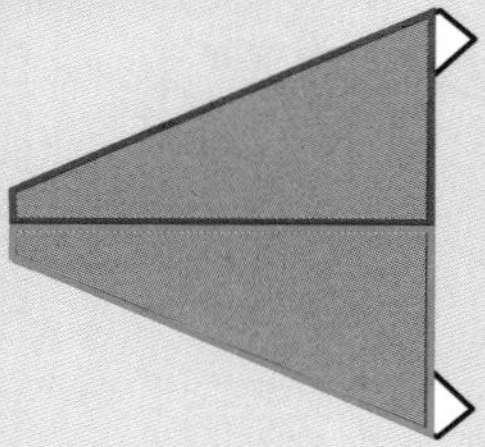

The shape outlined in blue here is exactly the same as the one outlined in red. We know this because the shapes have the same number of sides with the same lengths—they're just flipped in opposite directions.

Boxy Balloon (p. 18)

The origami paper in step 3 is ¼ the size of the paper in step 1.

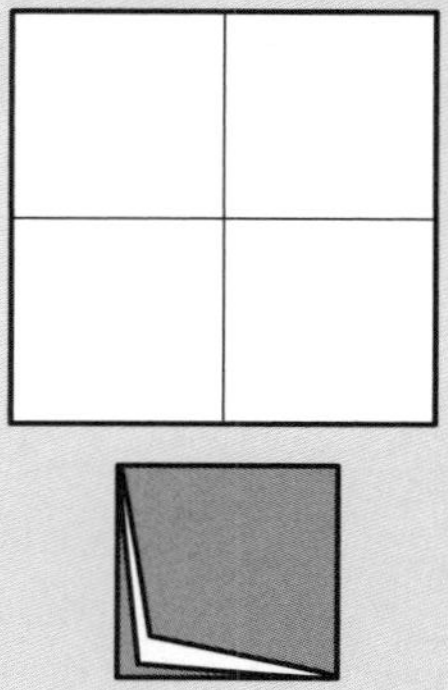

Jet Plane (p. 14)

This shape is called a quadrilateral because it has 4 sides, and it's irregular because all of its sides are not the same length.

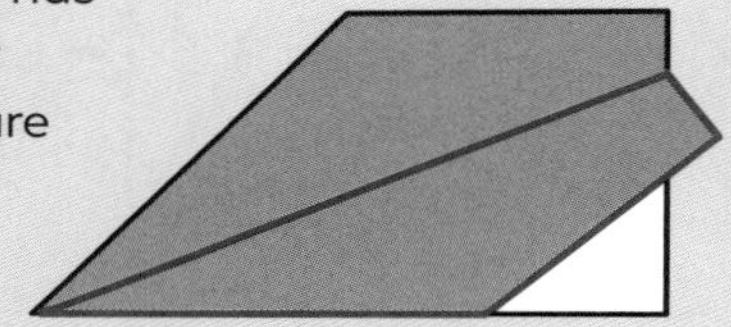

Winged Balloon (p. 21)

It would take 12 of the red triangles to fill up the whole origami paper. That means that 1 triangle is 1⁄12 of the paper.

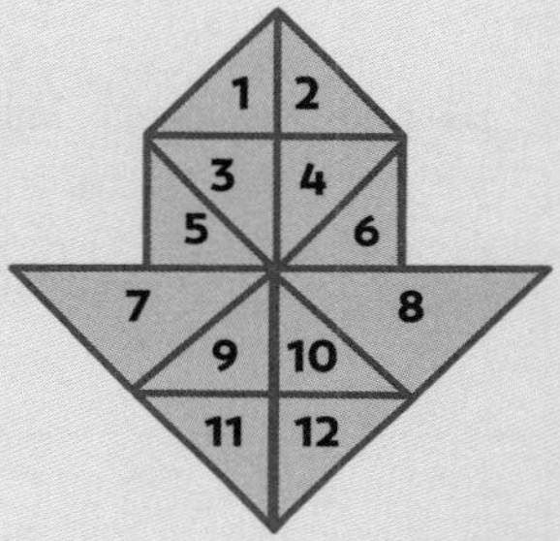

Flying Squid (p. 16)

The 2 triangle pairs are outlined in red and blue. When the paper is folded along the dotted line, both of the pairs match up exactly.

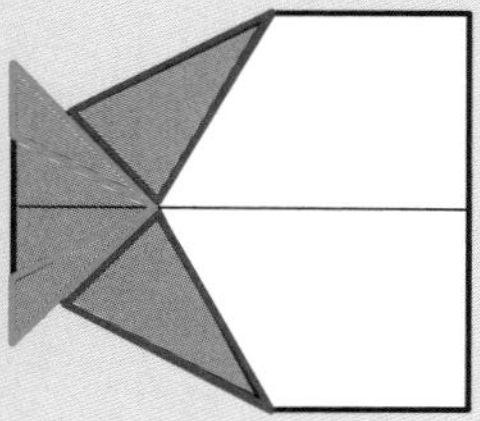

Propeller (p. 24)

The 3 shapes outlined in blue are the same shape as the one outlined in red, meaning that all 4 are congruent.

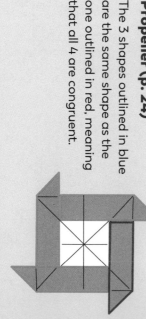

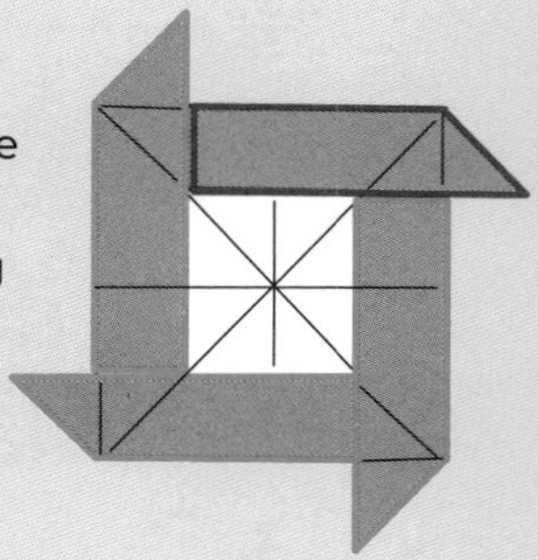

Catapult (p. 26)

This shape is called a pentagon because it has 5 sides.

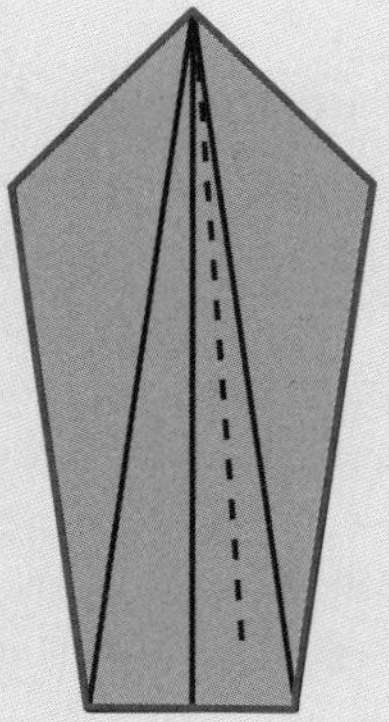

Roaring Dinosaur (p. 36)

The 3 triangles outlined in blue are the same as the one outlined in red. They're all the same size and shape even though one of them is turned upside down.

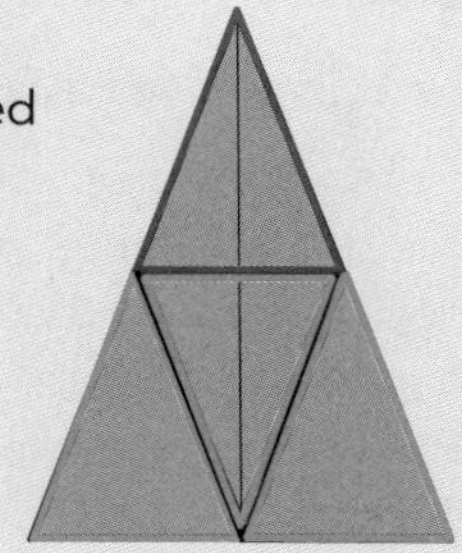

Flapping Bird (p. 30)

These triangles are all right triangles. They have this name because they each have a 90°, or right, angle.

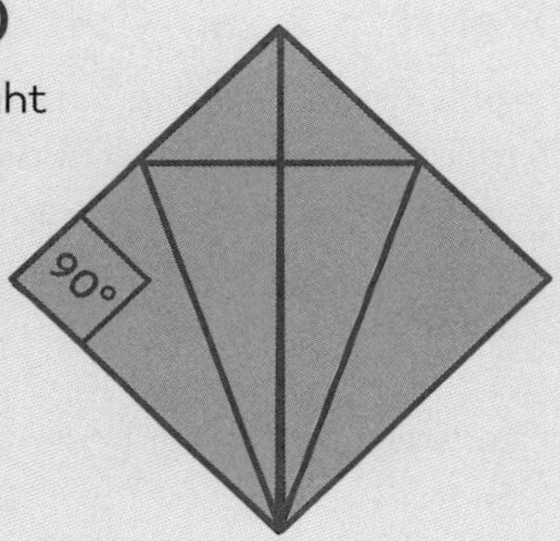

Hungry Raven (p. 38)

The corner outlined in blue is a 45° angle. This is because 2 of these corners make a 90° angle, and 45 + 45 = 90.

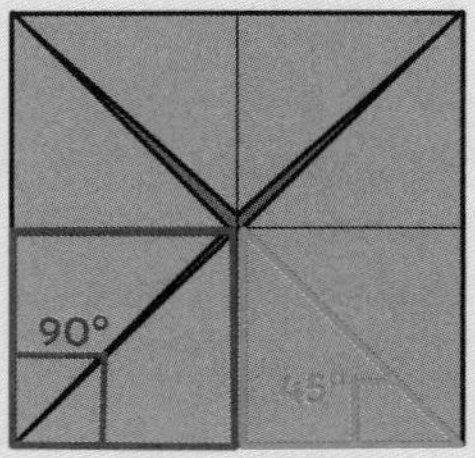

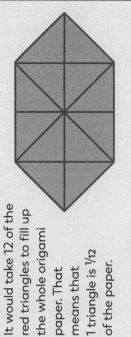

Fluttering Bird (p. 33)

This shape has 6 sides, so it's called a hexagon.

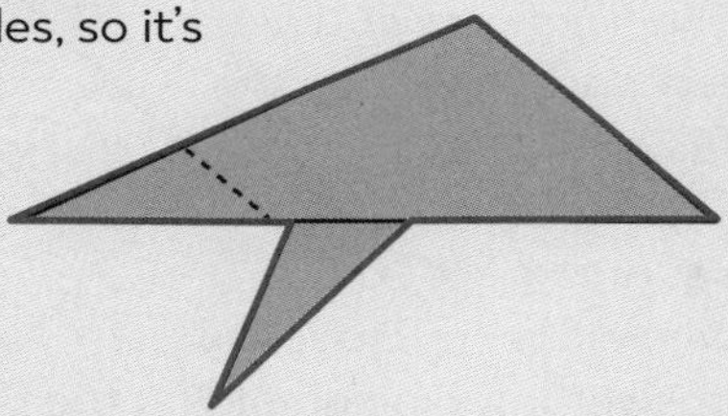

Croaking Toad (p. 40)

It would take 12 of the red triangles to fill up the whole origami paper. That means that 1 triangle is $\frac{1}{12}$ of the paper.

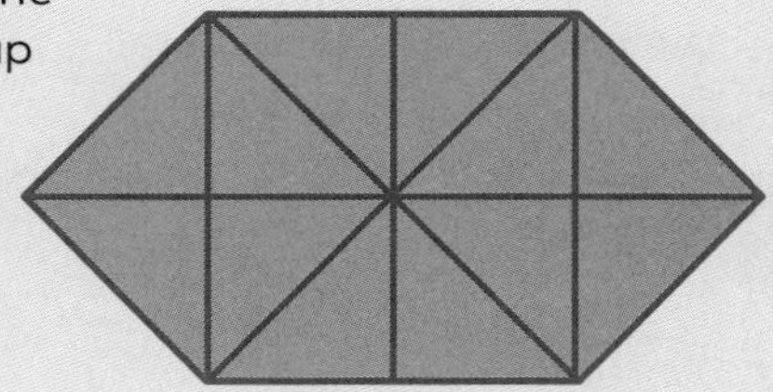

Find the Math! Answers

Beating Heart (p. 42)

These 5 triangles outlined in blue are different sizes, but they're all the same shape as the triangle outlined in red. All 6 are isosceles right triangles!

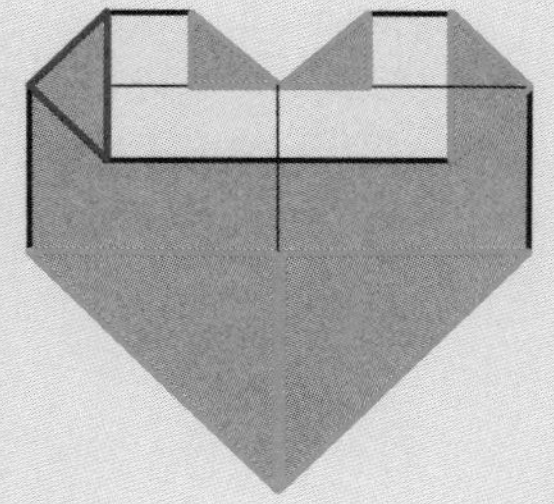

Jumping Frog (p. 44)

Because 2 of the rectangles could fit inside the square, 1 rectangle is ½ of the square. The folds in steps 6 and 7 give you a clue.

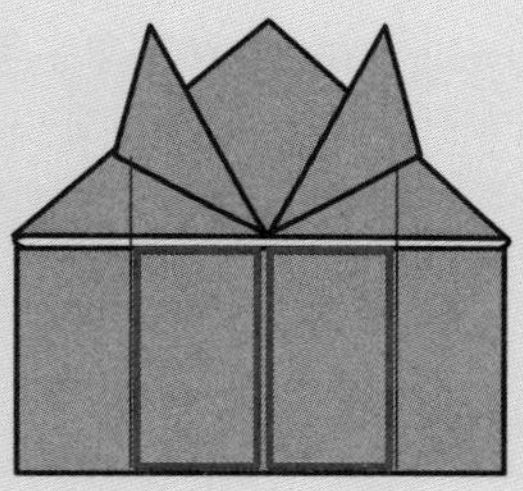

Hopping Crow (p. 46)

Adding ¼ + ¼ gets you ½ of the total paper. You can tell this is true because the left half of the paper is made of 2 quarters.

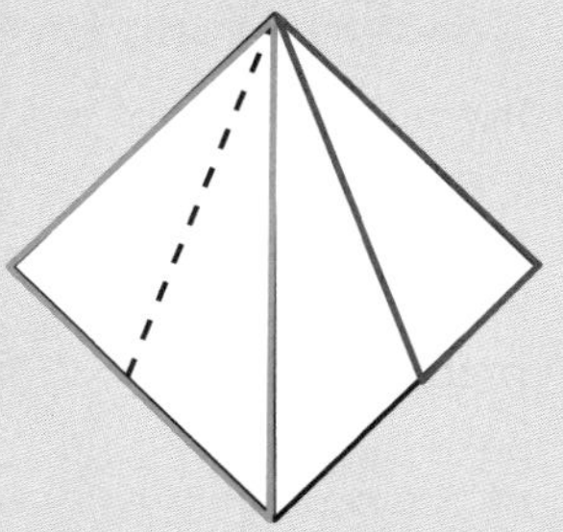

Creeping Mouse (p. 48)

The four corners of a piece of origami paper are always right (90°) angles because origami paper is square. And because 2 of the sides are the same length, too, the shape outlined in red is called an isosceles right triangle.

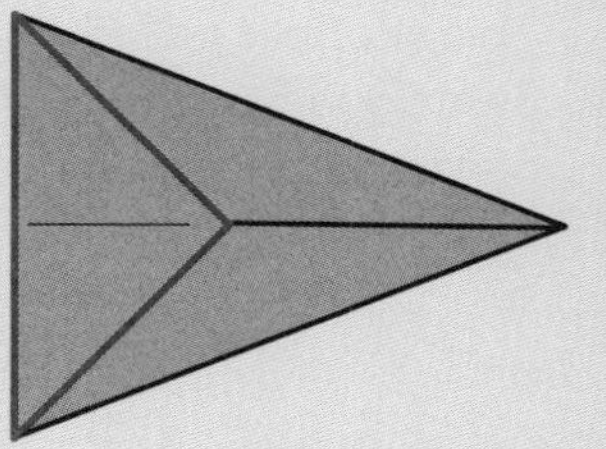

Fighting Sumo Wrestler (p. 50)

The triangle outlined in blue is similar to the one outlined in red, because they're the same shape but not the same size. There aren't any triangles that are the exact same shape and size, so none are congruent.

Grasshoppers (p. 54)

The 4 squares outlined in red would fit inside the full origami paper. This means 1 of the squares is ¼ of the whole paper. To get the answer, imagine unfolding the piece of paper that the square is a part of.

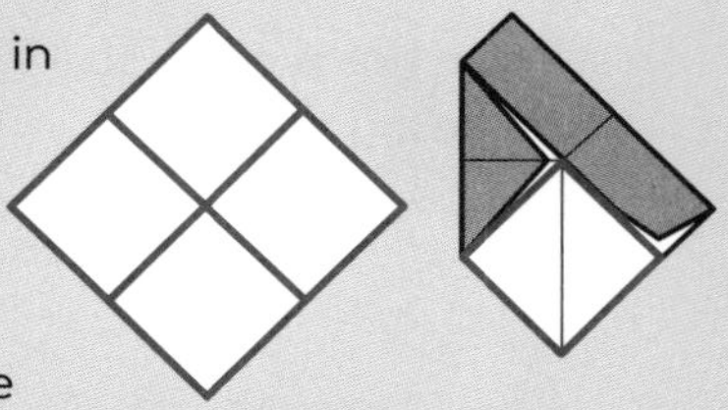

Bear and Cub (p. 56)

There are 6 total triangles in the Bear and Cub.

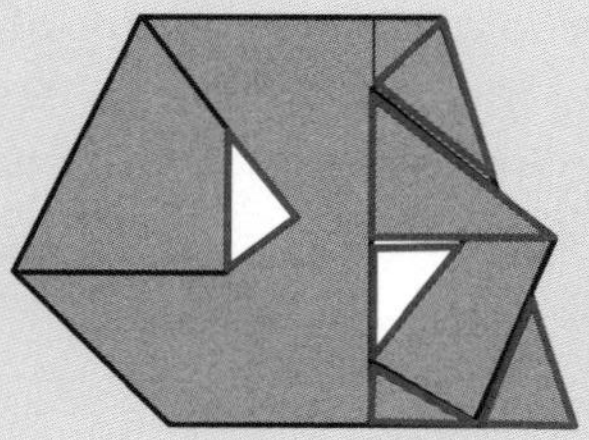

Tortoise and Hare (p. 62)

The rectangle outlined in red is 1/8 of the origami paper. To get the answer, count how many rectangles like this make up the whole piece of paper.

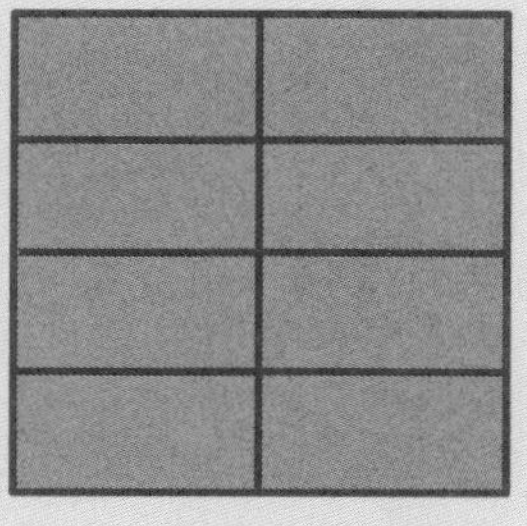

Penguin and Chick (p. 58)

This shape is a pentagon. You can tell because it has 5 sides.

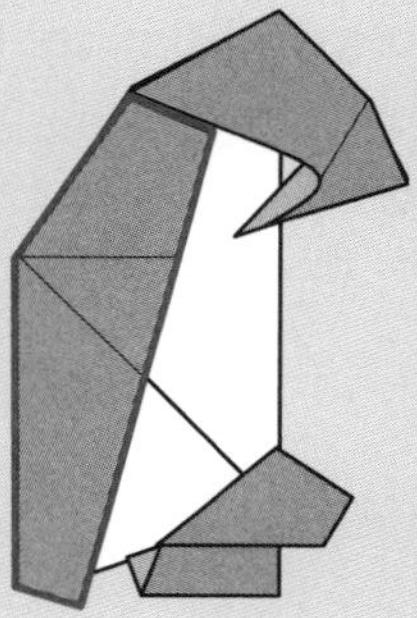

Cat and Dog (p. 65)

This shape is called a trapezoid. Trapezoids are 4-sided shapes (quadrilaterals) with 1 pair of parallel sides and 1 pair of slanted sides.

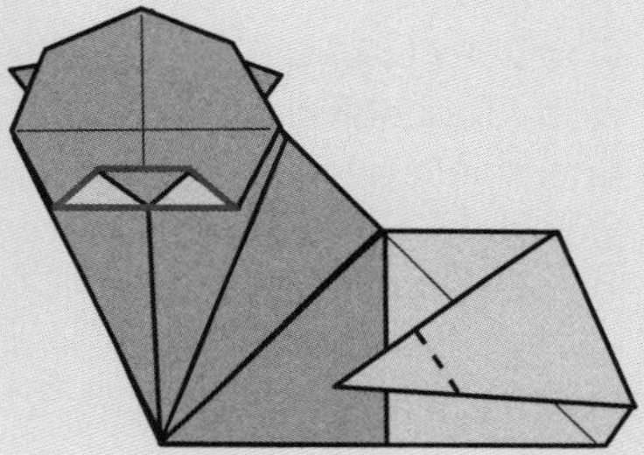

Ladybugs (p. 60)

When one half of a shape is a "reflection" of the other, it has reflection symmetry.

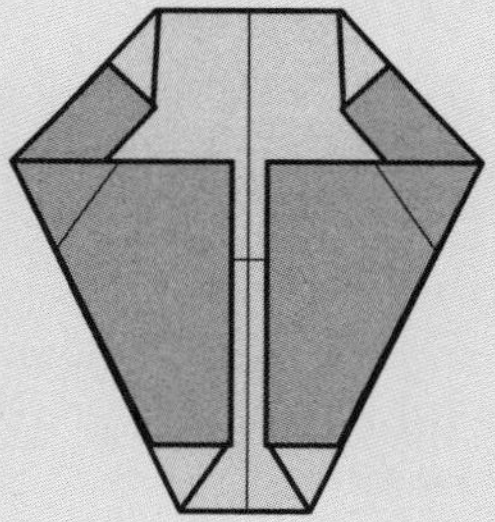

Four Frogs (p. 68)

The Four Frogs have 8 total eyes. 2 + 2 + 2 + 2 (2 eyes for each of the 4 frogs) = 8.

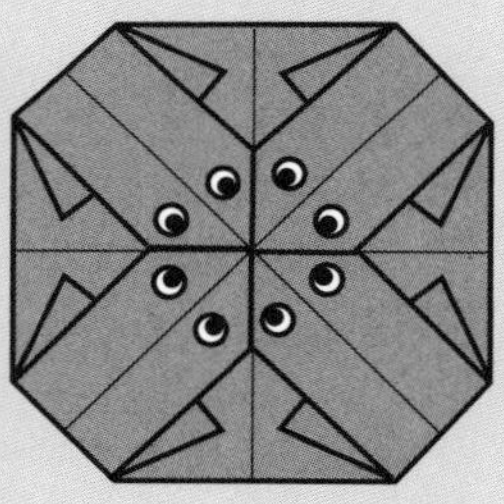

Find the Math! Answers

Six Turtles (p. 71)

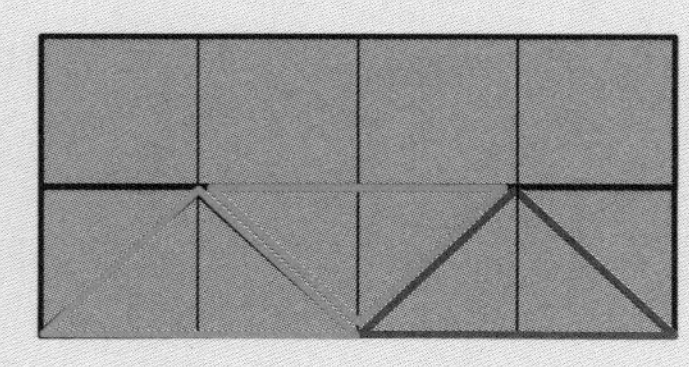

The 2 triangles outlined in blue are the same size and shape as the one outlined in red, meaning they're congruent (even though one of them is upside down).

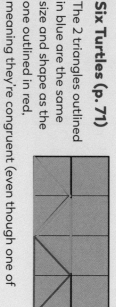

Dogs on Boats (p. 74)

The 2 parts of this triangle are not equal halves. The dotted line would need to cut straight down the middle for them to be equal.

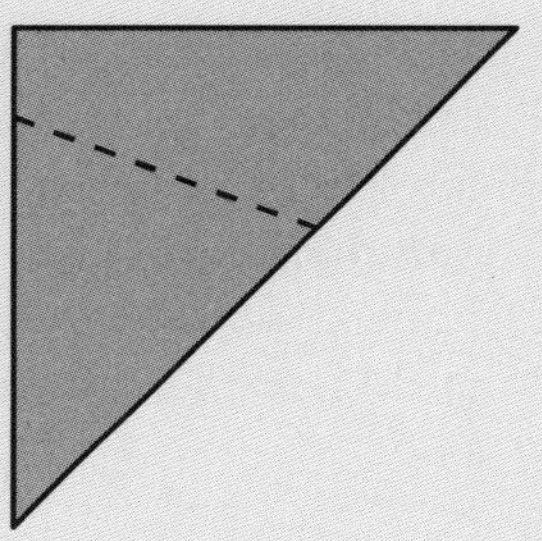

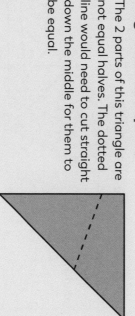

Cat on a Mat (p. 76)

Because 2 of the triangles outlined in red will fit inside the square outlined in blue, 1 triangle is ½ of the square.

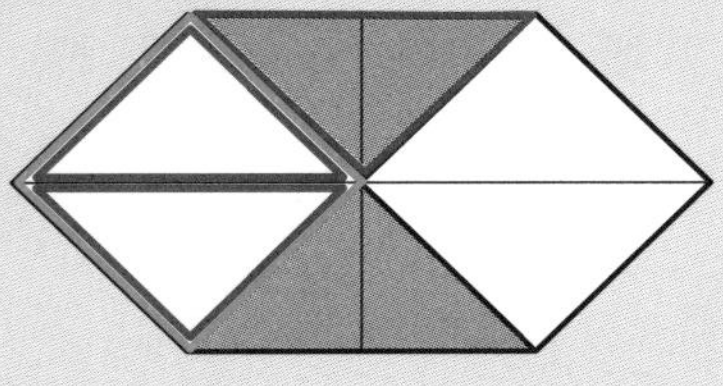

Spinning Top (p. 80)

The 3 triangles outlined in blue are the same size and shape as the one outlined in red, meaning they're all congruent.

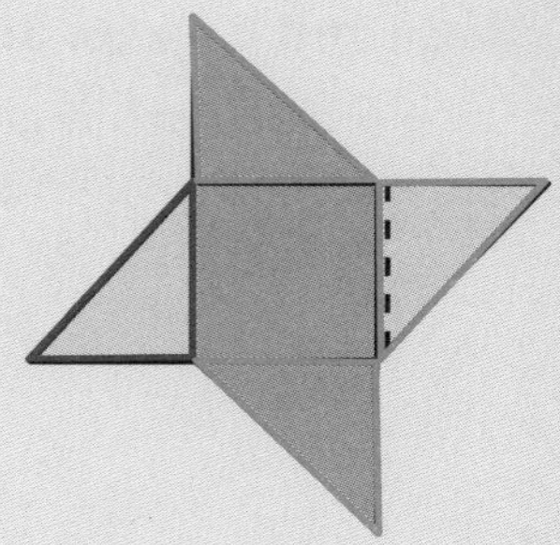

Ninja Star (p. 82)

Because the 6 triangles fit into the whole shape, 1 triangle is ⅙ of the whole shape.

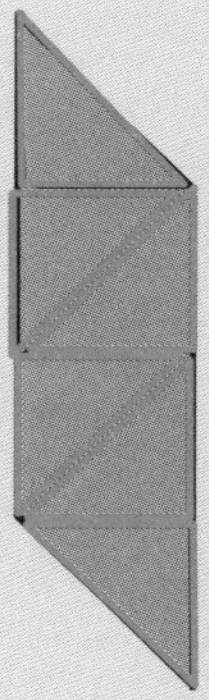

Star (p. 84)

All of the blue triangles in this shape are similar to the one outlined in red. (The other small triangle is both similar and congruent!)

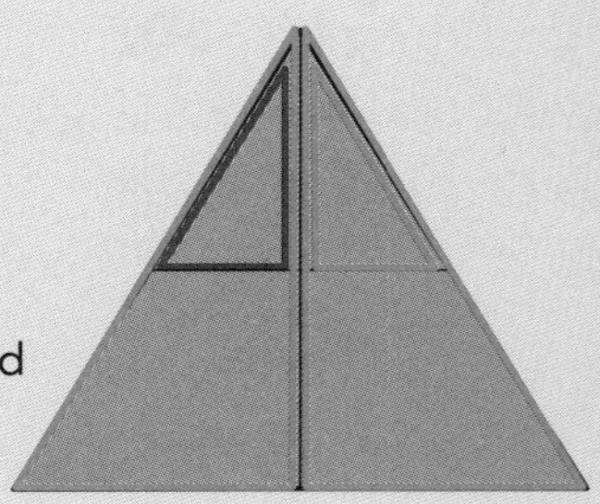

Kitty Candy Box (p. 86)

Not all of the triangles here are right triangles. The 2 outlined in red don't have 90° (right) angles. They're scalene triangles, meaning all 3 of their sides are different lengths.

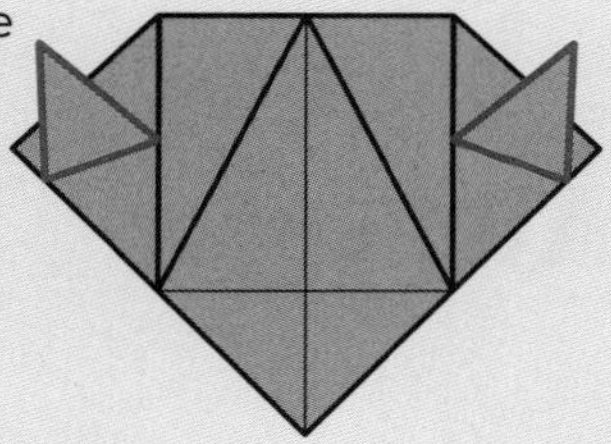

Fancy Letters (p. 92)

Shapes that are the same shape but different sizes (like the ones outlined here) are called similar shapes.

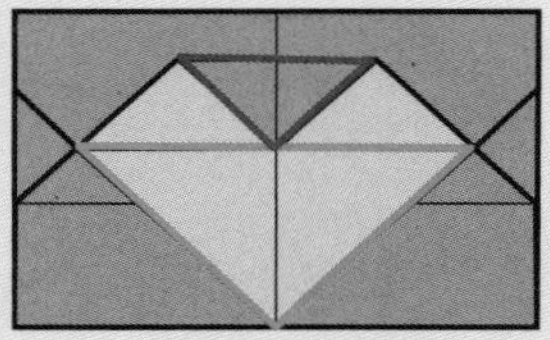

Little Candy Dish (p. 88)

The red triangle is 2 times as large as the blue triangle. This means that the blue triangle is also ½ the size of the red triangle.

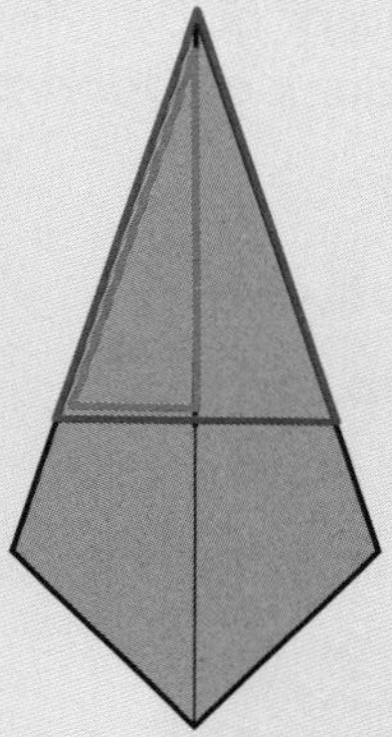

Flower Ornament (p. 94)

When 2 shapes are the exact same shape and size, they are called congruent shapes.

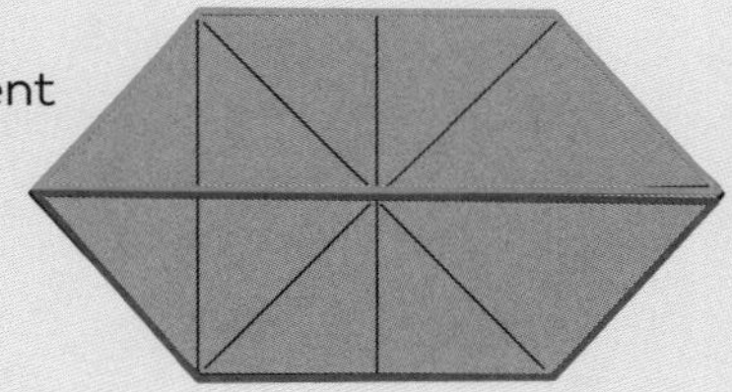

Spiral Envelope (p. 90)

There are 5 other triangles that are similar to the one outlined in red.

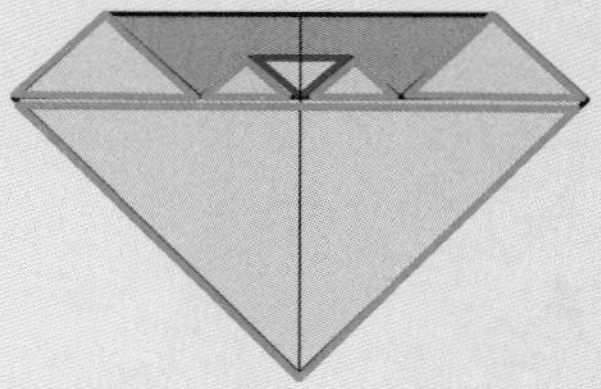

About the Author

FUMIAKI SHINGU was born in Fukuoka, Japan, in 1953. He moved to Tokyo after graduating from design school, and he founded a graphic design company in 1984. His origami kits have been sold in Toys"R"Us and other major outlets in Japan. He is also the author of *The Ultimate Book of Origami Animals*.

en.Origami-Club.com

origamiclub_cp

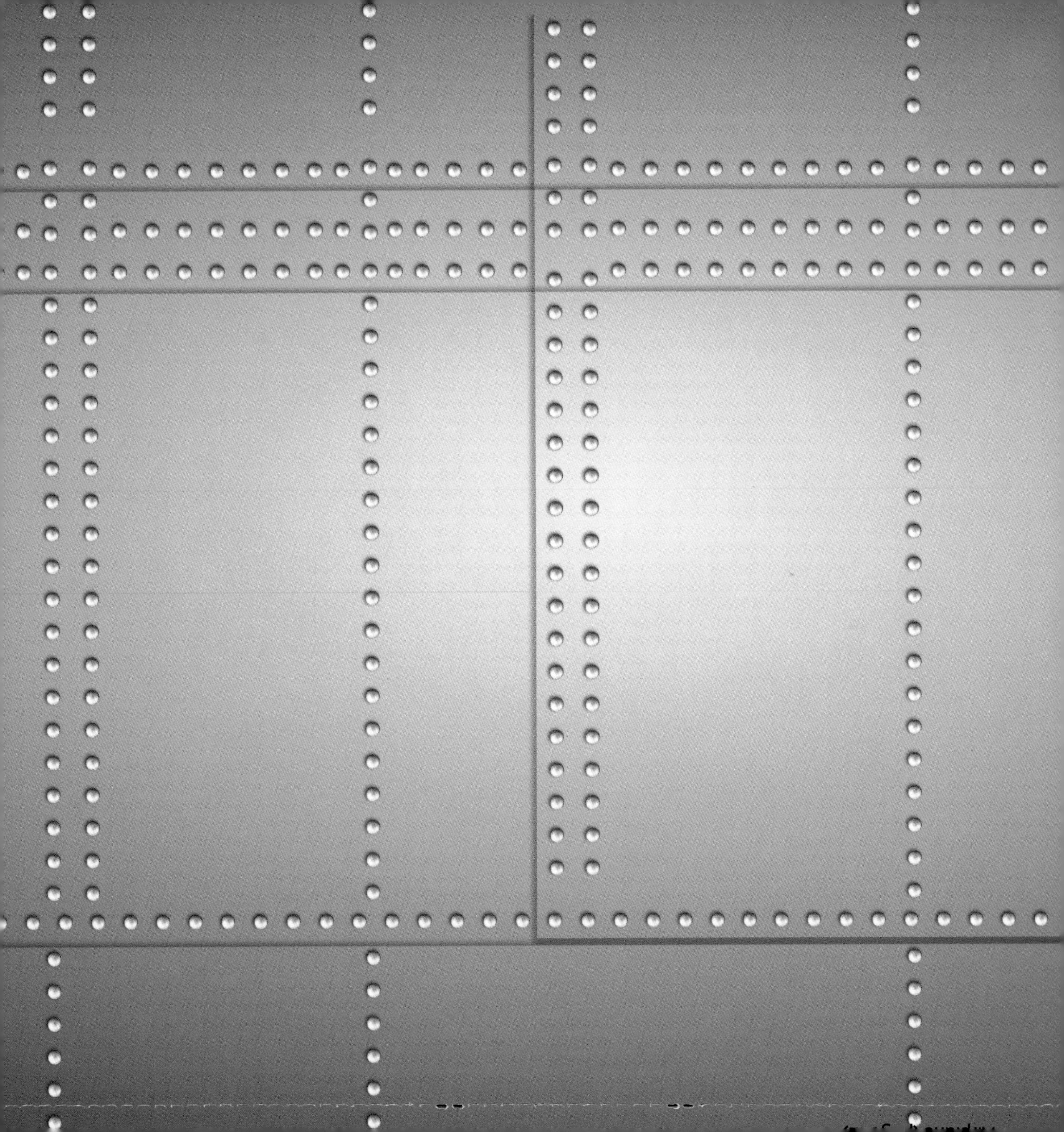

Flying Squid (page 1[illegible])

Flying Squid (page 10)

Flying Squid (page 16)

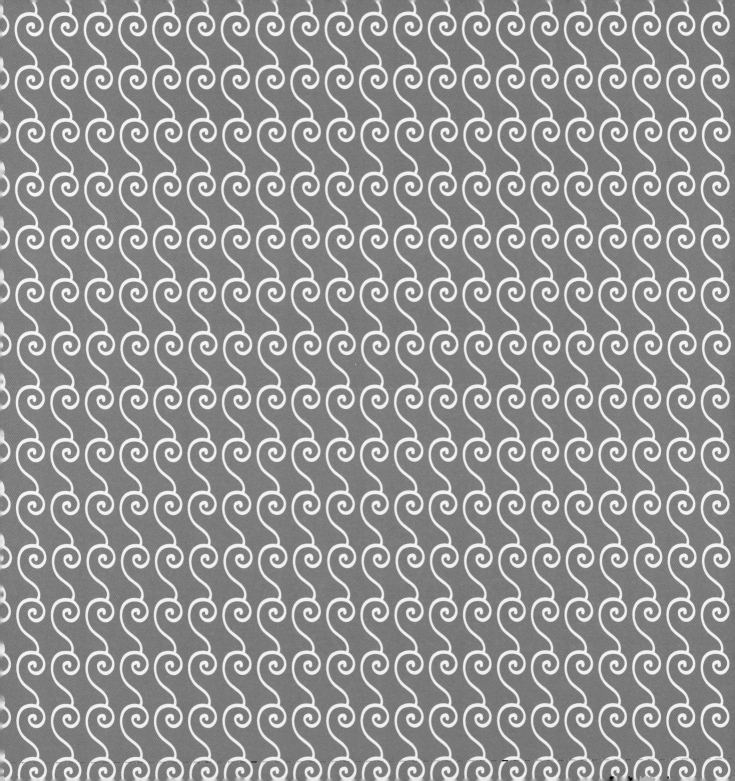

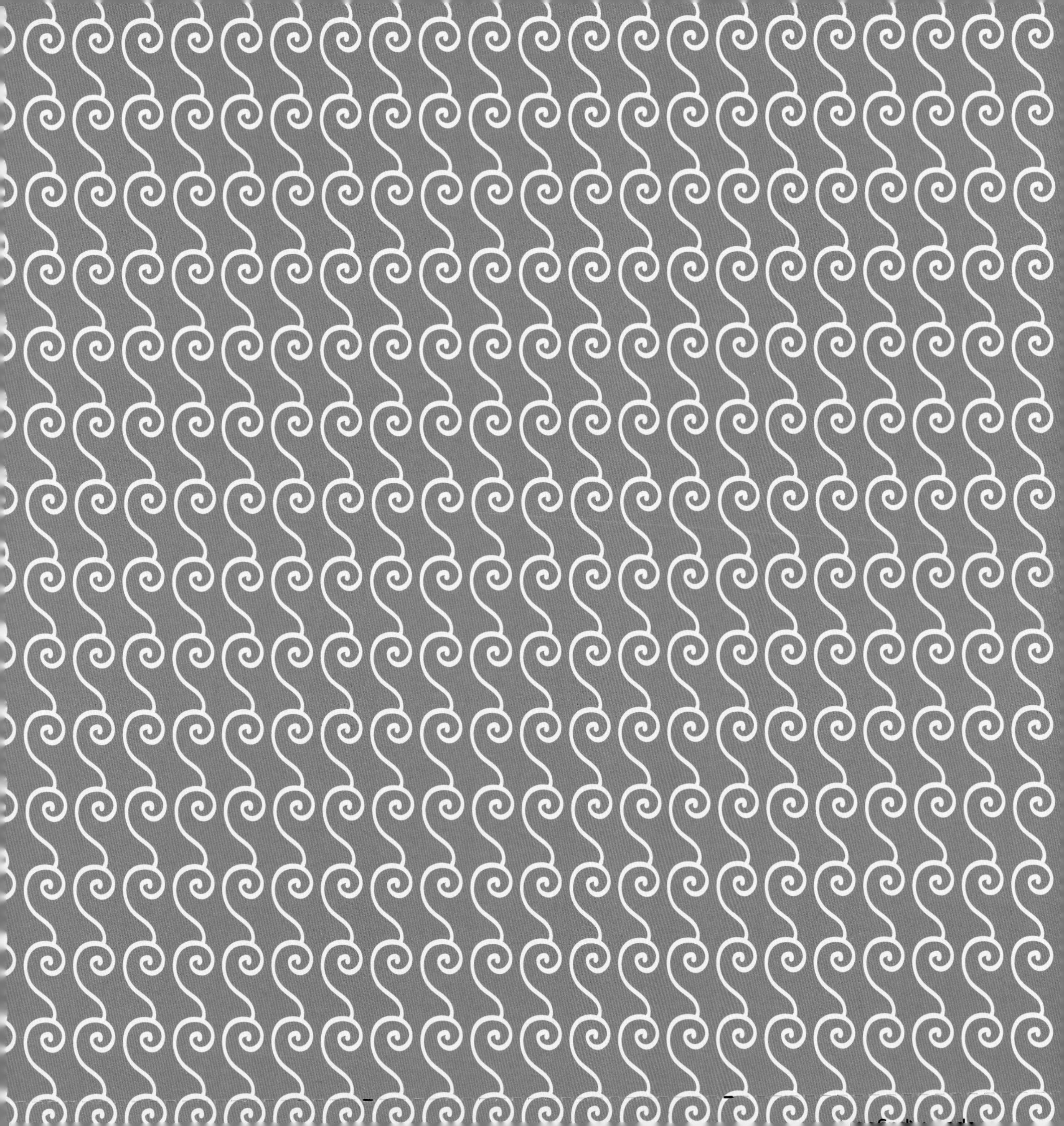

Cutout (page 25)

Catapult (page 2[illegible])

Catapult (page 20)

Fluttering Bird (page [illegible])

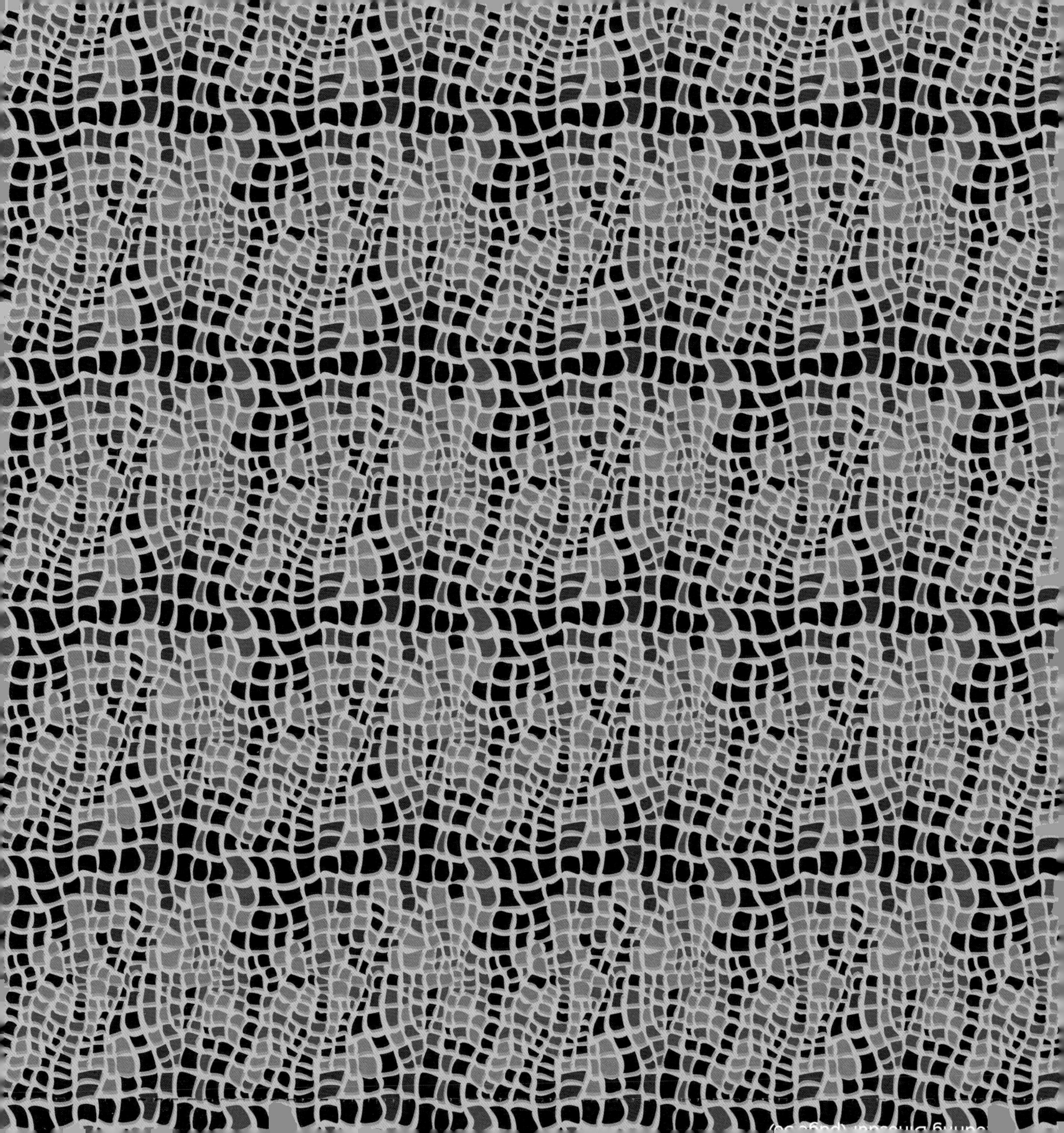

Roaring Dinosaur (page 30)

Hungry Raven (page 38)

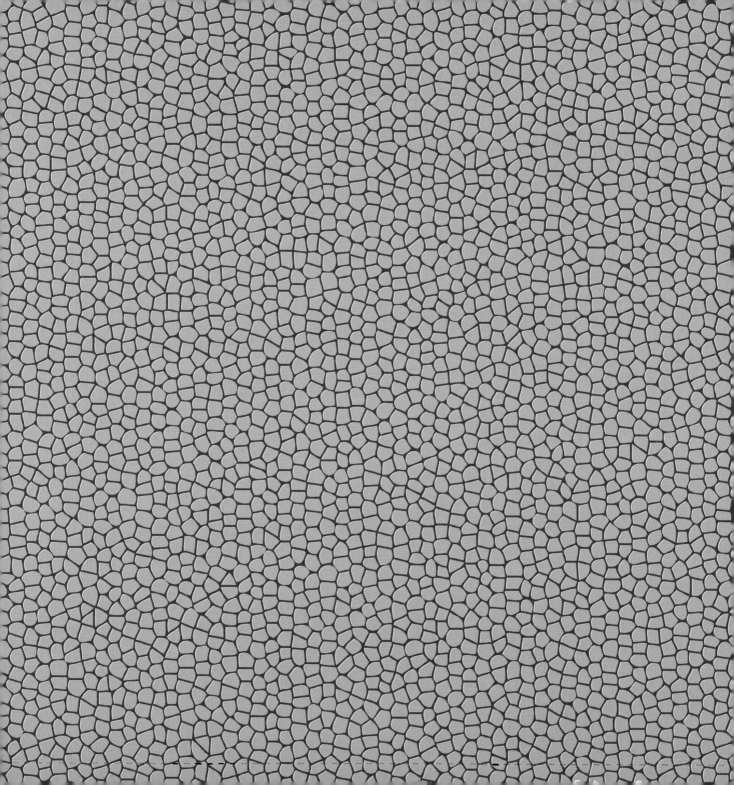

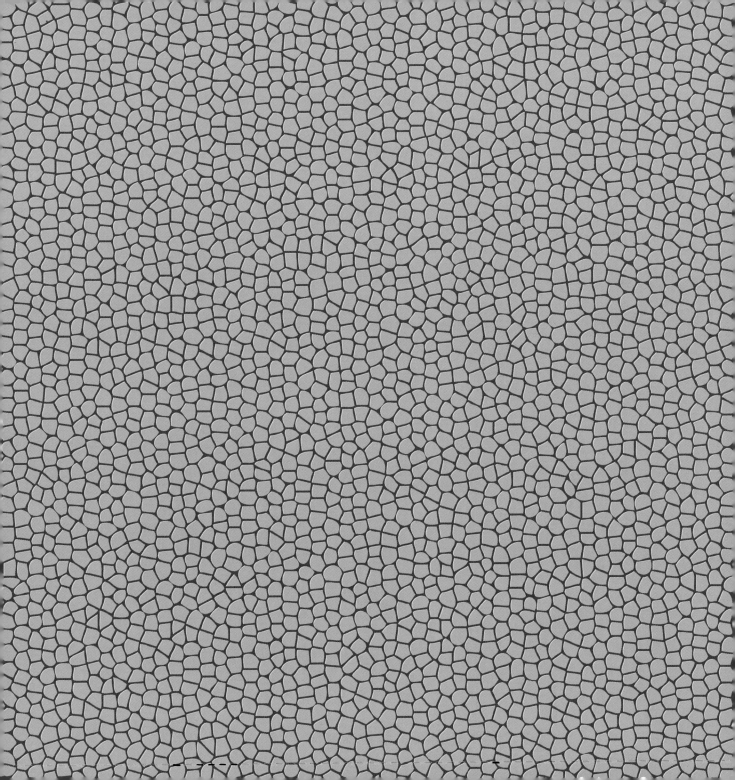

[illegible]

[illegible]

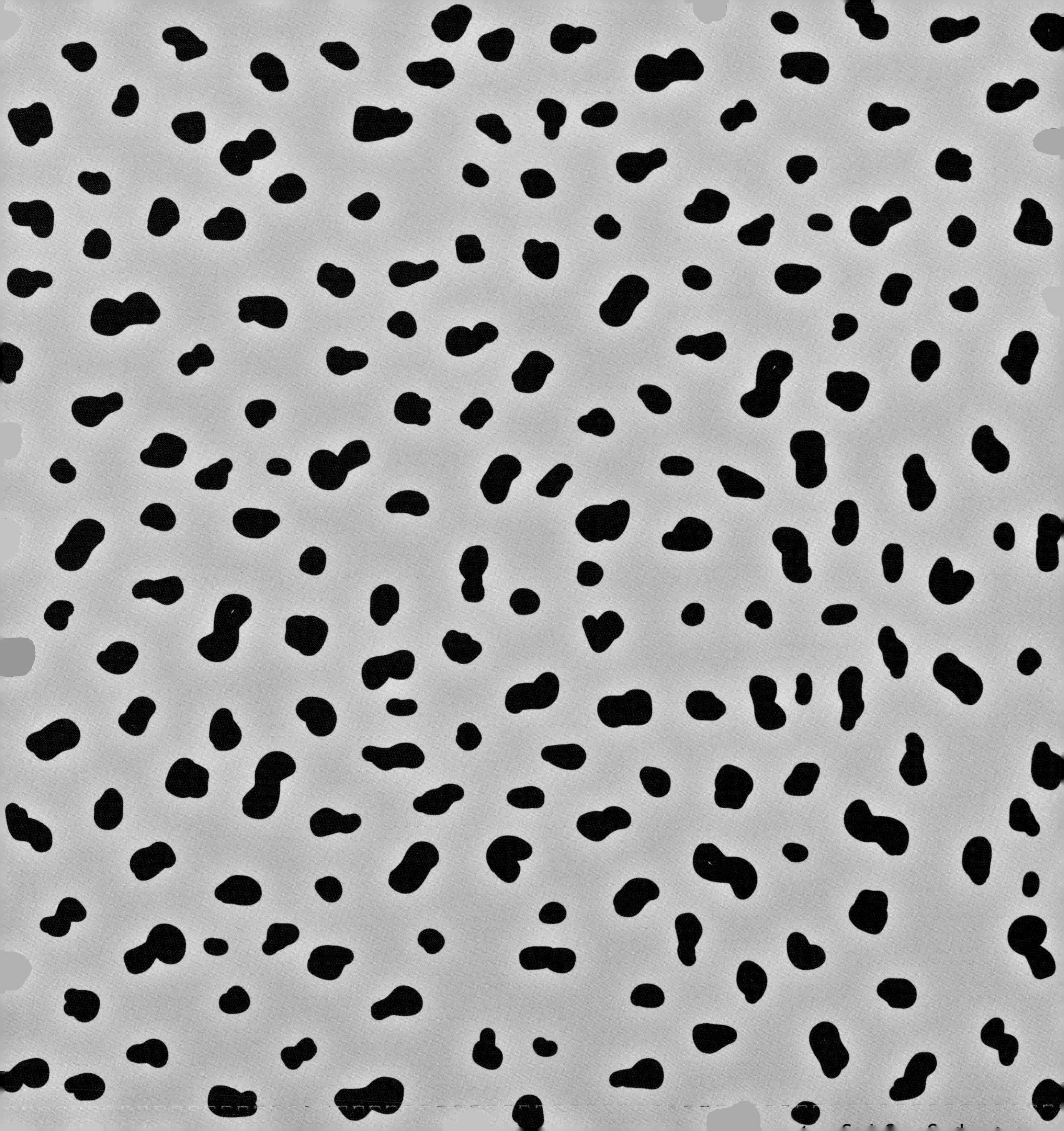

Hopping Crow (page [illegible])

Hopping Crow (page 4[illegible])

Hopping Crow (page 40)

Hopping Crow (page 40)

Fighting Sumo Wrestler (page [illegible])